Zbigniew Woźniak

The Elderly in Social Policy

Development in Humanities

edited by

Zbigniew Drozdowicz
(General Editor)

and Sławomir Sztajer

Volume 4

LIT

Zbigniew Woźniak

The Elderly in Social Policy

Towards a New Architecture of Gerontological Programmes

LIT

NARODOWY PROGRAM
ROZWOJU HUMANISTYKI

The present thesis has been financed as a part of a programme of the Ministry of Science and Higher Education, which is called: the National Programme for the Development of Humanities (NPRH)

Typeset by Michał Staniszewski

This book is printed on acid-free paper.

Bibliographic information published by the Deutsche Nationalbibliothek
The Deutsche Nationalbibliothek lists this publication in the Deutsche Nationalbibliografie; detailed bibliographic data are available in the Internet at http://dnb.d-nb.de.

ISBN 978-3-643-90373-0

A catalogue record for this book is available from the British Library

Klosbachstr. 107
CH-8032 Zürich
Tel. +41 (0) 44-251 75 05
Fax +41 (0) 44-251 75 06
E-Mail: zuerich@lit-verlag.ch
http://www.lit-verlag.ch

LIT VERLAG Dr. W. Hopf
Berlin 2013
Fresnostr. 2
D-48159 Münster
Tel. +49 (0) 2 51-62 03 20
Fax +49 (0) 2 51-23 19 72
E-Mail: lit@lit-verlag.de
http://www.lit-verlag.de

Distribution:
In Germany: LIT Verlag Fresnostr. 2, D-48159 Münster
Tel. +49 (0) 2 51-620 32 22, Fax +49 (0) 2 51-922 60 99, E-mail: vertrieb@lit-verlag.de

In Austria: Medienlogistik Pichler-ÖBZ, e-mail: mlo@medien-logistik.at
In the UK: Global Book Marketing, e-mail: mo@centralbooks.com
In North America: International Specialized Book Services, e-mail: orders@isbs.com
e-books are available at www.litwebshop.de

Contents

Introduction

The ageing of the world's population is an inevitable and irreversible process. However, it is also a part of human existence: as natural and valuable as childhood, youth and middle age. Every life phase heralds developments in various domains as well as the prospect of facing some functional limitations, the loss of certain rights and obligations, or even an increase in susceptibility to disease. Thus, every stage of human life is characterised by its specific risks and advantages.

While ageing is primarily an individual process, not everyone experiences it at the same time and in the same way; moreover, its individual and social consequences change depending on living conditions, place, time, gender and social status of the ageing individual. Therefore, instead of one process, we must speak of multiple processes, which can be measured by:

– number of years lived (demographic ageing),
– somatic changes and ability levels (biological ageing),
– intellectual and personality changes (psychological aspect of ageing),
– transformation of social roles, changes in family relations and relations within larger social communities (social ageing).

Ageing may cause personal problems concerning individuals (such as poor health and disabilities) or within their close environment. Not each and every difficult situation becomes a public issue, but a public issue may affect personal life. From such a perspective, ageing is not a social problem *sensu stricto*,[1] but the consequences of population ageing may lead to social problems

[1] Social problems are phenomena, conditions and situations which impede or prevent individuals from achieving social goals, disrupt the functioning of a society or its segments – communities or social groups and/or disrupt the equilibrium of social life. Social problems demonstrate that there are things which need to be changed or, at least, that values and goals should be better preserved. The main source of social problems is the organisation of society (life of a community), that is, the way social systems and institutions work.

demanding the intervention of various individual and collective subjects in order to solve, erase or at least alleviate them.

Someone aptly noted that while child was a new focus of in-depth, biological, psychological, social and pedagogic studies in the 19th century, the 20th century had to – theoretically and practically – face up to the needs of the elderly. The first decades of the 21st century are likely to be dominated by the search for appropriate methods to provide the elderly and the disabled with care and a respectable social position.

Besides, longer life expectancy will increase the importance of middle age, which may be necessary to revise past achievements, make future plans, consider lifestyle choices and prepare a person to be an active member of society during their old age (anticipation and foresight).[2]

A lot is already known about the contribution of different life stages to the process of ageing. Therefore, it is important to consider how to make this process satisfactory and favourable to longevity; also, how to improve the quality of the life of the elderly. This issue is gaining increasing importance and international experts have been drawing global attention towards the problem of inadequate social policies on ageing. While recommending flexible procedures for shifting from an active to a passive labour market, advising open access to permanent learning, encouraging the elderly to take on volunteer work and developing various forms of support families who provide care to the eldest family members, in fact, social policies (particularly in transition economies) tend to focus almost exclusively on providing the dependent elderly with financial support and care.[3]

Nowadays, public authorities are expected to design a new architecture of social ageing programmes, which would include, first of all, creating integrated forms of senior healthcare and projects devoted to preventing discrimination, marginalisation and social isolation of the elderly (particularly elderly women) as well as combining and uniting projects on ageing devoted to the problems of the elderly and the disabled.[4]

---

[2] *Averting the Old Age Crisis*, The World Bank Publication, 1994. See also *Lifelong Preparation for Old Age in Asia and the Pacific*, ESCAP, 1996.

[3] In 1999, The World Bank announced a quasi-crusade entitled *Averting the old age crisis: policies to protect the old and promote growth*. Important suggestions for social policy can be found in the following publications: *Older People and Transition Economies: An Overview of their Plight in the ECA Region*, Environmentally and Sustainable Development, World Bank, Washington, D.C. 1999; R. Holzmann, J. Stiglitz (eds.), *New Ideas about Social Security*, World Bank, Washington, D.C. 2001.

[4] It was assumed in the Madrid International Plan of Action on Ageing and the Political Declaration, which particularly recommended developing two global programmes: *Active and healthy ageing* and *A society for all ages*. The Commissioner Anna Diamantopoulou,

These programmes have the potential to increase the chances that the oldest generation will lead an active, independent and self-sufficient life as long as it is possible, considering their individual health, capabilities and needs.

Later in this book, drawing from research results on gerontology, sociology, social work and political studies, and deriving arguments based on his own deliberations and experience in designing and implementing social policies on regional and local levels,[5] the author will reflect upon social politics devoted to the oldest generation.

The proposed theory of designing social policy on ageing – an inevitable element of any development strategy – is based on a "philosophy" which is different to persistently replicated, so-called "model" strategies. The idea of this project is to take maximum advantage of all possible resources of regional and local social policies, regardless of whether statutory regulations explicitly define how to support and expand programmes, services and funds addressed to the elderly.

The author's theory of designing gerontology policies, presented in this book, attempts to answer the following questions:

1. What efforts should be taken in particular communities/societies to decrease the chance the elderly will be exposed to risks regarding their health care and social security?

2. What sort of systematic solutions must be implemented to reduce the risk that the elderly will lose the sense of security, confidence, stability and continual care – yet at the same time, to allow the elderly to hold enough autonomy and freedom to guarantee their independence and self-sufficient existence?

---

in her speech on ageing at UNECE on 8.04.2002 in Madrid, made a declaration about the cooperation between UE and UN.

[5] The theory developed by the author became the foundation of the urban policy (2003), and the regional policy strategy (2010). See Z. Woźniak, "Present Situation and Future Prospects of Social Policy Aimed at Senior Citizens Against the Background of the Globalization of Ageing," in M. Ziółkowski (ed.), *Ludzie przełomu tysiąclecia a cywilizacja przyszłości* [The People of the Turn of the Millennium vs. the Civilisation of the Future], Wydawnictwo Fundacji Humaniora, Poznan 2001, pp. 169–197; idem, "Priorytety w programach gerontologicznych i struktur europejskich jako przesłanka budowy polityki społecznej wobec starości i osób starszych" [Priorities in Gerontological and European Programmes as a Condition for the Construction of Social Policy Aimed at Aging and the Elderly], in M. Szlązak (ed.), *Starzenie się populacji wyzwaniem dla polityki społecznej* [Ageing Population: a Challenge for Social Policy], Regionalny Ośrodek Polityki Społecznej, Cracow 2003, pp. 14–33; idem, "Globalne cele polityki społecznej wobec seniorów priorytetem programów gerontologicznych" [Global Aims of Social Policy aimed at the Elderly as a Priority for Gerontological Programmes], in *Jesień, moja ulubiona pora roku – sprawdzone pomysły na twórczą i aktywną starość* [Autumn, my Favorite Time of Year – Proven Ideas for Creative and Active Ageing], Akademia Filantropii, Warsaw 2003, pp. 21–24.

3. Who must guarantee the durability and efficiency of systematic solutions aimed at minimising and/or eliminating the sources of threat to the social security of the elderly? Which administrative level should be responsible?

The author's intention was to specify which aspects of ageing and old age pose such a significant challenge to the elderly, their families and to the authorities, that they require common effort to build a long-term ageing programme on different state-levels (centre-region-local community).

From this perspective, an efficient social policy should give the authorities, as well as their partners and opponents, the opportunity to select various forms and directions of action. Not only should it be open to alternative ideas but also it should systematically stimulate them by incorporating a vast circle of partners into the process of designing and implementing projects. Instead of giving ready solutions, it should rather be a wide conceptual and strategic frame.

Some say that theory is the eye of practice. This book was intended to combine theoretical deliberations and implementation proposals. It analyses rules, aims, procedures and tools related to supporting and creating social policy programmes addressed to the elderly.

Although the proposed idea of social policy addressed to the elderly is partly based on existing knowledge about the qualities and determinants of social position, it also offers new models and solutions and seems to be innovative enough to be subjected to the evaluation of social policy makers – both theoreticians and practitioners.

Therefore, the readers are offered information and project proposals which are general but also specific enough to support current and future decisions about creating a comprehensive support system to improve the quality of life of the elderly.

The author hopes that the proposed multilayered and universal formula of ageing programmes will become a subject of public debate, gathering a wide range of potential actors in the public eye and that it will help build ageing programmes and strategies. Ideas presented in this book may help start the work on comprehensive legal regulations concerning the legal and social status of ageing citizens and facilitate the process of correcting current strategies and policies addressed to the elderly.

Chapter I

The premises of social policies on ageing

1. The globalisation of population ageing

> Since Thucydides, historians have observed the relationship between development and decline of great civilisations and demographic trends.
>
> Ken Dychtwald

We are experiencing an unprecedented revolution, creeping and waddling in the shadow of other global problems. Relatively slow, but incessant, it results from the permanently high proportion of elderly people in developed countries[1] and a fast pace of ageing in developing countries[2] (Focus box 1).

1. There are various reasons for the demographic ageing of societies. The following reasons are often mentioned:

2. Falling birth rate as a result of increasing life expectancy of women across the world who choose not to have large numbers of children and to delay first childbirth.

3. Declining mortality rates – particularly of younger age categories (including male overmortality rates).

4. Changing age structure of the population – particularly an increase in the proportion and number of older people and a decline in the proportion and number of younger people (changing dependency ratio).

---

[1] According to the UN criteria, aging society means that old people make up 7% of our total population; also, according to demographic criteria, population is old if people aged 65 and over make 12% and over of the whole population.

[2] It took France 115 years to double the number of the elderly – China needed only 37 years.

5. Longer human life span resulting in a growing number of older people, including the ageing of the older population (much more rapid growth rate of "the oldest old"[3] than elderly people in general).

6. Migration processes, which, in some parts of the world, lead to a significant decline in the proportion of younger people in a population.

The consequences of the persistent below-replacement fertility level (i.e. population decline as opposed to population growth).[4]

It is estimated that until the 17th century, people aged 65 or more constituted only 1.0% of the population and at the beginning of 20th century, only one quarter of the population could hope to live to be 65.[5] Nowadays, in highly industrialised countries, elderly people live much longer than ever before: human life expectancy has increased even to 80 years. In the most developed areas, a 60 year-old woman could live another 23 years and a man another 19, while in less developed countries it is 17 and 15 respectively.

The average life expectancy for the richest countries is expected to rise from 83 to 88 years in 2020. Almost 70% of the contemporary population of developed countries are expected to live to the age of 65 and 30.0–40.0% to the age of 80.[6]

At the moment, every ninth global citizen is 60 or more and the average age is 37. In 2050, it will be 46 (57 in Italy, 54 in Japan, 53 in West Germany). The oldest population is Europe (in 2008, the median was 40.4; in 2060 it will probably be 47.9). The oldest European countries are Greece, Sweden, Belgium and Italy while Ireland, the Netherlands and Finland are the youngest. By 2020, the biggest growth of people at retirement age will have been observed by (consecutively): Germany, Sweden, Japan, France, England and the USA.[7]

As a result of global demographic changes, histograms representing the number of people from different age groups have reshaped from a pyramid (1900) to an increasingly rectangular figure. In other words, population of progressive demographic structure (slim triangle shape) is transforming into a stationary population (the shape of a warning bell) and is moving towards a regressive model (the shape of a death urn[8]).

---

[3] The threshold for this age category shifted from 80 to 85.

[4] P. Harper, *Generations and Life Course: The Impact of Demographic Challenges on Education 2010–2050*, Institute of Aging, Oxford 2008, p. 2.

[5] K. Dychtwald, *Speculations on the Future of Aging*, INSIDE Magazine, 21st Century Publishers, Hawaii 1997.

[6] I. Hamilton, *The Psychology of Ageing: an Introduction,* Jessica Kingsley Publishers, London 2006.

[7] K. Giannakourris, "Aging Characterises the Demographic Perspectives of European Societies," *Eurostat. Statistics in Focus*, 2008, no. 72.

[8] Warning bell and death urn were terms used by Stanisław Waszak, a demographist from Adam Mickiewicz University, to describe demographic structures.

Scholars believe that after Stage Two of demographic transition,[9] Stage Three is approaching. It is supposed to result from international migration, which has been changing population structure in many parts of the world. Today, the gaps in the birth rate are filled due to *replacement migration*; however, the future fertility rate of global population is still uncertain, particularly in countries with a below-replacement fertility level. Will this process intensify or will there be attempts to rebuild the fertility rate by stabilising it? It is not certain what the pace of decline in birth rates in Europe and more developed Asian countries will be (a decline in family size, delaying childbirth, biomedical factors which may lead to fertility level below generation replacement), but it may bring dramatic consequences for the social and economic structure of many societies.[10] Therefore, it is hard to determine the number of migrants needed to compensate for the population shortage – experts estimate that Europe would need 23 million[11] but critics believe that by 2050, 100 million migrants will be necessary to avoid population decline, 161 million to maintain necessary labour force resources, and 1.4 billion to maintain appropriate proportions between those who are active and passive on the labour market.[12]

---

[9] *Stage One of the demographic transition* was characterised mostly by a decline in mortality rate as a result of progress in the field of medicine. It was the period of flourishing families, in which parents focused first of all on providing their children with well-being (King-child with parents era), playing their social roles and living according to cultural patterns. The processes of *the Second Stage* were signified by below-replacement fertility, favouring informal relationships, mortality decline, prolonged lifespan, intensified migration, aiming at maximum use of education and income, increased quality of life and life satisfaction. These phenomena result from political and worldview changes manifested in the increase of social egalitarianism, individual autonomy, social liberalisation. They are also related to better quality of life and conditions resulting from the development of service sector, modern technologies and medicine. Stage One was dominated by the care of family and offspring; the second puts emphasis on the individual right to self-realisation; the first was called *altruistic*, and the second *individualistic* (terms created by Dirk Jan van de Kaa). J. Jóźwiak, "Teorie przejścia van de Kaa" [Van de Kaa's Theory of Transitions], *Gazeta SGH*, 2003, no. 174.

[10] Already in 2000 the "official optimism" of the UN document was criticised: *Replacement Migration: Is It the? Solution to Declining and Aging Populations?* The criticism may be summarised by Joseph Chamie's words: This is the only time in history where people are living longer and populations are shrinking: B. Wattenberg, "European Union? European Ostrich!," *Jewish World Review*, 2000, no. 6, p. 1.

[11] Prof. Leszek Balcerowicz and his team calculated that Poland will need 160,000 migrants a year to "patch up" the holes in the labour market in the next couple of years.

[12] It is impossible to accomplish not only because of the rapid growth of population ageing in countries which migrate to areas of zero/negative population growth (particularly Europe), but also because of the growing dislike to migrants because of the problems on the labour market. See B. Wattenberg, "European Union?...," op. cit., p. 2.

Focus Box 1

Europe is grey – the world is turning grey
1. In 1950, the population aged 60 and over constituted 8.0% of the world population (205 million) – in 2006, the proportion increased to 11.0% (688 million). 2. The number of people aged 60 or over has increased by one million every month since 1995. It is estimated that the number of people aged 60 or over will have increased to 1 billion by 2020, will double in 2050 (22.0%) and become one-third of the global population in 2150. 3. The world population will have increased by half by 2050 compared to 2000 (up to 9 billion), and the senior population will increase threefold (even fourfold in developing countries). 4. Annual growth of global population now is 1.7–1.9%, while the number of people aged 65 or over increases every year by 2.5% – this category is expected to increase over the next 30 years, depending on the country, by 30.0 to 140.0%. 5. In 2030, people aged 50 or over will constitute half of the eu population. Every third person will be aged 60 or over. One third of the population of developed countries will be aged 65 or more. 6. Un demographists predict that in the next half a century the population of people aged 60 or over will increase: a. From 20.0% to 30.0% in developed countries, b. From 8.0% to 20.0% in developing countries, c. From 5.0% to 10.0% in the least developed parts of the world. 7. Since 1950, there has been a rapid growth of “the oldest old”: a. Since the beginning of the 1990s, the number of people aged 90 or over has increased threefold while the entire population of the elderly has only doubled,

   b. The proportion of people aged 80 or over has increased from 3.9% to 5.2% for the last 20 years – in the next 75 years there could be a 7-fold increase of the oldest old, while in developing countries this number will increase 3.5-fold,
   c. From 1950 to 2025 the number of the oldest old will have increased 10-fold – the population of the elderly will increase 8-fold,
   d. By 2025, the number of people aged 80 and over will constitute 11.0% of the elderly population – nearly 60.0% of them will live in developing countries.
   e. Starting from 1960, every ten years the number of centenarians has doubled. By 2050 the number of people aged 100 or over will have increased 14-fold (from 265,000 in 2005 to 3.7 million in 2050).
8. In 2025, more than 70.0% of people aged 60 or over will be living in developing countries – already more than a quarter of people aged 75 or over live in two countries: india and china.
9. In 2030, a quarter of the population of asia will be aged 60 or over.
10. The process of demographical ageing is and will be stronger in the female population – they already constitute two-thirds of the oldest old (aged 80 and over).

Source: *Active Ageing and Solidarity Between Generations. A Statistical Portrait of the European Union 2012*, Eurostat, Publications Office of the European Union, Luxembourg 2011; D. Beers, M. Mršnik, *Global Aging 2010: A Worldwide Challenge*, Standard & Poor's Financial Services, McGraw-Hill, New York 2010; K. Giannakourris, "Aging Characterises the Demographic Perspectives of European Societies," *Eurostat. Statistics in Focus,* 2008, no. 72; P. Harper, *Generations and Life Course: The Impact of Demographic Challenges on Education 2010–2050*, Institute of Aging, Oxford 2008, pp. 1–3; A. Kalache, S. Barreto, I. Keller, "Global Aging. The Demographic Revolution in All Cultures and Societies," in M. L. Johnson (ed.), *The Cambridge Handbook of Age and Aging,* Cambridge University Press, Cambridge – New York – Melbourne – Madrid – Cape Town – Singapore – São Paulo 2005, pp. 30–46.

It should be mentioned here that in 1880, when Otto von Bismarck decided the retirement age threshold should be 65, the average life expectancy was below 45. Today, in highly industrialised countries, elderly people live longer and longer and better and better – as a result of economic growth, better health conditions, and medicine and medical technology progress, and over the last 50 years life expectancy has increased by 20 years. That is why UN experts predict the following shifts of human life stages in the quite near future:

1. 18–24 years – youth,
2. 25–39 years – young adulthood (longer than before),
3. 40–59 years – middle age,
4. 60–79 years – late adulthood (delayed, postponed),
5. 80–99 years – old age (significant shift of the old age threshold),
6. 100 years and more – late old age (postponed).

Although uncertainty is a sign of the times today, demographic changes are certain. The ageing of the global population (particularly European) is an inevitable and irreversible process, and unprecedented in world history. Demography today is one of the few disciplines which enable long-term prognosis about population structure, because in normal circumstances – without cataclysms, wars, revolutions, epidemics, etc., demographic indicators and coefficients change very slowly. The population of people who will be old in 50 years has already been born – knowing today's demographic trends, one may predict with some likelihood the internal structure of the senior generation in a few dozen years. Thus, adequate social security systems can be planned and suitable services and support for the elderly can be developed.

Although it is easier to analyse demographic trends from a long-term perspective, they must be supplemented by numerous short-term prognoses. Demographic processes do not run in isolation from other factors of change which induce developments in production, consumption, saving and investing models and, consequently, lifestyles (economy, technology development, market, cultural changes, etc.). The causative power of these phenomena and processes may be significant when it comes to shaping particular areas of economic and social life. However, it is difficult to predict these processes more than a few, maybe a dozen years in advance.

The pace, depth and scope of changes in global population structure fully prove the theory of the global nature of the ageing of the world's population.[13]

---

[13] "Globalisation" defined after A. Giddens as "the intensification of worldwide social relations which link distant localities in such a way that local happenings are shaped by events occurring many miles away and vice versa." See M. Kearney, "The Local and Global: Anthropology of Globalisation and Transnationalism," *Annual Review of Anthropology*, 1995, no. 24, p. 547. For the purposes of this book, globalisation will be defined as a kind of strategy and

Sooner or later, global population ageing must initiate political, economic and social mobilisation, as the consequences of most populations' ageing have already resulted in the necessity to restructure the economy and redefine many policies (particularly social policy). In the near future, these consequences will initiate a cultural shift; from the apotheosis of youth to bringing back the important role of experience, epitomised largely by the oldest generation. In the next decades, all the processes and phenomena related to the globalisation of ageing will probably conduce *a relapse into gerontocracy* in economy and in politics and will surely cause very deep transformations in the family structure. The most radical gerontologists analysing future trends predict a re-arrangement of the global geopolitical order.[14]

Regardless of the attitude towards problems related to population ageing, ignoring it is no longer possible, particularly because of the growing number of elderly, which makes people around the world more aware than ever that they live in changing, multi-generational societies. What is more, there is a growing belief that senior citizens, as a significant part of these changes, should be/become their addressees (beneficiaries). Thus, it is necessary to observe the growing number of elderly and their social roles in families and larger communities from the perspective of the social, economic and political consequences of global ageing.

The co-existence of longevity and declining birth rate is a global phenomenon. It is thus safe to say that while the 20th century saw the end of the domination of youth in the global population structure,[15] the 21st century heralds a new era: the time of the matured. Certainly, the intensification of the process of population ageing will soon bring a system transition in all important spheres of social life – so deep that, in many key aspects, it will go beyond state, administrative and cultural borders.

Therefore, the resolution mentioned in the introduction will surely happen and afterwards, *nothing will be the same.*[16]

---

a basis for political, economic and social mobilisation triggered by general population changes in the world.

[14] The theories are further developed in the works of Dychtwald, Stuckelberger, Watson Wyatt Data.

[15] Already in 2000 there were more elderly people than children under 5; the proportion of people aged 0–14 is also expected to decrease from 17.6% to 14.5% in 2030. (Author's calculations based on: K. Giannakourris, "Aging Characterises the Demographic Perspectives...," op. cit., table 2 and 3).

[16] *Global Aging. The Challenge of the New Millenium*, Watson Wyatt Data Services, New York 2000.

2. Biological and medical aspects of human ageing

Be careful choosing your parents.
Anthony Smith
(author of the bestselling book *Body*)

Over the last decades, important advances have been made by scientists, which have contributed to a better understanding of the biological basis of ageing.[17] We have insight into the nature of genetic factors determining longevity, the cellular and molecular mechanisms underlying the ageing process and the environmental and lifestyle factors that can modify individual life trajectories through later life.[18]

The human body is made of a huge number of cells which are the building blocks of tissues and organs. The process of cellular renewal continues throughout life; as we grow older, this process begins to slow down. Individual cells and cell assemblies are subjected to damaging external influences (free radicals, parasites, ultraviolet radiation, etc.) and, as a result, the number of cells is reduced. Physiologically, a cell can be renewed by division – if it does not happen in a certain time, the cell degenerates and simply dies off.[19]

The lifespan of a cell differs depending on the type of cell and species, while the lifespan of a species is correlated with the "Hayflick limit": cells can divide only a limited number of times and when they reach a certain phase they undergo the process of a programmed cell death (*apoptosis*).[20] Apoptosis is also a positive process, eliminating unwanted, infected or defective cells. Inhibition of apoptosis can result in uncontrolled cell growth and tumour formation.

[17] For a long time, scholars have been trying to understand the mechanisms of ageing, to find the crucial elements that steer this process, to find the way to slow them down. At the moment, several hundred biological theories on the origin and mechanisms of ageing exist. Many of them overlap; biological processes of ageing and factors influencing them overlap as well.

[18] T. Kirkwood, "The Biological Science of Human Ageing," in M. L. Johnson (ed.), *The Cambridge Handbook of Age and Aging*, Cambridge University Press, Cambridge – New York – Melbourne – Madrid – Cape Town – Singapore – São Paulo 2005, p. 72.

[19] The most organised and heterogeneous cells (neurons and endocrine cells) are most subject to deterioration with age. The first to stop functioning are neurons – the process starts after 2 year of age. E. Tulle, "The Ageing Body and The Ontology of Ageing: Athletic Competence in Later Life," *Body & Society*, 2008, vol. 14, no. 3.

[20] From the Greek word for "falling leaves" or "falling petals." Sometimes, apoptosis occurs in the foetal period – for example, the differentiation of fingers and toes in a developing human embryo occurs because cells between the fingers apoptose.

From time to time, the media inform us about another sensational and promising discovery of a *longevity gene.* This may lead to a conviction that human life expectancy is programmed and it depends on individual genes (and telomeres). It also inclines people to hope that maybe at least there is a chance for a longer life, if immortality is not likely.[21] Biologists claim more and more firmly that there is nothing like a *longevity gene* or an *ageing gene.* Rather, there are certain genes which play a particularly important role in ageing and longevity by increasing somatic maintenance and repair and supporting the immune system.[22]

Without doubt, ageing is a process of polygenic inheritance; we do not know, however, which genes determine both growth and ageing. Genetic factors matter when we analyse the pace of ageing; therefore, we should not perceive genetic influence in terms of hereditary taint but only in terms of variations in human population.

A body ages because its cells age as a result of a limited number of divisions. In the end, all our cells must get old and die.[23] How long an individual can live is determined by joint action of many genes involved in various life processes from the moment we are born (in the foetal period, ageing is fastest),[24] and their products are very sensitive to environmental factors which complicate even mutual dependence of genes and environment effects.[25]

---

[21] Optimists assume that it will be soon possible to determine the physiological condition of a person studying a chosen group of genes. If we could learn about our weakest genes and be able to repair them, we would not "fail to work" in old age.

[22] Ewa Sikora, biochemist, Necki Institute of Experimental Biology, has no illusions: "Our body is disposable, given to us, so as it could serve the evolution of the species by mediating in the generation swap and increasing individual heterogeneity." M. Fikus, "Moja, twoja, nasza starość" [Ageing: Mine, Yours, Ours], *Wiedza i Życie*, 1998, no. 11, p. 11.

[23] Studying the number of all possible divisions of the cells grown in a laboratory, it was concluded that the number depends on a species. Human cells may divide about 60 times, mouse cells about 20; afterwards, they both age and die. It is not clear how this is related to longevity of a whole organism. One of the reasons is that different cells in a multicellular organism live differently. Some divide all our life, some we are born with (e.g. neurons) and they only diminish with time. M. Fikus, "Moja, twoja, nasza starość" [Ageing: Mine, Yours, Ours], op. cit.

[24] Biologists and geriatrists claim that the maturity and efficiency peak stage is about the age of 30. Afterwards, most physiological functions start to deteriorate. R. Chernoff, D. Lipschitz, *Health Promotion and Disease Prevention in The Elderly*, Raven Press, New York 1988, p. 6.

[25] Extending human life span can only partly be explained by genetic factors – there is scientific evidence that life expectancy is only 25.0% determined by genes. T. Kirkwood, "The Biological Science of Human Ageing," op. cit., pp. 72–81; G. McClearn, S. Petrill, "The Genetics of Behavioural Ageing," in M. L. Johnson (ed.), *The Cambridge Handbook...*, op. cit.; B. Jeune, K. Christensen, "Biodemography and Epidemiology of Longevity," in M. L. Johnson (ed.), *The Cambridge Handbook...*, op. cit, pp. 85–94.

In scientific environments, no one questions that ageing is an inevitable and irreversible biological process of all living organisms, a continuum on which consecutive changes are increasingly visible: from day to day, external signs of ageing may be of little significance, but the involution processes are gradual and incessant. Cumulative, developmental changes in the structure and functions of the human organism result from gradual efficiency loss of particular systems and/or their atrophy (when we grow older, the pace of the body integrity loss is 1% a year).

Although it is inevitable that our genotype determines our life to some extent, we can influence environmental factors and although we will not stop ageing, we may delay this process or at least make it more harmonious.

Ageing is not one but many processes, which today are known to be mouldable and, in many cases, modifiable.[26] Studies have shown that the condition of an old brain is better than the calculations of proportional loss would suggest. Due to the brain's flexibility, a myriad of newer and newer neuronal connections appear. Physiologically, the decline caused by the process of aging in organs, tissues and systems is gradual, which demonstrates the excesses and reserves of a body and its functional systems.

Considering all of the above, we should thus assume that biological ageing (senescence) is:

1. A natural, genetically-based process of change, resulting in the deterioration of cells, tissues and organs (consequence: disorganisation of their structure and function).
2. Another stage of body development and maturing – this process include changes in immune, nervous and hormonal systems.
3. A consequence of the accumulation of various maintenance failures leading to deterioration, a result of the lack of metabolic enzymes in the body.
4. A display of accumulated results of diseases and/or injuries.

It should be mentioned that ageing is an individual process, therefore:

1. Not every ageing person experiences all the above-mentioned changes and their consequences.
2. Not everyone experiences involution at the same stage of individual development.
3. Pace, profundity and extent of changes often vary more between people aged 65–90 than people aged 30–40.
4. The largest differences between the young and the old are observed on the level of interaction between functional systems.

[26] This was proved in 1980s in experimental research: J. Fries, L. Crapo, *Vitality and Aging. Implications of the Rectangular Curve*, W. H. Freeman and Co., San Francisco 1981.

5. Not all functional changes are caused by ageing – some result from pathology or overuse/underuse (lifestyle).

6. Most elderly people have constitutional reserves allowing them to meet the demands of everyday life.

Thus, physiological ageing is inevitable but also normal and healthy; however, it is only a model, almost unknown in everyday medical practice,[27] because in reality, ageing usually includes pathological elements. Ageing as a developmental process must be analysed with regard to the delayed effects of middle age and even younger periods of life. Numerous health problems may result from long-term, adverse living conditions – concerning individual lifestyles as well as natural and social environments.

For all these reasons, our old age is in fact premature and pathological. It is important to distinguish between primary changes, induced by normal, physiological processes, and secondary changes, which are caused by illnesses and which can be reversible. Therefore, it is more and more popular in gerontology to analyse ageing from a double perspective:

1. As a non-pathological condition, however, one that is vulnerable to age-related diseases.

2. As a highly functional status with little risk of disease, as opposed to pathological ageing resulting from non age-related diseases (Figure 1).

Such an approach became a stimulant to new directions of research devoted to the criteria and determinants of good ageing. For example, WHO has developed DALY (a disability-adjusted life year) – a measure of life expectancy expressed as the number of years lost due to ill-health, disability or early death and uses diverse aims of interventions addressed to people ageing in a normal or pathological way.

Secondary ageing (pathological ageing) may be accelerated by different factors such as: bad eating habits, ionising radiation, psychological stress, addictions and bad habits, sedentary lifestyle, noise, vibrations, bad microclimate.

The double nature of biological ageing makes diagnostic processes difficult. On the one hand, disease symptoms may be interpreted, also by doctors, as signals of a normal ageing process (underdiagnosis[28]). On the other hand,

---

[27] There are exceptional cases when a doctor can say about a dying person: *She faded away like a normal organism not contaminated by medicine* (this is how the head of a ward of a Warsaw hospital describe the condition of the dying Professor Barbara Skarga, Polish Radio Channel I, 3 September 2009).

[28] According to WHO, in many highly industrialised countries doctors are not aware of about 40–50% of their patients' medical problems, two-third of persons with difficulty walking are not known by family doctors and healthcare system is unaware of 20–50% people with urinary incontinence. See E. Heikkinen, "Health Implications of Population Aging in Europe,"

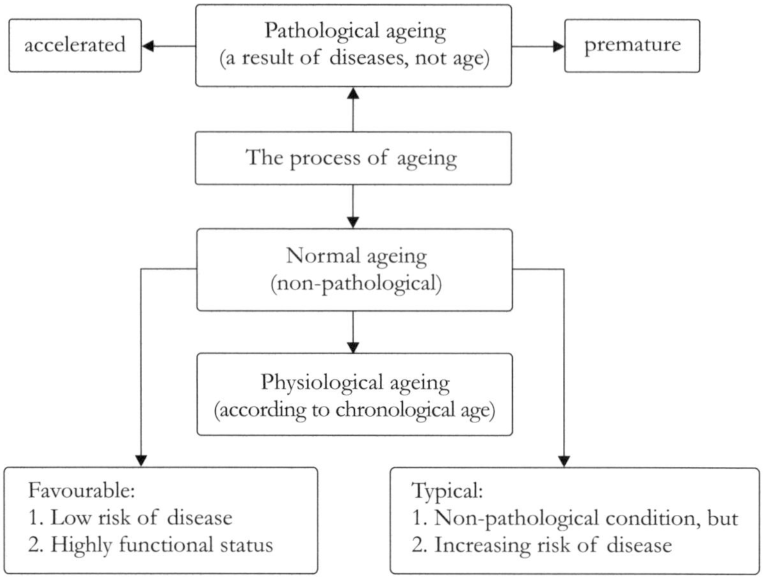

Figure 1. Types of ageing

Source: own elaboration.

it is even worse when some changes in the body are wrongly interpreted by doctors as pathological changes (overdiagnosis).

We should not lose sight of two additional and significant facts related to the health of the elderly which cause pathological conditions and accelerate the process of ageing:

1. Genetically inherited diseases exposed to the influence of environmental factors.
2. The organism of an elderly person is less immune to diseases, thus the body organs and processes are less able to maintain equilibrium.

Therefore, if we assume that ageing is a genetically programmed process and a result of accumulated environmental influences on the organism, the following aspects become important:

1. Biological potential of parents whose genes we inherit.
2. The environment in which we live and grow older.
3. The quality of life and not only its length.

World Health Statistics. The Impact of Demographic Trends on Health, 1987, vol. 40, no. 1, pp. 25, 33; *The World Aging Situation*, United Nations, New York 1991, p. 22 and other.

Although the old age is not a disease, ageing increases the likelihood of illness. The nature of elderly people's health problems is determined by the following factors:[29]

1. More severe effects of acute diseases and slower recovery.
2. Complications in many diseases hinder or prevent reversing the malfunction, and the aim is no longer recovery but simply maintaining the current condition.
3. Frequency and chronicity of diseases, multiple diseases.[30]
4. Changes in body composition and the function of organs – often resulting in organ damage limiting functional independence.
5. Weak response to disease and medical intervention; stress.
6. Disorders caused by malnutrition – bad diet, tooth loss, impaired taste, slowing digestive system as well as financial difficulties and loneliness which discourages from regular preparation of food.
7. Accidents and injuries[31] are the fastest growing cause of deaths and disabilities among the elderly – they result from hearing and vision impairment, slowing of responses, difficulty walking intensified by architectural barriers

---

[29] A comprehensive analysis of the questions related to the health problems of the elderly can be found in R. Chernoff, D. Lipschitz, *Health Promotion...*, op. cit.

[30] Almost two-thirds of chronic diseases requiring treatment afflicts people aged 65 or over: In a number of different European countries, the number of diseases reported by elderly people under medical treatment was 2–3 per person. In England, at least 50.0% of the population aged 60 and over were reported as suffering from at least 3 diseases. In western Germany, an in-depth clinical research revealed 10 ailments for each person aged 75 and over. ("Ageing and Health," *The International Journal of Public Health,* Bulletin of the World Health Organisation, Geneva 26.10.1999; P. Baltes, K. Mayer (eds.), *The Berlin Aging Study: Aging from 70 to 100*, Cambridge University Press, New York 1999; statistical data for Poland reveals that the most common chronic diseases among the elderly are: cardiovascular diseases (more common among women), musculoskeletal disorders (regardless of gender), respiratory diseases (more common among men), diabetes (mostly men), paresis and senility (much more common among women): M. Mossakowska, A. Więcek, P. Błędowski (eds.), *Aspekty medyczne, psychologiczne, socjologiczne i ekonomiczne starzenia się ludzi w Polsce* [Medical, Psychological, Social and Economic Aspects of Ageing in Poland], Termedia Wydawnictwo Medyczne, Poznan 2012; B. Żakowska-Wachelko, *Zarys medycyny geriatrycznej* [An Outline of Geriatric Medicine], Wydawnictwo Lekarskie PZWL, Warsaw 2000; J. Kocemba, "Biologiczne wyznaczniki starości" [Biological Determinants of Ageing], in A. Panek, Z. Szarota (eds.), *Zrozumieć starość* [Understanding Old Age], Test, Cracow 2000.

[31] Almost 90.0% of the fractures suffered by the elderly are caused by falls. Not only are accidents individual health problems, but also a financial problem for the health care system: C. Scanaill, Ch. Garattini, B. Greene, M. McGrath, "Technology Innovation Enabling Falls Risk Assessment in a Community Setting," *Ageing International,* 2011, no. 36, p. 228; R. Kenny, "Mobility and falls," in M. L. Johnson (ed.), *The Cambridge Handbook...*, op. cit.

in the environment, also home environment (bad light, slippery or uneven surfaces, dangerous places unmarked or not clearly marked, etc.).

Substance abuse called an invisible epidemic or late onset addiction (the Austrian gerontologist, Rosenmayr, calls it late onset freedom) is better recognised in the USA than Europe. Alcohol consumption among the elderly (more common among men) is a response to environmental changes, stress or emotional disorders caused by depression, insomnia or somatic problems – alcohol abuse may be also caused by problems related to hospitalisation, moving to a nursing home, and/or financial and family problems. Doctors are often unaware of the problem – their ignorance of elderly patients' history of alcohol abuse hinders diagnosis and the resolution of other medical problems. The seemingly low proportions of alcoholism among the elderly are believed to be caused by high premature mortality among younger alcoholics, unwillingness of the family to reveal the problem, as well as quitting the addiction due to medical reasons or repressive actions of the environment (hospital, nursing home, family, etc.).[32]

Drug addiction – it is common knowledge that the elderly are the main consumers of medication, however, there are more and more research findings revealing that the number of elderly people taking addictive substances is increasing and the number of addicted elderly people is rising as well. What is more, also the number of senior citizens addicted to both alcohol and medications is increasing (this concerns mostly psychotropic drugs taken more and more often by ageing women.[33]

---

[32] According to very careful estimations (data disproportions), alcoholics may constitute 2.0–12.0% of the elderly not living in nursing homes (depending on the amount of alcohol consumed in the general population). This number may increase up to 20.0–25.0% among residents of care and nursing homes. See *Substance Abuse Among Older Adults*, Center for Substance Abuse Treatment, Substance Abuse Among Older Adults, Rockville (MD): *Substance Abuse and Mental Health Services Administration* (US), Treatment Improvement Protocol (TIP) Series, 2008, no. 26; *Substance abuse treatment: Addressing the Specific Needs of Women*, TIP Series – Treatment Improvement Protocols, 2009, no. 12; A. Staab, M. Lyles, *Manual of Geriatric Nursing*, Gleneview, London 1990, p. 547 and next; D. Eyde, J. Rich, *Psychological Distress on Aging. Family Management Mode*, Rockville 1983, p. 143 and next.

[33] For example, a study from 1980s, representative of the German population aged 65–74, revealed that 25.0% of women and 12.0% of men used psychotropic medicines (P. Ellinger--Weber, "Medikamentengebrauch und Medikamentenabhangigkeit im Alter – unter besonderer alterer Frauen," in *Alter und Sucht*, Hamburg 1990, p. 28 and next). Other researchers (Gurland) suggest that 5.0–10.0% of the elderly take sleeping pills and benzodiazepines. Bron's and Lowack's study found that 30.0–40.0% of psychiatric wards patients are double addicted: from alcohol and medicines. See J. Corry, P. Cimbolik, *Drugs. Facts, Alternatives, Decisions*, Belmont, Ca 1985; *Alter und Sucht*, op. cit., p. 18 and next.

An increasing number of suicides as a cause of death of the elderly[34] – suicides of the oldest old are one quarter (women are majority) of all suicides.[35]

The main causes of suicide amongst the elderly are thought to be (in order):

– depression,

– avoidance tendencies (withdrawal),

– mourning (particularly in the first year after a loss – among men, the suicide rate increases four-fold at this time),

– social isolation (widowhood, single living),

– expecting their own death for some specific reason,

– problems with organising and completing actions,

– sense of hopelessness,

– institutionalisation,

– somatic disorders,

– a desire to prevent the family from financial catastrophe which longer treatment and care would cause,

– existential reasons: lack of joy, pleasures, life goals,

– sense of worthlessness of one's life, a lack of respect for oneself,

– organic disorders,

– sleeping disorders (nightmares).

A suicide decision may be made very quickly or may be prolonged (desisting from food, medication, therapy, contacts with doctors; very risky behaviour, deep alcoholism, etc.). There is a lot of evidence proving that suicide attempts by the elderly are related more to the subjective assessment of one's situation and negative expectations about the future than some objective conditions determined by disease, disability, widowhood, retirement or isolation.[36]

In many cases, it is hard to distinguish the manifestations of normal ageing from a pathological condition. The elderly may change their health assessment criteria over time and consider some symptoms as normal signals of ageing

---

[34] In the USA, suicide is one of the 10 main reasons of deaths of the elderly – Polish statistic hides it under a general category: external causes of injuries and poisoning, but suicide rates rise according to age, particularly among aged 65 and over.

[35] In Poland, 28.0% of all suicides are people aged 50–71; 7.0% are 71 and over; for women it is 32.0% and 11.0% respectively. Source author's calculations based on General Headquarters of Police data for 2011.

[36] See R. Butler, M. Lewis, *Aging and Mental Health. Positive Psychosocial and Biomedical Approaches*, London 1986, p. 251 and next; A. Staab, M. Lyles, *Manual of Geriatric Nursing...*, op. cit., p. 138, also: A. Schmidtke, B. Weinacker, "Suizidraten, Suizidmethoden und unklare Todesursachen alter Menschen," *Zeitschrift fur Gerontologie*, 1991, no. 24 (1), pp. 3–11; G. Dankwarth, K. Puschel, "Suizide im Senium," *Zeitschrift fur Gerontologie*, 1991, no. 24 (1), pp. 12–16.

– pain and discomfort tolerance increases, anxiety caused by the symptoms is ignored (*I will die soon anyway*), etc.

Studies conducted for several years have demonstrated that although the criteria of health self-evaluation are relatively unknown, self-evaluation is hardly a worse prognostic than clinical research when it comes to estimating an individual's state of health – particularly as regards the oldest age categories. There is a lot of evidence demonstrating that health and mood self-evaluation among the elderly influences functional abilities more than the prevalence of chronic diseases.[37]

In the 1960s, the first diagnoses of functional abilities appeared, which were based on several measurement methods:

1. Qualities determining the so-called functional age – based on a correlation with chronological age, which allowed for comparisons between individuals.

2. Measuring Activities of Daily Living (ADL) – scale originally developed for the use of rehabilitation and for chronically diseased patients and as one of the important criteria of classifying patients for closed institutions. Constantly improved, the scale is a recognised tool to assist medical diagnosis, very helpful in planning a budget for the care of people with limited abilities.[38]

---

[37] What influences health self-evaluation in different countries are cultural factors (knowledge, health socialisation, experience of playing the patient's role, etc. E.g. Finns from Tampere proved that health self evaluation correlated with the number of diseases, symptoms and functional ability level as well general life satisfaction (E. Heikkinen, "Health Implications of Population Aging in Europe," op. cit., p. 28). Also, Bonn longitudinal research (H. Thomae) demonstrated that persons who evaluated their health higher were more active with optimistic attitude and a weaker sense of loneliness, more interested in what happened around them. Besides, Polish research on a representative sample conducted in 1973 by J. Piotrowski showed that a quarter of elderly people evaluated their health as good for their age while 41% evaluated it as bad (J. Piotrowski, *Miejsce człowieka starego w rodzinie i społeczeństwie* [The position of the elderly within the family and the society], PWN, Warsaw 1974, p. 86); also in 1980–1991 about every fourth retired person evaluated their health condition as good [B. Synak (ed.), *Polska starość* [Polish Old Age], Wydawnictwo Uniwersytetu Gdańskiego, Gdansk 2002]. It is worth noticing that Poles at retirement age living in the USA evaluated their health better than those living in Poland – one-third considered it good (A. Zych, *Człowiek wobec starości. Szkice z gerontologii społecznej* [Facing old age. Outlines of social gerontology], Warsaw 1995, ed. 2: BPS, "Śląsk" Katowice 1999, p. 49 and next). In comparison, in the 1980s in the former Soviet Union, 13.6% of the elderly regarded their health condition good while in the former West Germany the figure was 30.0%. In the USA, 68.9% respondents assessed their health condition as very good or good, while 13.7%, 13.7% and 8.6% respectively saw their health as bad (S. Clemen-Stone, D. Eigisti, S. McGuire, *Comprehensive Family and Community Health Nursing*, McGraw-Hill, St. Louis 1991).

[38] Nowadays, many research centres conduct multidimensional studies about functional abilities – the author of this book has also designed some tools to measure ability levels for

A review of numerous representative studies conducted in many countries and concerning functional abilities allow us to conclude the following:

1. Functional ability decreases with age; nonetheless, almost half of the elderly people living in developed countries do not manifest any limitations in performing ADL.

2. Such abilities as transporting or housework become limited between 70 and 75 year of age,[39] while personal hygiene, meal preparation and self feeding, clothing and managing things outside one's home (shopping, offices, etc.) become limited after 75 year of age. In addition, almost 50% of people aged 85 and over need outside help.

3. The abilities of women, particularly aged 80 and over, are lower than men's – however, some research findings suggest that despite lower ability levels, women much more rarely need outside help.

4. In most countries, older women are less active than men and more prone to a sense of loneliness.

5. Old age is characterised by sensory impairment – European studies show that 50.0–60.0% of the elderly have hearing problems and 30.0 to 50.0% difficulty reading.

6. With age, motor responses slow down and the ability to control one's centre of gravity decreases.

7. Among the oldest old, most body responses and task performing significantly slow down; mobility decreases, body coordination deteriorates.

8. Between 30.0 to 50.0% of people aged 85–89 have difficulties with chewing.[40]

Considering the most effective solutions in geriatric care, one should not ignore economic barriers and, generally, limited resources[41] posing numerous

---

different age categories: Z. Woźniak, *Niepełnosprawność i niepełnosprawni w polityce społecznej. Społeczny kontekst medycznego problemu* [Disability and Disabled in Social Policy. Social Context of a Medical Problem], Wydawnictwo Szkoły Wyższej Psychologii Społecznej "Academica," Warsaw 2008; idem, *Najstarsi z poznańskich seniorów. Jesień życia w perspektywie gerontologicznej* [The Oldest of Poznan Senior Citizens. The Autumn of Life from Gerontological Perspective], Wydawnictwo Miejskie, Poznan 1997.

[39] Ageing and chronic diseases related to this process manifest most intensively in particular organs and body systems after 75 years of age – accompanied by rapid decline of numerous life functions (particularly among women).

[40] E. Heikkinen, "Health Implications of Population Aging in Europe," op. cit., p. 29 and next; Th. Abelin, D. Schlettwein-Gsell, "Behinderungen und Bedurfnisse Betagter," *Schweizerische Medizinische Wochenschrift*, 1986, no. 116, pp. 1524–1542.

[41] A resource is anything that serves to achieve goals, solve problems, eliminate threats and allows people to realise their life tasks, aspirations or values. Resources may be very tangible (money, housing, food, home and institutional care, transport, clothing) or immaterial (knowledge, courage, ingenuity, initiative, encouragement, humanism, love, etc.). Therefore,

moral dilemmas to people professionally obliged to fulfil the needs of the oldest citizens.

In many countries with experience in designing ageing programmes, the following factors determining effective action have been noticed:

1. Around the world, economists (mostly accountants) are the leading opponents of expanding the range and forms of geriatric care (particularly widening the range of preventive actions) – they argue that elderly people:

– occupy almost 40.0% of hospital beds (particularly emergency departments – therefore the phenomenon is sometimes called a geriatrisation of emergency services),

– consume a quarter of all prescribed medication,

– use up almost 30.0% of the state health budget: medical treatment of a person at retirement age is three times more expensive than younger patients.[42]

2. Therefore, people responsible for public finances ask whether it is reasonable to spend such large sums with no certainty about the effects.

3. Medical technology development and narrow specialisations resulted in the erosion of ethics and dehumanising of the nursing function of health services – the problem is even deepened as a result of the therapeutic nihilism[43] manifested in the behaviour of some members of the medical staff.

4. Low status of the jobs related to housework, help and care of the elderly or the disabled (low salaries, no prospects, difficult and unattractive work, and risk of job burnout) results in the shortage of trained staff and negative selection to such jobs. In consequence, additional training costs are necessary and there is a growing risk of abuse against caretakers.

5. Sense of hopelessness among the professionals facing openly political and purely economic motivations behind the allocation of means and resources to the care of the elderly.[44]

In the search for non-expensive methods of locating different forms of help and care as close to their potential recipients as possible, huge reserves have been noticed in the current geriatric care system, that is, 24-hour nursing

---

resources include individuals with their personal qualities and possessions, their closest social environment (family, friends, and neighbours), as well formal and informal groups, organisations, associations and institutions.

[42] *Aging in OECD Countries. A Critical Policy Challenge*, OECD Publishing, Paris 1996.

[43] Manifested in a simple formula: *Does it hurt? Are you unwell? And how old are you? Seventy? Oh, then it must hurt!*

[44] Time will verify the viewpoint of the opponents to environmental care; however, gerontology studies may prove very helpful in terms of everyday practice – not only do they provide polemic arguments, but also a base for effective actions such as data about the ability levels and about meeting needs of the elderly who live on their own.

homes. A few years ago, Scandinavian experts calculated that the cost of one place in such a facility equals 2 hours of nursing service and 3 hours of related services at a person's home, 365 days a year.[45]

The above-mentioned findings of gerontology research demonstrate that despite common chronic conditions of the elderly, most senior citizens feel well – even the representatives of oldest age category. Thus, we may conclude that there are numerous normally-functioning elderly people who, however, cannot be regarded as healthy from a medical point of view[46] – thus, if we consider correct resource location and the effectiveness of ageing programmes, it is important to distinguish between different categories of senior citizens and estimate the size of these groups, including:

1. Fit and independent elderly people who only need periodical medical check-ups.
2. Fit and independent elderly people whose ailments, however, demand ambulatory care.
3. Chronically ill, disabled elderly people who need permanent treatment.
4. Chronically ill elderly people with permanent impairments who need permanent, specialist care (medical nursing), and in case of disease exacerbation, hospitalisation (increased risk of institutionalisation).

What has been discussed in this chapter inclines to conclude that human life expectancy is not entirely determined by biological processes, particularly in the final stages of life. Investing in maintaining somatic health in late old age becomes less important, while an increasingly significant role in creating well-being is played by social and cultural factors. What matters in the ageing process is not only the length, but also quality of life (which Baltes called *co-evolution*).

Ageing and death are inevitable. It seems that while denying these two unavoidable facts, people deliberate deep inside how long and burdensome their old age will be and whether there is any way to make this last stage dignified and satisfactory. Therefore, it is very important to monitor the state of health and abilities of senior citizens, taking into account their social position as well as infrastructural resources and the organisation of their social life.

[45] The total monthly cost of the maintenance of one resident in a nursing home in Poland oscillates between 2200 and 3000 PLN depending on the amount of money spent on modernising the institution and expanding its functions.

[46] Between 70.0 and 80.0% of elderly people, despite some difficulties, are able to live on their own and only 2.0–3.0% are bedridden because of chronic disease or disability. The remaining 17.0–28.0% need some form of support. See R. Chernoff, D. Lipschitz, *Health Promotion...*, op. cit.; Z. Woźniak, *Niepełnosprawność i niepełnosprawni...* [Disability and Disabled...], op. cit.; M. Mossakowska, A. Więcek, P. Błędowski (eds.), *Aspekty medyczne, psychologiczne...* [Medical, Psychological...], op. cit.

3. Psychosocial determinants of the social status of the elderly

Not years but strains make you look old
(Polish proverb)

Although the primary impulses which initiate the process of ageing are certainly biological – these first stimuli activate the senior wheel of fortune – the final effects of ageing and the social status[47] of the elderly result from numerous non-biological processes of a psychosocial, cultural and economic nature (Figure 2).

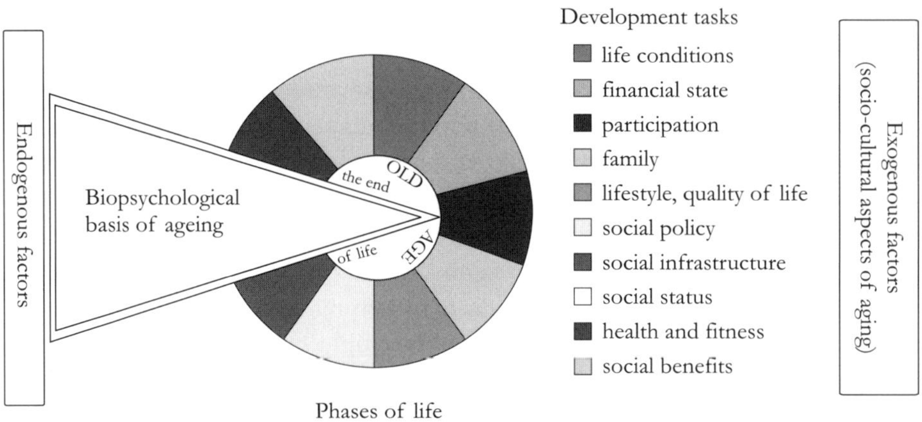

Figure 2. The senior wheel of fortune

Source: own elaboration.

From a sociological perspective, ageing is a series of changes triggered by responses to social environment. Social age reflects the social situation of the elderly; therefore it is usually calculated through analysis of the social roles performed by an individual, which change their character, scope and hierarchy in different life phases, changing also the social position of the elderly person (Table 1).

In the pre-industrial society, the status of the eldest generations was dependent on the position and role of parents in a family:

[47] Sociologists define social status as prestige attached to one's position in society. It is a synthesis of social evaluations of an individual in a given group.

– their powerful position gave control over the ascending generation and conditioning the future of the offspring,

– their carefully guarded monopoly on knowledge and skills (experience and so-called life wisdom),

– support of tradition, grounded in religious rules,

– the power of kinship and obligations within the extended family, the level of dependence and the range of mutual help among the community members.

Since the end of 18th century, the increase in the number of elderly has been accompanied by a decrease in their social position, both within their family and global society. What caused the decline of the social status of the elderly were the processes underlying social modernisation (industrialisation, urbanisation, dissemination of education, developments in the field of medicine, and wider access to health care).[48]

As a result of the lower social position of the oldest generation, the contemporary elderly are believed to be a generation which is moved from one status to another. Senior citizens are stereotypically perceived as inflexible, unproductive, sickly and inefficient, thus burdensome and costly; being old is identified with mental conservatism, inflexibility in social interactions, loneliness, isolation, the negligence of their closest family members, the end of meaningful activities and withdrawal from almost all social roles. According to a popular stereotype, old age is the exact opposite of growth and development; the complete antithesis of health, independence, vitality and vigour and the reverse of the values created by the mass culture, such as youth, consumerism, hedonism, moral freedom and relativism. Stereotypes focusing on the manifestations of pathólogies related to ageing hinder access to information about normal ageing processes. Not counting occasional, propagandist and instrumental instances of drawing public attention to the problem of ageing (deficiencies, dramas, shortages, abuses), there are hardly any political or media actions which would help objectify the position of the elderly, or particularly expose the positive aspects of ageing and thus present the problem of the "third age" as universal for the whole human population. This question becomes even more important if one considers that ageing is partly dependent on what we believe is important for a person in the last phases of their life.[49]

[48] The concept based on a repeatedly-modified theory of modernisation by D. Cowgill, "Aging and Modernization: A Revision on the Theory," in J. F. Gubrium (ed.), *Late Life. Communities and Environmental Policy*, Thomas, Springfield, Ill 1974, pp. 123–146; idem, *Ageing Around the World*, Wadsworth, Belmont, Ca 1986.

[49] What may also be stereotypical are some generalisations of gerontology theories and concepts, grounded in a specific period of development of a specific society and narrowed to one cultural area.

Table 1. Key changes of social position of an ageing individual and corresponding supporting action

50–64 years	65–74 years	75–84 years	85 or over
– gradual restriction of the time spent with friends – restriction/loss of interactions with people from younger age categories – children leaving home – the empty nest syndrome – loss of the role of a carer and an educator of one's child – restriction/loss of interactions with children's friends – reduced role of an active neighbour – flat is too big but the costs are bearable	– gradual loss of roles providing a sense of identity including the professional role (the retirement guillotine – mandatory retirement, regulated by law) – weakening/loss of the relations with workplace and social interactions with colleagues – necessity to adjust to lowered income after retiring – risk of widowhood (particularly among women) – deaths of peers – health disorders which may turn into chronic conditions	– health deterioration – gradual loss of vitality – weakening/loss of everyday skills – increasing difficulties with personal care, personal hygiene, performing harder household tasks, repairs, etc. – decrease in mobility – more peer deaths – no strong bonds with the local community – financial and technical problems related to payment of accommodation costs (particularly the costs of houses)	– severe health damage (accumulation of physiological effects of ageing and diseases) – difficulties in accessing the health care system – disorders/loss of space orientation – severe financial problems (treatment, care and convalescence costs) – restriction/loss of interactions within the neighbourhood – loss of people providing support (risk of social isolation) – increasing dependence on the help of other people, organise actions and institutions in everyday activities

– first serious symptoms of health disorders (effects of the lifestyle in middle age)	– difficulties in managing accommodation costs	– necessity/inclination to look for domestic help – insufficient knowledge of the social support resources – risk of losing independence and self-reliance	– likelihood of sharing home with family – increased risk of moving into a nursing home (particularly among women)

ROLE REORIENTATION

fields: recreation, education, employment, opportunity of voluntary work, transformation of social roles within family, neighbours and friendship circles

SOCIAL SUPPORT POTENTIAL

social security programmes: pension systems, social welfare, healthcare, rent supplement, reduced transport fees, lower telecommunication prices, etc.; third sector resources

INTERVENTION OF INFORMAL CIRCLES

maximising independence: services within intergenerational/neighbour circles

SUPPORTIVE ACTIONS FOR INDIVIDUALS

institutional infrastructure of social welfare, healthcare, volunteer workers)

Source: own elaboration.

Stereotypes about ageing can produce intergenerational barriers, leading to the limitation or avoidance of contact with the elderly and generating negative attitudes towards both senior citizens and their advocates.[50] What is worse, the elderly population is quite often uncritically perceived as a homogenous category, as if after reaching some magic age, former diversity and cherished individual features disappear and age makes everybody alike.

All in all, the social sense of being old is undoubtedly a product of social expectations (norms, patterns, values and attitudes) and the organisation of a community or global society which defines the rules and methods of meeting the needs of senior citizens and their access to the mainstream of social life and resources. In this way, society defines the rules of social participation (discrimination-equality) and sets out conditions determining the position and social status of this age category (social position and prestige). For this reason, the principle behind the choice of the potential purpose of action and/or the purpose of any social policy programme is the estimation of needs of a given social category (e.g. the elderly). The needs result from a dysfunction, embedded in individuals or their environment, and related to the operation of some system (environmental, cultural, normative or organisational).[51]

According to sociological and psychological research, the more people are alike in age, social status and participation in social life, the less varied the range of their needs. However, this fact does not entail the elimination of individual aspects in the process of expressing and satisfying needs. Therefore, the needs of the elderly cannot be analysed without considering the needs of people representing other age categories and without the role of the society as a whole. Over 50 years ago, a group of experts under the guidance of C. Tibbitts[52] determined a list of needs of the elderly which would be difficult to undermine. It included the need to perform socially meaningful actions, to be acknowledged as a part of community/society and to perform certain roles, to spend an increased volume of time in a satisfactory way; to have a normal social life; to be acknowledged as a human being; to have opportunities and possibilities for self-expression

---

[50] In extreme cases, it may lead to generating "gerontophobia and ageism" (a set of beliefs and attitudes based on stereotypes and prejudice about ageing and attributing competences and needs to people depending on their age.

[51] Needs may be classified into two categories: satisfied needs, which are manifested by symbols of satisfaction and expressed needs, and are impossible to satisfy at a given moment and remain in the aspiration sphere. There are more and more secondary needs in the everyday life which have all the features of primary needs. A comprehensive review of the contemporary theories and methods of needs can be found in A. Lisowski, *Badanie potrzeb społecznych* [Studying Social Needs], Warsaw 1996.

[52] C. Tibbitts (ed.), *Handbook of Social Gerontology. Societal Apects of Aging*, University of Chicago, Chicago 1960. So far, Tibbitt's list has not been questioned or corrected.

and a sense of achievement; to be provided with proper mental stimulation; to access to healthcare and health promotion; to have a regular daily routine, be in touch with family and experience spiritual satisfaction.

The above-mentioned needs list could be assigned to representatives of any age category. However, the elderly are characterised by an increased level of dissatisfaction when their needs are not met and the increased influence of economic and socio-cultural conditions on this process. In the older age, a need for financial security, a sense of safety and emotional support are gaining more importance. Their expression does not necessarily receive a proper response from the community and primary groups, as it usually competes with the needs of younger generations. Apart from socially justified material needs, the satisfaction of which is necessary for an elderly person to function properly, it is also essential to meet psychosocial needs.

The needs of the oldest generation, like the needs of other age categories, are as varied as its representatives – their biographies, personalities and the pace of ageing. The oldest citizens do not have very many needs or expectations from their environment – they lower with age and deteriorating health and abilities. Limiting secondary needs with age may actually make the senior citizens' life easier, as they can concentrate their focus and attention on what is essential, on the most important needs. The process of minimising needs with age is also affected by early socialisation, during which one learns that the old age is not a period that entitles one to have demands. Furthermore, the private character of family life and idealising of the integrity of the family system became a barrier to the critical evaluation of the level of care provided to the oldest generation in a family, and made senior citizens look for support outside their family circles.

Biological, psychological and social aspects of ageing are not always synchronised, which poses another adaptability challenge. Elderly people attempt to sustain a balance between their human needs and external expectations (*nuisances*) and their possibilities. In other words: successful adjustment to ageing depends on the ability to restore balance between cognitive and motivational structures (H. Thomae). Weakened social bonds result in changes in the lifestyle of an elderly person – with age, they more and more often concentrate on personal issues, particularly their health. Thus, an important question is to what extent the world surrounding an elderly person is willing to accept the limits of ageing people's adaptability. If the ability of an elderly person to adapt in their social world is limited, the senior citizen is liable to social exclusion. According to H. Thomae's findings,[53] elderly people adopt a strategy of

[53] H. Thomae (ed.), *Patterns of Aging. Findings from the Bonn Longitudinal Study of Aging*, Basel 1976, pp. 157–160.

perceptive restructuring of social position to deal with problems that are impossible to solve by making changes in social reality (there is no other way, it is just the way it is). This restructuring may take the form of identification with the achievements and goals of children and grandchildren, positive interpretation (*I am in a better position than X or Y*), revision of expectations (*You can win or achieve things as long as you're young. Once you're old, learn to enjoy things*), self-restriction related to the ability to delay gratification and accepting the reality "as it is" (could be worse – who knows whether it could be better). When the surroundings are not willing to accept an elderly person or help him/her adapt, he or she is inclined to take up the behaviour stereotypically attached to the elderly, which could even be considered pathological (e.g. aggression, alcoholism, homelessness, violence).

One of the processes accompanying ageing and the adaptation strategies and patterns related to it are characteristic changes in interpersonal relations. Decreased vitality causes the necessity of re-evaluating social bonds. Usually, only the most significant are kept, while for people who used to have most of their friends at their workplace, retirement often means the sudden end of their social life. With age, it is quality and not quantity that matters when it comes to interactions and relations with others. While active and sociable people will do the best they can to maintain existing ties, even if with less intensity or in other forms (letters, phone calls, internet), people who prefer family life in the older age may reduce their social life outside the family circle, rarely attempt to make new friends and their previous ties may weaken. This category of senior citizens will often live outside the mainstream social events which can accelerate and hasten the ageing process.[54]

The older people become, the more often "the world" comes to them while they less often go out "to the world." Thus, new activities are rarely taken by senior citizens. Instead, we observe:

– relative stability and little variability in behaviour leading to ultimate durability,

– continuing or (sometimes) extending interests and activities developed in earlier life phases,

– after the initial phase of increased engagement in performing social roles in the first years of retirement (particularly family roles), late old age brings the phase of deliberate resignation from non-familial forms of activities,

– after entering the last phase of life, performing family roles becomes less significant.

---

[54] Maintaining or developing physical and psychosocial activity is usually a necessary condition of successful ageing: H. Thomae (ed.), *Patterns of Aging...*, op. cit., p. 115.

The often-observed lower level and scope of activity of the elderly may be related to the higher level of involvement in performing other (particularly family) roles. Sometimes, the occupying of social roles by the elderly involves compensatory engagement (e.g. widowers/singles may compensate for their lack of family by being an active friend; friendship circles may even replicate family structures) or selective engagement-disengagement (e.g. reducing the role of a worker or colleague in favour of increasing involvement in a family role; temporary disengagement from less satisfactory roles). Relative stability is also reflected in the free time of the elderly. Along with ageing, the variety in form and scope of leisure time activities is less intensive.[55] Chronological age, however, is not the only factor responsible for this variety. What modifies or limits the activity of the elderly is health, fitness, education level, financial resources, sense of control over one's life and adaptability patterns developed in earlier life phases (particularly, middle age).

Summing up, varied forms of activities result in increased morale and life satisfaction[56] and improved chances for attaching new social roles to the rather static position of a retired person.[57] For instance, physical activity fosters good health, fitness and vitality, and thus independence and self-reliability when they are most needed, while interpersonal activity enables the elderly to receive support after losing one or many life roles (substitution). Intellectual activity maintains what has been gained earlier and adapts experiences to the previously developed frame of reference and helps continue varied forms

---

[55] The presented theories related to the forms and scopes of the activity of the elderly have been repeatedly confirmed by many authors; e.g. M. Halicka, E. Kramkowska, "Uczestnictwo ludzi starych w życiu społecznym" [The Participation of the Elderly in Social Life], in J. Hrynkiewicz (ed.), *O sytuacji ludzi starszych* [About the Situation of the Elderly], Rządowa Rada Ludnościowa, GUS, Warsaw 2012, pp. 33–50; F. Bijnen, E. Feskens, C. Caspersen, W. Mosterd, D. Kromhout, "Age, Period, and Cohort Effects on Physical Activity Among Elderly Men During 10 Years of Follow-up: The Zutphen Elderly Study," *Journals of Gerontology Series A: Biological Sciences and Medical Sciences*, 1998, vol. 53 (3), pp. 235–241; H. Thomae (ed.), *Patterns of Aging...*, op. cit.; R. Atchley, A. Barusch, *Social Forces and Aging. Introduction to Social Gerontology*, Wadsworth Publishing Co., Belmont, Ca 2005; P. Wehr, "Die Freizeit der 'Neuen Alten.' Daten Fakten," *Freizeit-Padagogik. Zeitschrift fur Kritische Kulturarbeit, Freizeitpolitik und Tourismusforschung*, 1990, no. 3–4, p. 103 and next; F. Poggeler, "Zwischen Isolation und Emantzipation – Zur Zeitfreizeit im Alter," *Zeitschrift fur Kritische Kulturarbeit, Freizeitpolitik und Tourismusforschung*, 1990, no. 3–4, p. 114 and next.

[56] One should not ignore the large category of inactive elderly people who have sufficient good health and income to feel satisfied.

[57] Experts stress that we should be balanced and cautious when promoting the idea of active ageing and fighting against the separation and isolation of the elderly, and avoid "extreme activism," which can turn out to be beyond the capabilities of some senior citizens. It mostly refers to professional work at retirement, and physical activity.

of intellectual activities as well as taking on new challenges offered by the contemporary world (modern technologies, new institutional solutions, new forms and tools of communication, media). Intellectual capacities (cognitive functions of higher order) do not necessarily decline with age. First of all, the decline starts before entering advanced age and involves all adults (particularly if they gave up intellectual activity). Secondly, the so-called crystallised intelligence (the ability to use skills, knowledge, and experience) continues and even develops with age.[58]

In mature and old age, intellectual activity relies on acquired techniques and adjusts experiences to the previously developed frame of reference. However, in later life stages, cognitive structure may reach the overload condition which requires simplification and selection and can lead to "selective intensity" or "selective attention" as well as "selective response to environmental stimuli." Scholars argue that selective intensity can be wrongly interpreted as withdrawal.

The result of human intelligence, personality[59] and experience is wisdom,[60] often attributed to the elderly and strongly related to their life satisfaction.

In the end, however, every ageing person reaches the final phase of social existence, when, due to the loss of vitality and fitness, the social roles they

---

[58] Psychogerontologists are careful in determining the influence of age on the IQ level, particularly on inductive reasoning, noticing relations and correlations, learning and short memory and reasoning speed. They are rather inclined to acknowledge age as the differentiating factor which influences specific skills (language, education, social/technical knowledge) and non-specific skills (perception speed, precision and carefulness). It is generally agreed that the IQ level of the elderly is lower than the IQ of younger people. However, unless IQ is supported by cognitive systems developed through years of experience, it declines along with age, as do intellectual achievements which are a result of both psyche and culture. Pitt directly states that the process of ageing influences intellect and personality, although it is not certain to what extent it results from the process of brain ageing, and to what extent from the social position of the elderly. B. Pitt, *Psychogeriatrics*, Churchill Livingstone, Edinburgh 1976. See also D. Bromley, *The Psychology of Human Ageing*, Penguin, London 1966.

[59] Old age may be defined as crystallisation/intensification of personality traits developed in earlier phases of socialisation.

[60] Although wisdom requires intellectual (mental) abilities/capabilities, other characteristics of wisdom are more frequently stressed. They are: sensibility, information resources, experience-based pragmatic knowledge and "fundamental pragmatics of life" including judgement and advice about difficult matters of life and knowledge and judgement about the course, variations, conduct, conditions and meaning of life. See P. Baltes, J. Smith, "Toward a Psychology of Wisdom and Its Ontogenesis," in R. Sternberg (ed.), *Wisdom: Its Nature, Origins and Development*, Cambridge University Press, Cambridge 1990, pp. 87–120; U. Lindenberger, P. Baltes, "Intellectual Functioning in Old and Very Old Age: Cross-sectional Results from the Berlin Aging Study," *Psychology and Aging*, 1997, no. 12; R. Sternberg, E. Grigorenko, "Intelligence and Wisdom," in M. L. Johnson (ed.), *The Cambridge Handbook...*, op. cit.

performed become less significant and are replaced with the role of a patient or of a disabled person. Usually, this is a gradual and multistage process, but in case of the institutionalised care of the elderly, the pace of identity degradation is faster and the freedom of choice and independence is more limited.

Ageing is a universal, biological and sociological phenomenon and the care of the elderly and respect for them are one of the few common values of human culture. An important role in the process of stabilising the social position of an elderly person is played by their family, because:

– interactions with family members may be the only kind of social relations the elderly have,

– activities within the family system are the most common form of human activity,

– for an elderly person, being part of a family unit – the elementary social group – is a source of emotional equilibrium and, more generally, mental health. Moreover, it helps the process of adapting to the life changes brought about by retirement,

– relations with family members may have inhibitory/stimulatory effect on activating the elderly by the way the members behave towards each other and towards familial responsibilities.

In patriarchal family models, the elderly used to enjoy greater authority and certainty of care. The 20th century modified the family structure and shook the position of the oldest generation. A nuclear, two-generation family emerged, which, while often staying in close touch with the elderly members living apart, could not guarantee durability or continuity in the event of chronic disease and/or disability. Today, neither the classic, extended (multi-generation) family nor the emancipated, nuclear family is the most functional, considering challenges posed by the globalisation of population ageing.

The most functional family type today is a coalition of small families, partly dependent on each other. This dependence means that members of the nuclear families exchange important services and goods (not necessarily material), with no economic or territorial limitations. Not only does such a model keep all the advantages of a family but also has larger resources, lower tendencies to converge power and more flexibility in satisfying the needs of its members. Family communities are more and more often the result of choice and mutual agreement between generations. These significant changes are not accompanied, however, by any concepts of the social roles which would be adequate for the new types of family membership and intergenerational configurations. Fortunately, the results of gerontological research demonstrate that despite all fears, the process of emancipation of the nuclear family has not come far enough to threaten to put the elderly at risk of complete isolation from the family circle.[61]

Each generation has to deal with the transformation and restructuring of intergenerational relations accompanying the process of ageing (Table 2). Intergenerational solidarity can manifest itself in various ways: emotional and territorial closeness (increasing the chance of interaction), community of ideas, norms and values; mutual exchange of emotions, goods, services and support (instrumental and emotional support); connections between the representatives of different generations and obligations of offspring to their ageing parents and grandparents.

Intergenerational solidarity includes, on the one hand, specific behaviour and the feeling of categorical belonging, and on the other hand, close relationships between generations on a personal and family level and within larger social entities. Various forms of support within the family system have been noted in many countries. They include different forms of intergenerational exchange – services provided to the elderly, financial support, ceremonial and ritual contacts, etc.

Considering changes caused by population ageing, it is important to note that there are more downward (parents-children) than upward (children-parents) family transfers and services – and not necessarily in case of financial threat to day-to-day existence.

According to gerontologists, supporting ageing relatives, although voluntarily initiated, sometimes seem to play an instrumental role in shaping the emotional content of intergenerational relations. It mostly affects some parents, who subtly buy future familial security by providing help to their children.

Contrary to the repeated stereotypes about the widespread abandoning of the elderly by their offspring, family values are rediscovered, as well as the solidarity potential which is an important source of social resources, alleviation for the labour market and the basic structure of satisfying emotional, material and caring needs.[62]

Caring for ageing parents, especially those suffering from chronic or terminal diseases, may require external help. Some caregivers desperately look

---

[61] Demonstrated by research: M. Silverstein, V. L. Bengtson, "Intergenerational Solidarity and the Structure of Adult Child-Parent Relationships in American Families," *American Journal of Sociology*, 1997, vol. 103, no. 2, p. 444. M. Silverstein, V. Burholt, V. L. Bengtson, "Parent-Child Relations Among Very Old Parents in Wales and the United States," *Journal of Aging Studies*, 1998, vol. 12, no. 4, pp. 387–409.

[62] *Active Ageing and Solidarity Between Generations. A Statistical Portrait of the European Union 2012,* Eurostat, Publications Office of the European Union, Luxembourg 2011; H. Bartlett, P. Harper, *Intergenerational Relations Research Workshop. Report*, Research Network in Ageing Well, University of Quinsland, Brisbane 2006.

for support which would allow them to rest and have a break in the often round-the-clock duty. Families experience stress particularly due to prolonging the caring phase. It is thus related more to the adaptive skills of a family system than to specific health problems of the oldest generation. Such a situation lowers the level of inter-family relations, becoming one of the main reasons adults pass on the care of their ageing parents to nursing homes (we have to do something about dad, mum can't stay there/at her place in such conditions, etc.).

Therefore, we can say that the things that lower the level and scope of intergenerational relations are not specific health problems and/or disabilities of the elderly but rather adaptive capacities (abilities) of the family system dealing with changes in functioning of ageing parents. Families lack full knowledge concerning proper care of the oldest generation (tradition, following patterns); carers face uncertainty as to whether they satisfy the needs of the eldest family members (particularly disabled). The elderly, on the other hand, lack certainty over what they can expect (require) of their offspring and relatives. They also lack the ability and readiness to accept care when it is needed.

It is hard to determine what changes in social position and function of the elderly will be brought about by the ageing baby boomers generation.[63] What makes it different from previous generations of the elderly is lower fertility, better education, better health awareness (but worse health in the case of the first phase of the demographic boom), considerable economic stratification which poses a risk of a larger increase in retired people with low socio-economic status than in pension schemes, and prognosis would suggest considerable geographic (journeys) and social (migrations) mobility, lifestyle expectations exceeding pension level, preferring to live at one's home, more individual use of social resources and expecting or even demanding a high level of public services and benefits (objections to segregating benefits/services), and – more than anything else – claiming participation in decision making and control over authorities and public expenses.[64]

Further prolonging of human life will be a scant reward if longevity is not accompanied by an improvement in the quality of life, understood as

[63] Top positions in politics, economy and media are taken by 50-year-olds, who, while entering the retirement age, are still interested in maintaining their positions and power. Thus, it is easier today to modify the way we think about ageing and old age (fashion, advertisement, consumption, position in social structure) due to pure categorical selfishness. As a result, the position of the elderly as consumers and labour market resources will be strengthened (silver economy).

[64] More on this subject: Winters (2005), Quine (2006), Quine and Carter (2006), after H. Bartlett, *Ageing Well and Maintaining Independence into the Future*, Australasian Centre of Aging, University of Queensland, Brisbane 2007, pp. 3–4.

Table 2. Advantages and risks of intergenerational relations

Benefits of intergenerational relations	
For senior citizens	For young people
– reduction in the likelihood of depression – strengthening of the general immune system – provision of a sense of purpose and meaning of life – building the sense of being needed – invigoration and energising of older adults (transfer of knowledge) – satisfaction of the social needs of older people without families and/or grandchildren available to them – frequent and varied transfers in both directions, (children to parents and parents to children) reduce fears – what today may seem a demographic challenge, tomorrow can transform into new opportunities in many spheres (today's needs: tomorrow's possibilities)	– help to alleviate/reduce fears of ageing – help young people understand the nature and manifestations of ageing and later accept their own ageing – fill a void for children who do not have grandparents available to them – young generations learn new skills, gain new knowledge and the so-called "wisdom of life" – co-responsibility for others is strengthened; not only as a norm of rational exchange but also as a civic virtue. – strengthening of social and emotional intelligence – a chance to build altruistic attitudes – future intergenerational relations will increasingly depend on the policy dedicated to young people, families and the oldest generation

Barriers to intergenerational relations	
Social	Developmental
– domination of small families – increasing number of one person households of senior citizens, particularly women – individualisation and changes in the structure and functions of families – grandchildren do not know their grandparents very well despite longer lives of the latter – particularly when the intergenerational contacts are not very frequent (large cultural and status differences, geographical distance) – apotheosis of youth and media images of old age reinforce the negative stereotype of the old age as something to fear – family transfers may increase social inequalities – women have to choose between professional career and care of the dependent members of the family – financial matters can cause conflicts between family members	– if children don't interact with older adults, they will have difficulty understanding them – children's negative perceptions about the elderly – increase as they grow older, so developing positive relationships at an early age helps reduce negative perceptions – relating to older adults can be particularly challenging for adolescents – adolescents tend to be focused on the present, and think mainly about themselves, so they may be less interested in learning about older adults – adolescents will need guidance and encouragement to help them relate to older adults and understand the implications of aging.

Source: based on L. Spence, H. Radunovich, *Developing Intergenerational Relationships*, University of Florida, Gainesville 2010; M. Kalmijn, *Theories About Intergenerational Solidarity*, Department of Social Cultural Sciences. Tilburg University, Tilburg 2005; A. Hatton-Yeo, T. Ohsako, *Intergenerational Programmes: Public Policy and Research Implications an International Perspective*, The UNESCO Institute for Education, The Beth Johnson Foundation, Hamburg 2000.

a personal balance of positive and negative features, social statuses, situations, states and events characterising a person's life and including experience related to biological, psychological, interpersonal, social and economic spheres.

Quality of life is the lability of an elderly person to be independent and autonomous.[65] What maximises it is an increased knowledge of alternative options, various possible attitudes and behaviour, as well as the awareness of barriers and limitations in these spheres. Quality of life also means reaping benefits and having satisfaction with an efficient institutional system, an unbroken sense of general and – in particular – social security: good housing conditions, a good social environment, access to health care, recreation and social support resources.

Although there are no particular differences between studying the quality of life of senior citizens and other social categories (Table 3), research results demonstrate that the key roles in shaping QOL are played by physical health; sufficient and steady income allowing one to meet one's needs; living space adequate to one's needs, sociability, friends and social life; happy family life; functional health and fitness, capability for self-service and self-help, experiencing love, attachment and care of offspring.

The analysis of social position and prestige of the elderly indicates that in case of senior citizens, ascribed status (assigned by society/group on the basis of characteristics not acquired by a person according to one's merit) is more important than achieved status (assigned by society/group on the basis of characteristics acquired by a person according to one's merit; for instance, education, earnings, family situation, etc.). The reason for this phenomenon is the unique aspect of the position of elderly, that is, their asymmetric dependence[66] on younger generations, which increases with time and becomes more and more permanent. Dependence is a particular form of physical vulnerability or helplessness concerning social relations with other people and/or

---

[65] Independence and autonomy are values and behavioural patterns which are most favourable to individuals and their life choices. These terms, however, are not identical – independence is an ability to perform roles, functions and tasks according to the requirements of everyday life, while autonomy means individual freedom in being guided by one's own, personal rules and pursuing desires and ideals. It means that social partners (e.g. carers and support providers) need to respect personal choices of the elderly even if they are conflicting with their own views. See *Active Ageing. A Policy Framework*, A Contribution of the World Health Organization to the Second United Nations World Assembly on Aging, Madrid, April 2002; *Preparing for the 21st Century. Focusing on Quality in a Changing Health Care System*, http://www.nas.edu/21/health.html [accessed: 23.09.2009].

[66] Dependence in its psychosocial aspect is a complex manoeuvre of an individual who perceives him or herself as weak in relations with other individuals perceived as strong and able to provide help (Goldfarb).

institutions which increases together with the decline of physical and mental powers. Everyone is somehow dependant but the form and extent of dependence changes over the life course: from complete dependence of a little baby to a relative independence of an adult and stronger dependence of an elderly person. The fear of losing life independence may cause an increasing sense of insecurity in many life spheres, starting a vicious circle of finding new – real or imaginary – barriers in normal, everyday functioning. It particularly regards older people without life capitals, allowing them to reach sufficient level of education, broad social contacts and good family relations, who meet additional barriers in their attempts to adjust to changing social and economic conditions. These obstacles make it difficult for the elderly to maintain the social position they once had. In consequence, they live in worse economic conditions (material poverty) and are more often among those touched by the effects of unfavourable social and economic processes. Moreover, they usually lack access to suitable institutions which help gain, develop and increase life capital, as a result of the underdevelopement of these institutions caused by short supply of public resources, low efficiency, etc.

To conclude, one of the key priorities of future gerontologist programmes and the only way to weaken the negative effect of the minority position of the elderly is to counteract the decline of their social status and, at the same time, to use the potential of senior citizens and their contribution into the culture of community.

4. Factors conducive to marginalisation and social isolation of senior citizens

> Perhaps individuals are as old as they feel they are – but the way they feel is significantly determined by the social expectations and social positions they have.
>
> Leonard Breen

Among the key factors which may make social functioning of senior citizens more difficult are stereotypes about ageing – the tendency to attribute behaviour characteristics of a minority to this social category. The relationship between the minority and the majority may take the form of:

– conflict (contradictory interests and goals, discrimination, hostility, isolation),

– assimilation (pressure from the majority or minority desires to assimilate), or

– integration (cooperation, lack of prejudice, tolerance towards things that are different).

Elderly people meet a lot of the definitional criteria for a minority group as they are a part of population distinguished by some characteristics which

Table 3. Key domains of the quality of life – universal and categorial profiles

Existence	Existential aspect	
	Universal profile	Particularly important for senior citizens
Physical aspect *body and health*	somatic health personal hygiene nutrition physical exercise clothing general physical appearance	ability to move by oneself at home and outside self-service abilities proper, balanced diet
Mental aspect *thoughts and feelings*	mental health adaptability love life	ability to think logically dealing with everyday tasks and problems
Spiritual aspect *ideas and values*	shared values personal behaviour standards views and beliefs	sense of life achievement participation in spiritual and religious life
Social aspect *place in the social world*	social status social rules	chance for re-adaptation and attributing new roles to the social position of an elderly person
Belonging	Relations with social environment	
physical aspect *place to live, workplace*	home workplace/school neighbourhood community	private space home equipped with senior-friendly amenities
social aspect *surrounding people*	significant others family friends colleagues neighbourhood and community	family circle capable of providing help realistic chance of receiving neighbourly help
to a community *availability of community resources*	adequate earnings services and healthcare employment educational programmes recreational programmes events and actions on the community level	availability of health care and ability to use it using service points and shops in the neighbourhood (nearby)

Self satisfaction	Achieving personal goals, Satisfying wants and aspirations	
The practice of everyday life *activity* *everyday routine*	housework paid work education activity voluntary activity noticing and understanding health and welfare needs	care for the life partner support for other adults capacity for doing housework welfare activity
Spare time *enjoyment*	promoting activity and relaxation stress-reducing activities	hobby, interests participation in organised forms of recreation
Developmental aspect *activities facilitating dealing with life and changes*	promoting maintaining/ development of knowledge and skills adaptability to changes	improving/maintaining intellectual capacity and memory adjustment to life changes

Source: modified proposals elaborated by: *Quality of Life Research Unit*, University of Toronto; *Quality of Life*, http://www.utoronto.ca/qol/concepts.htm; M. Hodgins, V. McKenna, M. D'Eath, *Enhancing the Quality of life of Older People in Poverty (with particular reference to those living alone)*, Health Promotion Research Centre – NUI Galway: Combat Poverty Agency Research Seminar: 30 January 2007, p. 3, http://www.combatpoverty.ie/research/seminars/presentations/2007-01-30_MargaretHodginsEtAl.pdf [accessed: 15.06.2011].

can be negatively evaluated – such as physical appearance, behavioural patterns, lifestyle, social status and disproportions regarding access to wealth, power, prestige, privileges and rights.[67]

Stereotyping ageing and old age may form a basis for discrimination,[68] which, leading from words to violence, may create such phenomena as distancing (e.g. labelling, avoiding/limiting interpersonal contacts); devaluation (seemingly neutral conditions, criteria or practices that touch upon a particular category/group/individual which cannot be objectively justified); delegitimisation (limitation/deprivation of a citizen's rights, inequality in access to services and benefits and/or some institutions, labour market, etc.); segregation (banning/limiting contacts or close relations with some individu-

[67] This phenomenon was aptly described Simmel, who believed that minority exists as long as it is situated within a real, concrete social structure which determines its distinctive features.

[68] Discrimination is the distinguishing treatment of an individual/social category/group only on the basis of their "otherness," for example, age, gender, religion, race, illness, disability, financial status, sexual orientation, views, etc. – in some cases, it may take form of positive discrimination, which is limiting the rights of the majority in the name of interests of a potentially discriminated minority (e.g. legal protection of the status of people of different sexual orientation).

als or groups, housing discrimination leading to segregation); elimination [exclusion from access to some roles, institutions, social contacts (ostracising); in extreme cases: refusal of medical treatment].

Ageism, negative stereotypes and attitudes towards the elderly and ageing, as well as glorification of youth may turn into a severe form of violence and/or abuse of the elderly or open the way to such offences, or create intergenerational conflicts. Abuse is a way of treating others which causes harm or difficulty: from neglect, mistreatment, mental and physical torment, to an offence (burglary, theft, assault, etc.) or even murder. Such behaviour may also appear in relationships where there is an expectation of trust or care (behaviour of relatives, carers, neighbours and people working for institutions responsible for care of the elderly).

Violence against the elderly can take the form of an action or negligence. In extreme cases, it is aggressive and health-damaging behaviour which can even be a direct cause of death. There are several types of abuse of older adults, including: physical (hitting, restraining, exposure to cold, withholding food, poisoning, pushing, slapping); emotional and/or psychological (constant intimidation and insults, attacks on dignity, blaming, threatening, isolation, cursing and other forms of mental cruelty), financial (illegal and improper use of a person's money, property, or other valuables, financial exploitation, forcing power of attorney, forcing the elderly to make unnecessary financial transfers, forgeries, defalcations); sexual (direct or indirect sexual activity without the older person's consent: exposing, touching, photographing, forcing to watch pornography, forced nudity, rape); negligence (intentional or unintentional but harmful behaviour of formal or informal carers whom the elderly trust, lack of care, not meeting essential needs); symbolic violence (after P. Bourdieu: is the imposition of systems of symbolism and meaning, i.e. culture, upon groups or classes in such a way that they are experienced as legitimate).

It is very difficult to estimate the amount of violence and mistreatment involving the elderly;[69] however, the reports about elderly abuse demonstrate that:

---

[69] It is difficult to estimate the size of the phenomenon (it is the so called dark number), but research results show that the various forms of this phenomenon were noted in different countries ranging from 4.0–6.0% to 25.0% of cases. See *Elder Abuse fFact Sheet*, Administration on Aging and National Center on Elder Abuse, 2009, www.prodevmedia.com/.../elderAbuse-FactSheet [accessed: 1.10.2011]; *A Global Response to Elder Abuse and Neglect: Building Primary Health Care Capacity to Deal with the Problem Worldwide: Main Report*, World Health Organization Ageing and Life Course Family and Community Health. WHO Press, Geneva 2008; E. Krug, L. Dahlberg, J. Mercy, A. Zwi, R. Lozano (eds.), *World Report on Violence and Health*, World Health Organization, Geneva 2002. In Poland, research in this field has been conducted more intensively since the beginning of the 1990s. See M. Halicka, "Elder Abuse and Neglect in

– those who abuse and mistreat the elderly are usually the same people who provide them with care (informal and institutional carers),

– most victims are women and people with physical disabilities,

– the vast majority of the victims live with their oppressors,

– the vast majority of such abuse is committed by family members of the elderly.[70]

There have also been cases of abuse of the elderly living in nursing homes but they occur more rarely[71] in comparison to family homes and the places of residence of the elderly[72] and mostly concern physical constraint of the boarders, depriving them of dignity, the right to choose and decide about everyday matters as well as neglecting caring tasks (e.g. exposing them to the risk of injuries or pressure ulcers).

Stereotypes, discrimination, violence (particularly symbolic violence) are phenomena which, together with the atrophy of important institutions of social control (family, neighbourhood, legal system, educational system, etc.), trigger off the process of marginalisation.[73] As a result, the social status of the marginalised individuals/groups is characterised by:

– deprivation of power and access to decision-making,

– fewer rights – more duties,

Poland," *Journal Elder Abuse and Neglect*, 1995, vol. 6, no. 3–4, pp. 157–169; eadem, "Człowiek stary jako ofiara nadużyć" [Older people as victims of abuse], *Gerontologia Polska*, 1996, vol. 4, pp. XXXVI–XL; M. Halicka, J. Halicki (eds.), *Nadużycia i zaniedbania wobec osób dorosłych. Na przykładzie badań środowiskowych w województwie podlaskim* [Adult Abuse and Neglect. The Example of Field Research in Podlaskie Region], Temida2, Bialystok 2010; E. Rudnicka-Drożek, M. Latalski, "Rodzaje przemocy wobec kobiet po 65. roku życia" [Types of Violence against Women over 65], in J. Kowaleski, P. Szukalski (eds.), *Starość i starzenie się jako doświadczenie jednostek i zbiorowości ludzkich* [Ageing and Old Age as a Personal and Collective Experience], Zakład Demografii UŁ, Lodz 2006, pp. 186–189; B. Tobiasz-Adamczyk (ed.), *Przemoc wobec osób starszych* [Violence Against the Elderly], Wydawnictwo Uniwersytetu Jagiellońskiego, Cracow 2009.

[70] *Elder Abuse Fact Sheet*, op. cit.; *A Global Response to Elder Abuse...*, op. cit.; E. Krug, L. Dahlberg, J. Mercy, A. Zwi, R. Lozano (eds.), *World Report on Violence...*, op. cit.

[71] Studies on the subject are rare because it is difficult to give a reliable diagnosis (personnel concealing facts, threatening boarders, ignoring information given by families of the elderly). The interest of public opinion in violence in eldercare facilities is mainly aroused by the media.

[72] E.g., in 2002 in the USA, 36.0% of the staff of welfare institutions reported to have known at least one case of abuse against the elderly in the previous year, 10.0% committed such an offence, and 40.0% admitted to mental cruelty against the elderly in their care: E. Krug, L. Dahlberg, J. Mercy, A. Zwi, R. Lozano (eds.), *World Report on Violence...*, op. cit.

[73] Marginalisation is a decline in status of a social group or category, caused by the decreasing number of this group, weakening/loss of position/function, presenting views and/or taking actions which are unaccepted by the majority. It may result in inability/impossibility of participation in the mainstream of public life: economy, politics, culture and the life of community.

– smaller range of choice – more limitations,
– fewer economic possibilities – lower economic position,
– fewer educational, recreational and career possibilities,
– higher exposure to the effects of social pressure and crises,
– social and legal discrimination,
– social labelling (stigma) and discriminatory practices.

The majority of scholars refer to the problems of marginalisation and social exclusion together, suggesting the synonymy of the two terms, or their sequencing/overlapping, and thus perceiving exclusion to be a process. However, considering the current state of knowledge, marginalisation (process/source) should be distinguished from social exclusion (condition/result).[74] Social exclusion is a result (resultant) of a series of events/situations occurring in different phases of the dynamic, long-term process of expropriating groups/individuals of various civil roles and brushing them aside from social life – which always leads to marginalisation and exclusion (Figure 3).

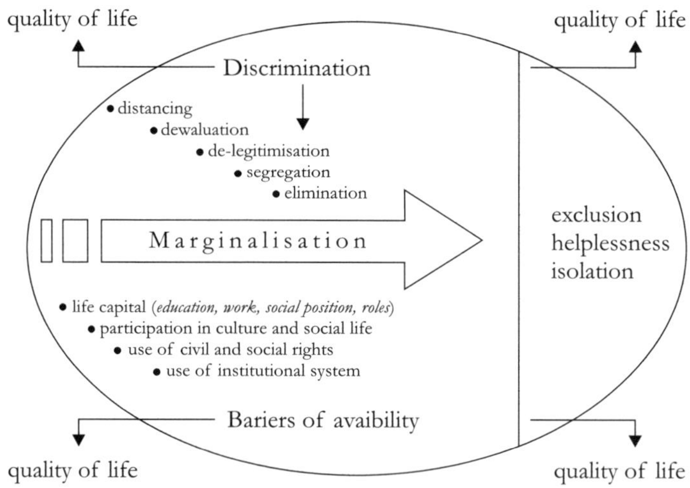

Figure 3. Marginalisation and social exclusion – the essence and the components of the phenomenon

Source: own elaboration.

Exclusion means not deviating from the socially accepted life path. It concerns individuals, families or groups that live in unfavourable economic conditions; have been afflicted by unfavourable social processes resulting from

[74] Similar stand is presented by R. Szarfenberg, *Marginalizacja i wykluczenie społeczne* [Marginalisation and Social Exclusion], Instytut Polityki Społecznej UW, Warsaw 2008, p. 6 and next.

mass and dynamic developmental changes; have not been equipped with life capital; do not have access to institutions which provide life capital; have characteristics (age, gender, disability, addictions, chronic disease, other individual features) which hinder them from accessing common social resources; rarely participate in socially significant spheres of public life; who are deprived of entitlements granted to other individuals or groups in a given society or don't have the opportunity to use their entitlements; are culturally different from their environment in a way which makes it impossible to communicate; became marginalised as a result of subjective judgements of an individual/group; are a subject to the destructive behaviour of others and their indoctrination; who are dominated by groups in the position of political, economic, cultural and media power.

Among a few dozen categories at risk of social exclusion, the elderly are ranked low in the lists created on the basis of international research results[75] and the findings of Polish sociologists (including the author of this publication[76]).

Although the above-mentioned data from Poznan studies undermine the stereotypes of ageing, and suggest that families with many children and the disabled are the categories particularly susceptible to marginalisation and social exclusion, they also demonstrate that phenomena generating the sense of uselessness, lack of control and influence pose a particular threat to shaping and controlling one's life.

Studies on marginalisation and social exclusion devoted only to the elderly are rarely carried out – the exception to the rule being the British research[77]

---

[75] See H. Silver, "Reconceptualizing Social Disadvantage: Three Paradigms of Social Exclusion," in G. Rogers, Ch. Gore, J. B. Figueiredo (eds.), *Social Exclusion: Rhetoric Reality Responses*, International Institute for Labour Studies, International Labour Organization, Geneva 1995, pp. 74–75; R. Steel, *Involving Marginalised and Vulnerable People in Research: A Consultation Document*, Promoting Public Involvement in NHS, Public Health, and Social Care Research, Involve 2004, p. 2; *Narodowa Strategia Integracji Społecznej dla Polski* [National Strategy of Social Integration for Poland], Ministerstwo Pracy i Polityki Społecznej, Zespół Zadaniowy ds. Reintegracji Społecznej, Warsaw 2003.

[76] Z. Woźniak, R. Cichocki, P. Jabkowski, A. Siatkowski, *Jakość życia mieszkańców Poznania zagrożonych marginalizacją i wykluczeniem społecznym (badania wybranych kategorii wysokiego ryzyka wykluczenia). Raport z badań wykonanych na zlecenie Urzędu Miasta Poznania* [Quality of Life of Poznan Citizens at Risk of Marginalisation and Social Exclusion (the study of selected high-risk categories of exclusion). Research report on the studies conducted for the Poznan Municipal Office], Centrum Badania Jakości Życia Uniwersytetu im. Adama Mickiewicza w Poznaniu, Poznan 2009.

[77] Data gathered from the research commissioned by the British government and conducted on a sample of 9901 people aged 50 and more. See M. Barnes, A. Blom, K. Cox, C. Lessof, A. Walker, *The Social Exclusion of Older People: Evidence from the First Wave of the English*

carried out using data gathered during the English Longitudinal Study of Ageing. The quoted studies demonstrate that there are no universal risk factors – they are the same for each dimension of social exclusion (the dimensions are: income deprivation; employment deprivation; health deprivation and disability; education, skills and training deprivation; barriers to housing and services; living environment deprivation; and crime) However, there is also no simple domino effect where exclusion in one area appears to link to exclusion in another and so on.[78] Some dimensions of exclusion increase the risk of exclusion in another area but there are also some which do not involve any other risk factors, or only one of them. According to the British research findings, the factors with the widest influence over the dimensions are: depression, poor health, living alone, membership of non-white ethnic origin, rented accommodation, transport problems/barriers, low income, being female.[79] Age itself is not strongly connected to every dimension. It is a risk factor for the older-old with regard to exclusion from basic services, financial products and material goods. Variables most strongly related to an older person experiencing multiple exclusion turned out to be: advanced age (being 80 or over), living alone, having no children, poor psychophysical health, rented accommodation/social housing, very low income, lack of own means of transport and no access to a telephone.[80]

Exploring risk factors related to marginalisation and exclusion of senior citizens for different dimensions of exclusion allows the presentation of precise correlations:

1. Being older-old is associated with an increased risk of exclusion from basic services, material goods and social relationships. An additional factor increasing the risk of exclusion is living alone. In comparison, the younger-old much more rarely experience exclusion from social relationships, basic services and material goods.

2. Women are generally more likely than men to be excluded from cultural and civic activities, to experience financial exclusion because of a lack of

---

Longitudinal Study of Aging (ELSA). Final Raport, Office of the Deputy Prime Minister (Creating sustainable communities), London 2006; J. Banks, E. Breeze, C. Lessof, J. Nazroo, *Living in the 21st Century: Older People in England – The 2006 English Longitudinal Study of Ageing (Wave 2 and 3)*, Institute for Fiscal Studies, London 2006. The analysis was based on correctly filled questionnaires.

[78] Ibidem.

[79] Around half of older people are not excluded on any of the dimensions but 29.0% are excluded on one dimension, 13% on two dimensions, and 7% on three or more dimensions. M. Barnes, A. Blom, K. Cox, C. Lessof, A. Walker, *The Social Exclusion of Older People...*, op. cit., p. 8.

[80] Ibidem, pp. 8–9.

access to financial tools to manage their own money, and be excluded from basic services and from material goods.

3. There is only one dimension in which a greater percentage of men are excluded than women – social relationships.[81]

4. Living alone is associated with high rates of exclusion on all dimensions while having a life partner, particularly a partner and children, significantly lowers the likelihood of exclusion. Living with children (and no partner) is associated with high rates of exclusion on all dimensions, except for exclusion from material goods. People with no living children are more likely to be excluded from material goods than all older people.

5. There is no strong difference between those that are married for the first time or have a second or later marriage: all are less excluded on almost all dimensions, while individuals who are widowed or divorced are also overrepresented among those who are excluded from social relationships. Also, almost one half of individuals who are single and never married are excluded from social relationships.

6. Older people living in towns are more likely to be excluded from social relationships (particularly neighbourly relations).

7. Those with no living siblings are more likely to be socially excluded due to the fact that the indicator was based on contact with family and friends. However, these people are also more likely to be excluded from basic services.

8. Those who are employed or self-employed are less likely to be excluded on almost all dimensions.

9. People who are retired are more likely to be excluded from social relationships, material goods and basic services but less likely to be excluded from cultural and civic activities.

10. People describing themselves as permanently sick or disabled experience a wide range of types of exclusion: the worse their health and abilities, the more likely they are to be excluded on all dimensions. Those with mobility difficulties are particularly likely to be excluded on all dimensions. Having poor eyesight is associated with higher levels of exclusion on most of the dimensions. Although this is less true of people with difficulties with hearing, they are still significantly more likely to be excluded on the social relationships, civic activities and basic services dimensions.

11. Those who have experienced falls are more likely to experience exclusion in terms of social relationships, access to basic services and material goods.

---

[81] This regularity was also demonstrated by Davidson and Arber in their study from 2004: K. Davidson, S. Arber, "Older Men: Their Health Behaviours and Partnership Status," in A. Walker, C. Hagan Hennessy (eds.), *Growing Older: Quality of Life in Old Age*, McGraw-Hill, Maidenhead 2004, pp. 127–148.

12. Older people with the lowest income are significantly more likely to be excluded on many dimensions, particularly if low income is accompanied by a lack of access to day-to-day money management and a lack of material goods, and when they suffer neighbourhood exclusion and are generally excluded from from social relationships.

13. Those on a state pension or other benefits as their primary source of income are more likely to be excluded across all dimensions than people whose main source of income is a private pension.

14. Nowadays, the important sources of exclusion of the elderly are communications devices and devices that increase mobility. The absence of a telephone, the lack of use of a car or van is a sign of deprivation, which increases the likelihood of exclusion, particularly in rural areas.

15. Physical activity quite effectively protects senior citizens from social exclusion.[82]

In extreme cases, social exclusion may lead to helplessness, that is, a condition of an individual that believes they have lost control over their life (events, situations and issues), usually accompanied by powerlessness. People are helpless when there is no "good choice" and they feel forced to choose a bad, non-promising possibility. In such cases, people have a growing belief that whatever they do, it will not influence in any way what happens to them. Helplessness signals an inability to deal with a given situation and is a manifestation of the belief that one does not have enough knowledge to overcome problems and there are no solutions to help oneself or no ideas for how to get rid of the problem. This attitude leads to giving up actions or taking up an action doomed to failure.[83]

Helplessness occurs regardless of actual powerlessness and is a result of previous life events and experiences (unemployment, addictions, deviations and pathologies, illnesses, disabilities, poverty, etc.), degree of suffered "injuries," previous adjustment patterns, efficiency of actions taken, current methods of adjustment to the situational demands and the availability of support resources in a social environment. Individual or group helplessness may be accompanied or increased by existing law regulations, institutional dysfunctions and global or environmental norms, action and communication patterns (institutional-normative helplessness).

[82] On the basis of: M. Barnes, A. Blom, K. Cox, C. Lessof, A. Walker, *The Social Exclusion of Older People...*, op. cit., pp. 24–32.

[83] The accepted definition of helplessness is close to the theories of M. Seligman, *Learned Optimism: How to Change Your Mind and Your Life*, Knopf Doubleday Publishing Group, New York 2011; S. Kluczyńska, "Aby chciało się chcieć. Teoria wyuczonej bezradności" [Care to Care. The Theory of Learned Helplessness], *Niebieska Linia*, 1999, no. 5.

Marginalisation and social exclusion, helplessness, violence and abuse: they all signal an imbalance in the relationship between the elderly and their environment. In such a case, individuals too easily give up their preserved elements of control over life events (autonomy and independence), which poses a risk of losing bonds with the community, loneliness, pretensions, being "pushed into" a process that leads to learned helplessness,[84] and, finally, to social isolation, meaning a long-lasting stay outside basic social relations and resources, and the inability to communicate with the outside world.

First definitions of isolation were close to the meaning of anomy and alienation. A breakthrough definition proposal was given by P. Townsend (1957), who stressed the necessity of distinguishing between isolation (an objective state of deprivation of social contacts (external factors) and loneliness (a subjective state of the individual, intrapersonal factors related to psychological loss).

It is now generally agreed that social isolation is a process that involves the loss of the sense of personal integrity and/or links to other social resources.[85] Therefore, the people who are particularly susceptible to isolation are ageing citizens of limited activity, who are emotionally inaccessible, with access to a limited stream of information, who used to perform very narrow, specialised roles, who have high expectations of their self image and without strong family or social support.

Isolation poses a threat to socialisation and adjustment processes and decreases the level of independence of the elderly and becomes a barrier in searching for help. Therefore, we should be aware of many concurrent and accumulated factors which, without quick intervention, will decrease the adjustment level and the involvement with social relations which sometimes leads to social isolation. Needless to say, factors fostering isolation do not affect all ageing persons to the same extent.

Review of gerontologist research findings allows us to surmise that social isolation of the elderly is not as much a categorical as an individual phenomenon. It is also overestimated, even with regard to the oldest old and interrelated with earlier life stages.[86] Therefore, far-reaching generalisations

---

[84] Seligman: learned helplessness is the giving-up reaction, the quitting response that follows from the belief that whatever you do, doesn't matter (M. Seligman, *Learned Optimism...*, op. cit., p. 14.) Helplessness is or can be a learned method to survive in a society/group which consists in confirming oneself, one's social environment and various institutions in a belief that as a result of unequal chances, discrimination or other important reasons, one cannot solve one's own problems, therefore one needs support and care from the state or other entities.

[85] Ibidem, pp. 1–2, 15.

[86] Literature review on the subject can be found e.g. in G. Wenger, R. Davies, S. Shahtahmasebi, A. Scott, "Social Isolation and Loneliness in Old Age: Review and Model Refinement,"

Table 4. Key factors contributing to the social isolation of the elderly

Types of "isolators"	Individual level	Environmental level
Biophysical		
Generally among senior citizens	generally, poor health and abilities decrease in vigour and physical endurance failing senses severe mobility limitations being unable to go out without help, intensified by an increasing sense of loneliness organic brain damage – progressing perception atrophy	few geriatrists uneven distribution of medical staff – difficulties in providing appropriate conditions in long-term care too little attention paid by medical staff to specific needs characteristic of the advanced age doctors focusing on acute rather than chronic diseases insufficiently developed network of rehabilitation/revitalisation services stress put on long-term care in specialised eldercare facilities geographic dispersion and uneven distribution of financial products and various forms of help
Also, among		
Women	wider spread of chronic, age-related diseases	few doctors with geriatric qualifications few male doctors recognise significant health problems of ageing women
Villagers	physical disability more often recorded among people geographically isolated	limited access to services and benefits of healthcare system
Alcoholics	addiction makes solving other life problems difficult alcoholism hinders diagnosis and treatment of other diseases multi-factor health threats	risk of pharmaceutical treatment without the knowledge of alcohol abuse or other intoxicants doctors unaware of the alcohol problem of their patients alcoholism interrupts the process of supporting patient
People with chronic mental diseases	higher coefficient of chronic somatic diseases	no specific risk factors

Victims of abuse and violence	deterioration of physical condition increases dependence on others and decreases the chance of self-care	no specific risk factors
People with Alzheimer's disease	degenerative disease, treatment effects little known	needs further studies on causes and new ways of treatment
Psychoemotional		
Generally among senior citizens	mental diseases; chronic or occurring with age changes in developmental tasks internalised social stereotypes of ageing: low self esteem fear of senility and being placed in a eldercare facility sense of losing control over life issues sense of being separated from others negative feelings caused by changes in the perception of the outer world fading sexual desires low morale related to the sense of loneliness	reinforcement of the negative stereotypes of the elderly – particularly generalisations with regard to gender roles and the ability to remain independent in old age limited and unevenly distributed personnel with gerontologist qualifications limited number of elderly treatment and care models – particularly those aimed at maximising potential and functioning of the chronically ill
Also, among		
Women	internalised stereotypes limit the number of alternatives physiological changes related to ageing: source of distress	evaluating women on the basis of appearance
Villagers	conflicts related to the attempts to move senior citizens from a rural to an urban environment philosophy of relying on oneself can make it difficult to gain acceptance in local environment sense of being a burden for family/friends	no specific risk factors
Alcoholics	denying problems with alcohol limited awareness of other life problems alcoholism – symptom of depression and/or loneliness	limited interest among professionals in treating elderly alcoholics limited efficiency of the treatment regime due to age

People with chronic mental diseases	unsuccessful treatment limited mental resources limited interpersonal skills long lasting mental disorders (senile psychosis)	limited development of the models of treatment of chronic mental disorders limited interest among professionals in working with people with chronic mental disorders
Victims of abuse and violence	fear of carers sense of shame at the behaviour of family depression caused by current status	frustration of carers unsolved problems from previous phases of family life long-lasting domestic violence embarrassment of carers who do not want to admit they need help and block the search for other sources of support
people with Alzheimer's disease	awareness of the atrophy of cognitive functions distress caused by "brain death"	insufficient development of forms of treatment aimed at maximising the functioning of patients
Social		
Generally among senior citizens	loss of professional role widowhood (and sense of loneliness) death of relatives and/or friends no children being single – living alone lower education level in comparison to younger people low social status lack of knowledge of social resources being a victim of criminal attack	lack of sufficient forms and means of social support deteriorating environmental living conditions forced displacement – mainly due to modernisation of urban areas different treatment on the grounds of age communication problems and lack of understanding in a family
Also, among		
Women	more likely to be widowed decreased likelihood of re-marriage or finding a new life partner increased likelihood of moving into eldercare facility or using day care centres	low expectations of the sexual role of ageing women negative social reactions towards marriages of older women with younger men

Villagers	decreased acceptance of care from outside the family increased sense of estrangement from the world of closed systems	poor availability of various services and products – institutional networks and infrastructure usually far from potential customers-villagers hospitals and care facilities located far away, discouraging friends and relatives from visiting patients/boarders informal sources of support may be unable to satisfy the needs of people living in rural areas
Alcoholics	withdrawing from social contacts and activities in order to conceal the problem with alcohol inadequate choices of forms and means of overcoming the addiction	lack of social awareness of the alcoholism of the elderly strong social labelling/sanctioning of alcoholics family belittle the problem/feel ashamed or break off contacts
People with chronic mental diseases	collapse of family relations and friendships limited abilities to deal with life problems low education level and limited educational opportunity little chance of employment	uncoordinated provision of services and products shortages in the services and products in a community negative effects of deinstitutionalisation of patients negative attitudes towards people with mental disorders unwanted boarders in eldercare facilities – aimed at "normal" boarders
Victims of abuse and violence	absence of a person willing to take care of the older person misunderstanding of family problems	improper ways of dealing with the problems of the elderly employed by families insufficient resources and improper help in the care of people dependent on others – low supply of care services insufficient legal protection of people threatened by violence
People with Alzheimer's disease	behavioural changes are off-putting for the social environment inability to perform social roles	insufficient support resources for family carers family carers close to exhaustion

Economic		
Generally among senior citizens	Low income or living on the dole Insufficient financial resources limiting/blocking: – access to services and products – paying bills – proper diet – social contacts – recreation and transport	conservative political climate (family and own activity as main resource) social benefits inadequate for needs inequality of pension limiting the income of people getting pension benefits taxing pensions
Also, among		
Women	deep deprivation caused by lack of means of support in older age	discriminatory pension schemes (ignoring the work of housewives and periods of bringing up children) difficulties in finding jobs which would improve living conditions
Villagers	worse access to the pension benefit system or lower pension	economic help from the “centre” rarely directed to rural area dwellers
Alcoholics	costs of buying alcohol further lower the income level	no specific risk factors
People with chronic mental diseases	very limited sources of income and means of support	central funds favour institutionalisation in care facilities and limiting psychiatric treatment
Victims of abuse and violence	senior citizens can neither benefit from resources they have, nor manage them lack of reliable resources	insufficient financial support of family or home care
People with Alzheimer’s disease	consuming all savings for medical help and care	insufficient support of home carers

Source: own elaboration based on: E. Rathbone-McCuan, J. Hashimi, *Isolated Elders. Health and Social Intervention,* An Aspen Publication, London 1982; G. Wenger, R. Davies, S. Shahtahmasebi, A. Scott, “Social Isolation and Loneliness in Old Age: Review and Model Refinement,” *Ageing and Society*, 1996, no. 16, pp. 333–358.

and overestimating the scale of social isolation of the elderly can preserve the myth about the alienation of the elderly in contemporary society.

That is why, later in this book, the reader will find a list of isolators[87] localised on an individual and environmental level. Their accumulation and intensity may weaken social relations and make the ageing person unable to communicate with his/her environment, which will eventually lead to the breaking/vanishing of the connection between the senior citizen and social resources (Table 4).

When analysing the table contents, it is important to remember that "isolators" do not appear in the life of the elderly just once – newer and newer risk factors may emerge and the whole process restarts. Each new "isolator," accumulating risk factors and their growing intensity and influence on a person's life make resources shrink, which gradually decreases the chance of solving the problem of isolation as all resources available are used to survive.

Although marginalisation, exclusion and social isolation are neither common nor the most important of all risks and problems the elderly have to deal with, failure to acknowledge the factors and conditions causing these phenomena may lead to some senior citizens being forced outside social structures, depriving their life of meaning and quality.

Admittedly, gerontology studies have demonstrated that the majority of older people maintain intensive, rewarding social contacts. Nevertheless, it is important to know what, when, in what conditions and with what intensity certain factors may contribute to the isolation of the elderly from the social world unless appropriate steps are taken.

Therefore, when building the fundamentals of gerontology programmes, the phenomena related to marginalisation and exclusion which may lead to helplessness or even, in extreme cases, to social isolation of the elderly, should be analysed in a multidimensional way considering them all as:

– a component shaping a general level of the quality of life of an individual,

– realising subjective and objective aspects of civil rights and participation in public life (normative perspective),

– a signal of barriers in access to resources, social and institutional systems, people and public goods as factors generating threats which lower the conditions of living (infrastructural perspective),

---

Ageing and Society, 1996, no. 16, pp. 334–335. Atchley, on the other hand, claims that reclusive retirement is rare and does not exceed 10.0% of senior population: R. Atchley, A. Barusch, *Social Forces and Aging...*, op. cit.

[87] Isolators are situations or events which may be regarded as a barrier to maintaining personal integrity and social involvement by an elderly person. Ibidem, p. 11

– a set of variables influencing the level and of limitations which lower the capacity for independent functioning (functional perspective).

The effects of social isolation of the elderly are and can be reversible (rehabilitating, re-motivating, reconstructing social relations). Therefore, the state, its institutions and social partners should monitor the social position of the oldest citizens, protect their civil rights, and counteract discrimination and estrangement of the elderly and intergenerational conflicts. Creating the conditions which help the elderly integrate and function properly in public life would be helpful in this process. This must be, however, a general rule and not a special form of legal protection of one social category.

Chapter II

Social consequences of population ageing. Possible scenarios

Introduction

> Mom, I don't want to see what's already gone, I want to see what's going to happen.
>
> (A girl occupying a rearward-facing seat on the bus)

Without doubt, the world is facing unprecedented revolution due to the fast pace of ageing in developing countries and persistently high percentage of the elderly in developed countries. The globalisation of population ageing heralds serious, unfavourable changes for:

1. The state – e.g. significant increase in pension and healthcare costs; widening gap between pension contributions and payments which may result in destabilisation of budget and tax increases; strong pressure to reduce pension rights; reduction of expenditures on national defence, infrastructure, education, healthcare and other public services and products significant for social life. Consequently, it is necessary to establish new political priorities and new social programmes to alleviate the growing tension between those who pay and those who are the beneficiaries of the social security system in their old age. Ultimately, the state authorities may withdraw from governmental guarantees concerning the pension system.

2. The economy – e.g. restricted labour market and consumer market; higher labour costs and capital costs; employing foreign labour forces (particularly highly qualified) or moving production abroad; oversupply in building

industry, real estate, retail and other key sectors of economy; intensification/aggravation of competition; growing pressure to bring control over capital back to the state, which may be intensified by the global financial crisis (particularly in the European Union).

3. The individual – e.g. increasing necessity for personal savings to help overcome risks and solve problems related to old age; cuts in pension rights and privileges (first step: raising the retirement age); growing dependence on the family system in case of long-term disease and/or loss of life independence; decreasing value of real property and other forms of possessions and dropping pensions (impoverishment of many social categories).

4. The family – the increasing number of older people have older and older children – as a result, more and more inner-family relations are between old people and other old people; the offspring of the oldest generation are sometimes already retired; the decreasing fertility rate results in grandparents and great grandparents outnumbering their grandchildren; the family system needs to be restructured into a more heterogeneous arrangement with new configurations of family structures: return to multi-generational households; three-four generations of relatives from reconstructed families (my children, your children and our children – weakening blood relations bring problems with family identity); older people attempt to create replicas of family relationships and/or make the offspring move in again to live with their ageing parents; increasing costs of living (changes in the tax system, shifting the healthcare costs onto citizens, indirect taxes, insurances, etc.); increase of intergenerational competition – dilemmas related to the process of setting priorities, purposes and tasks of a family; growing financial and temporal preoccupation with long-term care of the oldest generation (chronic disease, serious disability); disruptions in realising recreational, social and cultural functions due to the increase in caring and nursing tasks.[1]

[1] Elaborated on the basis of the World Bank prognosis and K. Dychtwald, *The Path to a Successful Retirement: Lessons from the trailblazers*, Healthy Living. AOL Lifestyle, 2011, www.huffingtonpost.com/...dychtwald/the-path-t [accessed: 8.02.2012]; *Raport o kapitale intelektualnym Polski* [Report on the Intellectual Capital in Poland], Zespół Doradców Strategicznych Prezesa Rady Ministrów, Warsaw 2008, www.slideshare.net/Polska2030/raport-o-kapitale- [accessed: 12.05.2009]; V. Bengston, P. Oyama, *Intergenerational Solidarity: Strenghten Economic and Social Ties. Expert Group Meeting*, United Nations Headquarters, Department of Economic and Social Affairs – Division for Social Policy and Development, New York 2007; K. Dychtwald, D. Kadlec, *The Power Years: A User's Guide to the Rest of Your Life*, John Wiley and Sons, New Jersey 2005; P. Baltes, J. Smith, *New Frontiers in the Future of Aging: from Successful Aging of the Young Old to the Dilemmas of the Fourth Age*, George Maddox Lecture Series, Duke University, Durham 2002; *Global Aging. The Challenge of the New Millenium*, Watson Wyatt Data Services, New York 2000; K. Dychtwald, *Speculations on the Future of Aging*, INSIDE magazine, 21st Century Publishers, Hawaii 1997; H. Moody, *Four Scenarios for an Aging Society*, Hastings Center Report, Sept-Oct 1994.

Not only does the progressing population ageing bring consequences to the economic sphere, it also poses ethical questions about equal access to resources and their just allocation; about improving the quality of life of the ageing citizens; the right choice of social and medical intervention adequate for their health; delaying or accelerating the moment of death of the ageing person. Moral dilemmas are also generated by the issues related to public and private expenditures on long-term care, its duration, the access to it, and the special protection of the civil rights of the poor and disabled elderly.

Therefore, today we already know that changes caused by population ageing of most societies entail the necessity of restructuring the economy and redefining many policies, particularly in the area of social policy. It is thus certain that population ageing in the near future will bring system transition in all important areas of social life – so deep and far-reaching that in many cases it will cross national, administrative and cultural borders.[2]

It is natural and common – but also tempting – to look ahead and sketch the profiles of future societies with an unprecedented number of ageing and old people. Incorrect prognosis from the 1960s and 1970s (particularly, the theories of the *Club of Rome*), however, demonstrate that moderation and caution are crucial in predicting future events related to such formations as complex as dynamically changing contemporary societies.[3] For that reason, today's *fortune-tellers* base their visions on an assumption that the only prognoses which are likely to come true are those which concern tendencies already noticeable at the time of announcing the prognosis and which are rather short or medium term (3–5 years). Such are the prognoses of social changes generated in response to global population ageing. There is a lot of evidence that these processes are not only hypotheses. On the contrary, changes in social and demographic structure, already observable today, provide empirical evidence showing that they are not isolated from other phenomena (economic and technological development, fluctuations in the labour and financial markets, etc.) but create the need to quickly rebuild the production-consumption and saving-investing models and to provide systemic, organisational solutions able to *serve* unprecedented social and individual challenges and needs.

---

[2] Already at the end of the 1990s, Ken Dychtwald recommended following socio-economic consequences of demographic changes, as the lack of deep functional and structural changes in the societies of old demographic structures could pose a risk of *re-arranging the global geopolitical order*. K. Dychtwald, *Speculations...*, op. cit., p. 5.

[3] The past is believed to have *compromised itself*, therefore even the most radical critics of futurology do not acknowledge such documents, claiming *if there is such a thing as growing human knowledge, then we cannot anticipate today what we shall know only tomorrow* (Karl R. Popper).

In predicting the consequences of changes generated by population ageing, scenarios seem safer than prognoses as they contain not predictions but narrative and coherent descriptions of the available options in the areas of risk and uncertainty.[4] Instead of classic forecasts, scenarios offer a possibility to estimate the influence of phenomena/processes *ex ante*; they may provide basic knowledge of varied possible courses of events, which can be useful for political deliberations and future decisions. Scenarios may be *linear* (accumulation of change) and *abrupt/disconnected* (response to sudden changes about the choice of criteria and processes), but as a changing system has more than one potential option, scenarios do not predetermine the future but provide numerous possible versions – should any of them turn out to be mistaken, they will become a prerequisite of intervention, gradually changing the initial assumptions.

Therefore, cautiously developing the visions of future and keeping in mind that *what is best today, tomorrow is only good*, we must continue to predict, even roughly, what might happen to societies with a substantial number of the oldest citizens. As John Galsworthy aptly noticed: *If you do not think about the future, you cannot have one.*[5]

[4] When it comes to *risk,* we know potential determinants of events/actions/decisions but we do not know the likelihood of their occurrence (this is a characteristic of stochastic/dynamic systems). In case of *uncertainty* we know little or hardly anything of the potential factors influencing events/actions/decisions, but we do have some concept/idea/suspicion about what may happen (this is a characteristic of poorly structured systems). More about the rules of writing scenarios in J. Spangenberg, *Scenarios and Decision Making: Finding Integration Synergies, Avoiding Risks*, Presentation at the SEIT anniversary, Tallinn, Estonia, 8 November 2007.

[5] Elaborated on the basis of the secondary analysis of prognostic materials from years 2000–2011: P. Henry, *Active Ageing and Intergenerational Solidarity: Findings, Issue and Perspectives*, Institute for Quality of Daily Life SODEXO, 2011; *Paying for the Past, Providing for the Future: Intergenerational Solidarity,* OECD Ministerial Meeting on Social Policy, Paris, 2–3 May 2011, Session 3., www.oecd.org/social/ministerial [accessed: 26.06.2011]; O. Kapella, A.-C. de Liedekerke, L. Spence, H. Radunovich, *Developing intergenerational relationships*, University of Florida, Florida 2010; *Future Scenarios*, Brussels, Family Platform, http://www.familyplatform.eu; S. Harper, *Generations and Life Course: The Impact of Demographic Challenges on Education 2010–2050,* Institute of Aging, Oxford 2008; A. Stuckelberg, A. Vikat (eds.), *A Society for All Ages. Challenges and Opportunities*, United Nations Economic Commission for Europe, New York – Geneva 2008; S. Steyaert, S. Eggermont, H. Vandebosch, *Towards the Desired Future of the Elderly and Information and Communications Technology (ICT): Policy Recommendations Based on a Dialogue with Senior Citizens*, Second International Seville Seminar on Future-oriented Technology Analysis: Impact of FTA Approaches on Policy and Decision-making – Seville 28–29 September 2006; *Future Ageing. Inquiry into Long-term Strategies to Address the Ageing of the Australian Population over the Next 40 Years*, The House of Representatives Standing Committee on Health and Ageing, Canberra 2005; A. Kalache, S. Barreto, I. Keller, "Global Aging. The Demographic Revolution in All Cultures and Societies," in M. L. Johnson (ed.), *The Cambridge Handbook of Age and Aging,*

1. Moderately optimistic scenario: The society of competitive generational interests

Processes and phenomena related to population ageing in the next decades will probably be conducive to *recidivism of gerontocracy*[6] and will lead to significant transitions of social systems and the structure and functions of family. Thus, age may achieve/maintain the influence, access to power, resources and enrichment as well as basic control over resources through its assigned status (a position available for people of certain age). What favours this situation is little activity or even passivity of state authorities in the face of challenges posed by changes in demographic structure, as well as the lack of changes in economy in response to new socioeconomic phenomena. Advocates of this scenario can be found among those keenly interested in keeping the systemic *status quo* (economic interests): wealthy retirees, elderly people in political or corporate power, etc.[7]

In societies where age categories are hierarchically ranked, similar to social classes or statuses which classify people into categories based on power, prestige or ownership:

1. Age divisions go *across* gender structure, social strata and other social categories (a risk of intensifying intergenerational conflicts).

2. Differences in income, prestige, power, social mobility, class relations and class consciousness, which appear in various age categories or age cohorts, create inequalities between generations:

– age is used as a criterion for *entering/exiting* the level of high social status;

– every generation lives "for itself" – dialogue and understanding are more and more difficult to achieve;

– young people demand faster generational rotations in economic and political power structures;

Cambridge University Press, Cambridge – New York – Melbourne – Madrid – Cape Town – Singapore – São Paulo 2005, pp. 30–46. I. Sohail, "Ageing: Alternative Futures and Policy Choices," *Foresight,* 2003, no. 5–6, pp. 8–17; other materials used, see chapter III.

[6] The cohorts of near retirees (*the boomers generation*), as well as Yuppies from the early 1990s will root into economic and political structures they've built, which are strong enough not to give up the power they once achieved.

[7] The above-mentioned scenario has been widely discussed; there are some pessimistic phrases to be found such as: *senile earthquake, geriatric tsunami, geriatric Pearl Harbour, Gerrasic Park*: e.g. P. Peterson, *Gray Dawn: How the Coming Age Wave will Transform America – And the World,* Times Books – Random House, New York 1999; P. Wallace, *Agequake: Riding the Demographic Rollercoaster Shaking Business, Finance and Our World*, Nicholas Brealey Publishing, Boston – London 2001.

– every category/cohort feels discriminated against by others;

– conflicts based on inequalities between generations are transferred into the family sphere;

3. Small, nuclear family is weakening – there are no alternative structures to take over its functions.

4. Ageing is regarded an important socio-economic problem – excessive benefits and privileges of the elderly are stressed more and more strongly; there is an increasing social expectation of a more even redistribution of national income and social resources:

– increasing financial needs and costs of elderly care are more and more difficult to cover – the needs of children and youths are disadvantaged;

– younger generation express growing objections and openly protest against raising taxation caused by increasing costs of pensions and care of the elderly;

5. Attempts to re-examine the role of age as a source of inequality in intergenerational relations "stiffen" the views and behaviours of the elderly and make the ascending generation more radical.

6. Economic barriers and reduced social support facilitate marginalisation and isolation of the oldest generation – senior citizens (particularly the oldest old) encounter barriers when accessing infrastructural resources and the mainstream of the life of a community and wider social relations.

7. Ageing becomes a difficult experience, particularly in case of people living in poor conditions and/or residential care for longer periods of time.

8. There is uneven, unjust access to information and resources, particularly to technological achievements. This afflicts senior citizens the most; their needs/problems are not taken into account.

Weakening/absent dialogue between generations and little support from the state and its agendas for the solutions which would balance social statuses of different generations creates frustration among young people and induces the generation and maintenance of the three plagues of old age:

– loneliness – the pain we suffer when we long for company but we lack it;

– helplessness – the pain we suffer when we need support but do not receive it;

– boredom – the pain we suffer when our life lacks spontaneity and variety.[8]

Demographic, economic and social processes in the quite near future will probably cause cultural reorientation: from today's *apotheosis of youth* towards

---

[8] A good example is Marek Koterski's film: *Dzień świra* [Day of the Wacko], 2002.

restoring the role of life wisdom and experience, which are characteristic of the oldest generation. A more balanced nature of intergenerational relations will depend on the depth and scope of authentic social dialogue and state authorities' initiatives to increase productivity and jobs for young people.

2. A scenario close to technocratic utopia: Generations in the virtual world: digital citizens – senior citizens in a network

The world, obsessed with the idea of developing advanced technologies (including information and communication technologies), with a knowledge-based economy and developed sector of innovative services, heralds the advent of an information society in next decades.[9] In an information society, technological development will be of the utmost importance and a key role will be played by knowledge and information (individualised education, lifelong learning), which altogether will make for unprecedented possibilities and further specialisation of work, production and entertainment. In such a society, culture will fully become a virtual reality, and the real world will be created by the media to a large extent. As a result, decentralisation and deinstitutionalisation of the society will increase; there will be a revival of local communities and social life will become more diversified.

Thus, the society of the future will be constituted by advanced technologies but may also involve a risk of anomie[10] caused by technological-innovative processes.

---

[9] See footnote 1 and 5; also: T. Goban-Klas, P. Sienkiewicz, *Społeczeństwo informacyjne: Szanse, zagrożenia, wyzwania* [The Information Society – Opportunities, Threats, Challenges], Wydawnictwo Fundacji Postępu Telekomunikacji, Cracow 1999; K. Kędziora-Kornatowska, A. Grzanka-Tykwińska, „Osoby starsze w społeczeństwie informacyjnym" [The Elderly in the information Society], *Gerontologia Polska,* 2011, no. 19 (2), pp. 107–111.

[10] According to Durkheim, anomie is common when the surrounding society has undergone significant changes and, more generally, when there is a significant discrepancy between ideological theories and values and what is actually achievable in everyday life. This produces a sense of futility, lack of purpose, and emotional emptiness and despair. According to Merton, anomie refers to social action and means the discrepancy between common social goals and the legitimate means to attain those goals. In other words, an individual suffering from *anomie* would strive to attain the common goals of a specific society, yet would not be able to reach these goals legitimately, according to the accepted norms. A definition of anomie which seems proper for the purpose of this book, is the feeling of instability of social solutions, futility and hopelessness as a result of changes in the contemporary world in which relatively permanent norms/standards lose their importance ("lack of 'moral compass'").

2.1. Phenomena and processes related to the technological-digital revolution

Boundaries of academic knowledge are expected to change, the number of inventions and discoveries will increase, the efficiency of scientific research (particularly of exact science) and technical processes should improve. Also, the expectations about education level and efficient services of highly automated systems will increase. Intellectualisation of work will decrease the role of physical effort as improved productivity reduces/eliminates the necessity of employing migrants.

Power will reside in technocrats' hands; there will be new techniques and ways to acquire professional and life experience. The prevailing structures of interests and social (particularly multigenerational) relations will change. Technology will alter the economy and bring social innovations; large sums will be spent on scientific studies combining genetics and artificial intelligence. Hopes for a "digital soul" will be aroused; biological aspects of ageing will be able to be "corrected" according to individual desires.

Ageing citizens, in different life phases, will enter the increasingly developed virtual world. Therefore, different scenarios have been elaborated which refer to different categories:

1. Senior citizens for whom advanced technology and related products are familiar – entering the ageing phase, they are equipped with experience gained in middle age. This group quickly adapts to new challenges, participates in all important spheres of social life, and is not discriminated against, whereas all others are threatened by the digital divide. Therefore, in this scenario, intergenerational differences are small.

2. Older people who encounter the technical and digital revolution after it has already entered its third/fourth developmental stage. Despite their substantial number, older people are marginalised, liable to social exclusion and discouraged by constantly appearing novelties. The image of contemporary *juvenilism* will be strengthened by the leaders of the information society – young people equipped with new competences "assist" seniors in management (if not take over their jobs), which makes the latter feel controlled. As a result, the intergenerational gap widens.

3. The situation of social resistance against advanced technologies governing everyday life, and the promotion of technology as if it were an unconditional necessity. Older people will be the first to struggle to restore authentic, direct relations between people from different generations. *Baby boomers* or the *hippie* generation may become the most active contestants of the extreme version of the overwhelming information society, as they were

once the ones who cleared the way for an open and democratic life for the next generations.[11]

4. A widening gap between the increasing population of the older generation, who are in good health and have a good financial state, and support and adapt to solutions which increase their comfort and quality of life, and those whose life is difficult, who have health problems and restricted abilities and are not capable of adapting to new technologies or gaining the benefits of an information society. What poses the key problem is not as much the differences between the young and the old as between the different categories of the elderly.

The first scenario is regarded as favourable to the elderly; however, it seems too idealistic or even utopian. The second is considered the least favourable or promising when it comes to the relationship between senior citizens and the world of new information and communication technology (ICT). The third, while favourable to the elderly, does not exclude further development of information and communication technology, and the fourth seems the most realistic in 2020.[12]

Human birth is a moment when life chances and trajectories are approximately possible to predict (mortality, morbidity, disability prognoses, etc.) due to the following factors:

1. Increase in specialist medical knowledge (access to online databases and knowledge; online consults), accuracy of medical diagnoses and general efficiency of healthcare.

2. Knowledge society anticipates health hazards and efficiently eliminates them – nanotechnologies, organ culture, brain surgery, studies on biological determinants of changes related to body ageing, plastic surgery and gene therapy bring further hope.

3. Development of ICT diagnostics and expert systems, expanding medications and illness databases, advancing "distant treatment," using multimedia systems (virtual reality) with medical assistance (e.g. surgeries) will allow people to live to be 120–140.

4. Direct medical information exchange between any two health centres (clinics) within one state or different countries in the whole world, at any time and in any scope and, in future, "distant treatment" and being given diagnosis and doctor's advice while at home, via ICT network, will increase the chance of preventing mass health threats and will help quick responses in emergency

[11] The conflict over ACTA at the beginning of 2012 indicates the breaking of intergenerational barriers in case of the penetration of society by an increasingly anonymous network society.

[12] This part of the scenario was elaborated upon based on: S. Steyaert, S. Eggermont, H. Vandebosch, *Towards the Desired Future...*, op. cit.

situations. Effect: improvement of health within society as a whole and further increase in life expectancy.

The already born generations of future retirees can expect improvements in health and a reverse of negative tendencies regarding health, considering the likelihood of successes in biomedical studies on ageing. For example, it is expected that:

1. Further significant advancements in the research on genetic determinants of diseases, meaning that diagnosis, prevention and treatment could begin long before the symptom of disease occurs.
2. Considerable decrease in risk and cost of expensive therapies will make it possible for a larger number of patients to access it (e.g. instead of expensive *by-pass* surgical procedure used in cardiology, less costly and less invasive chemical and mechanical ways of removing fatty deposits from arteries).
3. Perfecting laser surgery will improve effects of removing tumours.
4. Wider application of microprocessor technology in constructing prosthesis will help to compensate for or reconstruct lost abilities.
5. Development and improvement of diagnostic processes, preventing and treating Alzheimer's disease and other forms of senile dementia may significantly decrease the need for long-term care.[13]
6. Considerable progress in stimulating and controlling immunology (e.g. lowering the susceptibility to pneumonia) and endocrine system (improving physiological control mechanism, e.g. temperature control) and nerve conduction, delaying memory changes and keeping the speed of processing information), which would significantly improve the quality of life of the elderly.
7. Extension of human life span by 3 to 5 years thanks to decreasing morbidity and mortality caused by cardiovascular disease or cancer. Limiting the spread of AIDS will also be important for future generations of the elderly.

What gives us hope for decreasing the scale of disability in the oldest age categories is dissemination and widespread application of health promotion rules, particularly regarding the so-called *killer diseases* and implementation of regular check-ups.

In a developed information society, the state will be able to aptly recognise citizens' needs and correctly determine allocation resources. However, to be successful, such a project must be accompanied not only by technological development, but also by implementing social innovations and a balanced society based on both technology advancement and socio-cultural systems.[14]

[13] Alzheimer's disease, which leads to complete disability, is estimated to afflict 5% of population aged 65 or more and up to 20% of people aged 80 or more.

[14] Social innovations include successful implementation of social reforms and new forms of goal achievement, such as: new organisational forms, new rules, new lifestyles which help to

2.2. Phenomena and processes related to the threat of anomie

Possible changes caused by introducing advanced technologies will not be accompanied by cultural and social changes at the same pace. Cultural homogenisation will increase and the dominance of mass culture will strengthen.

The line of demarcation will be access to goods and services offered by advanced technologies; the distinction between the young and the old will be based on *technological criteria*: old is the one who loses the capacity to adapt to new conditions and challenges.

Technical and cultural generation gaps and technological barriers will bring social conflicts caused by a growing sense of electronic control and thus creating a feeling of limited freedom of individuals.

Differentiated access to knowledge, advanced technologies and healthcare may become a source of social inequalities and intergenerational conflicts.

A sense of alienation in the technicised world (developing the automated and robotised sphere) may result in increasing the risk of social conflicts.

Passive forms of entertainment in leisure time (in front of computer) and general decline in physical activity (lifestyle) risk the degradation of physical culture and, in consequence, a decrease in the physical fitness of the general populace. As a result of the entertainment in ICT network, new diseases of affluence will appear. Efficient action in moments of crisis will be much too dependent on technical systems (ICT, controlling and monitoring systems, etc.).

There will be a considerable reduction in employment, particularly in the case of blue collars – the number of jobs related to technological processes, trade and telecommuting, and the work itself will increase (effect: growing risk of boredom, burnout and atomisation of social life).

Instrumentalisation of the doctor-patient relations, already gone too far, as a result of the extension of technical possibilities will reduce face-to-face contact and could bring about the dehumanisation of healthcare.

The nuclear family with a small and planned number of offspring is only one of many forms of family life. There are a variety of informal relationships between men and women but the social support system outside public sector is poor.

Young people are needed – they are a "treasure" for the labour market characterised by severe generational gap. Young and affluent people may become a subject of envy and ICT can impede full social participation among senior citizens and their everyday functioning in the digital world.

---

solve problems more efficiently. They also mean creating openness to change and improvement not only of economic conditions but also the quality of life.

To summarise the proposals of the discussed scenario, we can say future societies will have to deal with technological change and the risk of anomie caused by the pace and intensity of the demographic ageing of the population. In other words, the discussed scenario will be co-determined by the expectations of the advocates of the *digital citizen* idea, innovative projects and the hopes of the elderly fearing senility and death. A chance to alleviate risks and increase the effectiveness of the technological revolution is to support it with political and civic structures and generate virtual and real agora.[15]

3. Manipulative scenario of social engineering: Instrumental and bureaucratic management of ageing and its problems

Authors of this scenario presume that social programmes addressed to the elderly are formulated in a language characteristic to marketing and public relations – older people are considered mainly as a re-election tool.

The fear of consequences of population ageing and of a crisis which could be induced by this process translates into formulating political aims, e.g. changes in the retirement age, reforms of the pension system, social security for the elderly, etc.

Real needs generated by an increasing number of senior citizens and the political interests of the power elite lead to an intensive development of the service system and other economic endeavours designed for citizens living longer and longer. New interest groups appear, which focus their actions on cataloguing senior needs, financing various forms of meeting these needs, monitoring the social status of the elderly, organising long-term care and evaluating sectoral policies (elderly needs – a lever for development).

Main political parties differ in their proposals of strategies aimed at solving the problems of ageing and the elderly: referring either to purely market mechanisms or to a monopolist role of the state (in both cases, intervention strategies prevail). As a result, the policy on ageing is inflexible and under the pressure of the needs of the growing number of the elderly and their social expectations.

The necessity of shifting and centralising political and executive decisions is explained by demographic crisis – the budgets of state agendas and ministerial departments, statutorily obliged to deal with the problems of elderly, are growing. One of the variants of this scenario may be a marriage of technological advancement with a strong state model (state interventionism).

[15] The term was coined by I. Sohail, *Ageing: Alternative...*, op. cit., pp. 13–17.

The weaker the state interventionism, the greater the chance that numerous other actors of the public scene will shape the social policy. In the event of a low level of technological advancement combined with state interventionism, social policy can be oriented towards justice and improvement/maintenance of the quality of life of all age categories (older generation benefits as well). In the worst version – low level of technology advancement and limited state intervention – citizens must look for solutions to the problems of older people by turning to non-public sectors: informal/private sector (family, social circles) or the third sector. Market forces set boundaries between generations and the risk of pension funds collapsing is increasing.

What can correct/alleviate the effects of global population ageing are centrally funded gerontology programmes, such as the protection of older people's access to healthcare in the face of increasing privatisation of medical services, use of pronatalist tools to improve demographic situations (social benefits for women who gave birth to children, particularly many children), support of scientific research on the position and functioning of senior citizens which are conducted by state agendas, universities and other academic institutions, etc.

Nuclear family is a preferred model but state interventionism weakens its tasks and functions. As a result, a demanding attitude towards and dependence on state bureaucracy is growing.

Social policies on ageing will become a necessity more than a choice. However, the bureaucratic corset will make their strategies, aims, structures and tools so inflexible that intervention will overshadow anticipation of events and most social programmes addressed to the elderly will be taken over by social welfare institutions (reactive policy).

Authority is legitimate but not eternal. Therefore, the potential success of the discussed scenario is believed to lie in established formulas of the rotation of political elites, guaranteed participation of the elderly in public debate and decision-making processes.

4. Optimistic-persuasive scenario: Society for all ages – senior citizens as a resource of the system revitalisation

Anticipated effects of ageing are important both for senior citizens and for those who are only now entering the last stage of life or are going to enter it in the next years. We all have to face transformation and restructuring of intergenerational relations, of the state and of social communities. It requires a redefinition of social roles and developmental tasks for the elderly and their social environment. Strategies to maintain intergenerational cohesion are expected and believed to be the only method to avoid intergenerational conflicts in the process of competing for ever-limited resources.

More generations than ever before will live next to each other; people will increasingly transfer income, care and support within and across generations. Intergenerational solidarity and justice will move to the fore of policy concern and will influence the new ethics of our societies.

Once people become aware of longevity, their individual life courses will change both professionally and personally. Individuals will have to rethink their own personal life courses and the question of when and how they wish to mix education and work.

The labour market will face increasing skills shortages and a large proportion of older workers, and adapt to train and retain older workers. New cohorts will expect and demand increasingly flexible working patterns. Home is likely to develop as a place of work, education and health care.[16]

Ageing societies will require the transfer of educational resources between young and old, even at the cost of young people. Education is likely to be a mix of formal group teaching (akin to current early learning in schools and universities), self-promoted learning using information and media technology, community learning, work-place learning and skills development. The role of *qualifications* will need to be re-examined – separation of education to enable personal development, to enhance employability and career progression, to develop skills, and to successfully contribute to wider society is likely to disappear. Permanent education is likely to be funded by individuals, communities, employers, governments and private enterprises.

Thus, education in years 2020–2050 will be a combination of:

- formative education,
- education as a lifestyle choice,
- education to enhance employment prospects,
- education to enable full participation in public life (citizenship).

New social hierarchies will be based on the difference between the groups of well educated people, adapted to new social structures and tasks and those who will not have enough knowledge, skills or abilities to face new challenges and interaction patterns. Educational tasks addressed to migrants will increase as well, particularly since people from different cultures may have very different expectations of what learning is.

In near future, education could play a key role in:

- recruitment, arrival and integration of new migrants,

[16] S. Harper, *Generations and Life Course...*, op. cit., pp. 4–6.

– increasing the employability of foreigners,
– recognition and updating of qualifications,
– cultural and social adjustment,
– social integration and cohesion.

It is hard to predict how the family, as the supportive environment for the elderly, will change. Most likely, care of dependent family members will require the help of second, third or even fourth partnerships within extended families.

Consumption will also change and vary between generations (silver economy) and within age categories (diversity within the target group). Disposable income will need to be distributed between increasing leisure, education, mobility, healthcare and other demands. Therefore, infrastructure and services (housing, transport, education, entertainment, tourism and healthcare) will need to adapt to a growing number of senior citizens, their needs and abilities.[17]

World experts draw attention to the fact that intergenerational relations in a world inhabited by a growing number of ageing people will require:

– recognition of senior citizens as a valuable part of social resources,

– scientifically supported strategies to overcome myths and stereotypes about ageing,

– enabling active participation of the elderly in development processes (including a guaranteed right of choice on when to leave the labour market),

– providing older people with proper care and support related to health and prevention of ageing,[18]

– conditions for lifelong learning and its promotion,

– promotion of intergenerational solidarity.

These challenges are expected to arise due to the changes in social structures and institutions portrayed in the vision of *Society for All Ages*, elaborated since 1999 by special UN agendas and numerous member states.[19] This idea introduces to the public scene a model of society which is intended to be

---

[17] Ibidem, pp. 5–10.

[18] See Z. Woźniak, "Profilaktyka starzenia się i starości – mrzonka czy konieczność?" [Ageing Prevention: Fantasy or Necessity?], *Ruch Prawniczy, Ekonomiczny i Socjologiczny*, 2011, no. 1, pp. 231–254.

[19] *Toward a Europe for All Ages. Promoting Prosperity and Integenerational Solidarity*, Commission of the European Communities, Brussels 1999, COM 221 final; "3 Steps Toward a Society for All Ages," in *Preparation for 1999 – Toward a Society for All Ages*. United Nations, www.un.org/esa/socdev/iyop/iyoppre3.htm [accessed: 5.09.2003]; Ch. Nusberg, *Strategies for a Society for All Ages*, American Association of Retired Persons, Washington, D.C. 1998; *Toward a European Society for All Ages*, Age statement for The European Year of Equal Opportunities for All, The European Older People's Platform, Brussel 2007; *Towards a Society for All Ages*, www.osc.govt.nz/positive-ageing-strategy/publication/towards-a-society.html) [accessed: 23.05.2008]; A. Stuckelberg, A. Vikat (eds.), *A Society for All Ages...*, op. cit.

friendly and functional for all its members. The authors refer to gerontological study results which demonstrate that the potential of healthy and active senior citizens is hard to overestimate. The more active they are the greater their contribution to society and different generations. Policy makers should thus perceive active, healthy ageing as a key factor in enhancing the chances for societal development. What is more, the elderly should not be regarded a problem but as a potential resource which can help increase the chances of solving other social problems (e.g. new jobs in service sectors for senior citizens, increased demand for caring and nursing services, seniors as consumers).

The global strategy for active and healthy ageing, proposed by international organisations and European structures, include:

- social policy addressed to the elderly,
- advocacy of needs, problems and issues of the elderly,
- educational and training programmes,
- dissemination of knowledge about ageing,
- gerontological research and dissemination of findings,
- extending the international gerontological database.

Therefore, the *optimistic scenario* is based on the following assumptions:

1. Not only does demographic ageing bring an increase in the number of the elderly, but also an increase in people living longer, in most cases increasingly active and healthy. What is more, the elderly, who have accumulated rich experience, knowledge and skills, become the ones who store social memory and wisdom: Lifelong education opportunities provide for this wealth to be distributed throughout our society.[20]

2. Ageing is not perceived only as a money-consuming burden – in the future, the elderly will not be considered a significant problem which societies have to face but rather as a resource: a source of social and cultural revitalisation.

3. Society for all ages adapts its structure, functionality, policy and planning to the needs and abilities of all citizens. In this way, it unlocks everyone's potential for the benefit of everyone (key role of sectoral policies: labour market, healthcare, housing, personal and social security to age actively and productively).

4. Applying the principle that the elderly can choose their own lifestyle freely and lead independent lives in familiar surroundings and cover preventive care and services in their homes will increase the chances of achieving and maintaining a sound financial situation and good health and delay the loss of independence and autonomy.

---

[20] S. Harper, *Generations and Life Course...*, op. cit., p. 11.

5. Understanding and accepting age differences are a chance to restore the equal position of the elderly in society (reducing/eliminating ageism from areas of social life).

6. Unlocking the potential of all age categories for the benefit of everyone according to the principle of reciprocity and equity enables self-investment and sharing the harvest of these investments:

– increasing income and savings are a chance for a variety of lifestyle choices during old age (flexible forms of employment for people who are about to retire and retirees; the increasing role of silver economy, senior citizens as a significant segment of consumer market – shifting the stress from achieving specific, traditional life goals to intrinsic values);

– transfers of resources from diverse, public, private, non-governmental and individual sources, also through international exchange, will help to meet the needs of the elderly in a more balanced way and will facilitate uncompetitive intergenerational relations;

– governmental support for the development and application of technologies will help intergenerational integration and avoid technological and digital exclusion of the elderly;

– wide state funding of research on ageing and old age – both the problems of health/fitness and social innovations or QOL – will help to elaborate upon and update diversified profiles of older people and to create gerontology programmes based on rational premises;

– promotion and implementation of programmes aimed at ageing prevention[21] and creating a holistic system of geriatric care[22] to improve health and fitness as the basis of QOL of the elderly;

– support for the potential and resources of the civic sector acting for and "with" older people (particularly expanding the resources of senior volunteering);

– provision of security and access to the public sphere for senior citizens, implementing programmes and active forms of preventing social isolation of the elderly (particularly those who are lonely and disabled).

---

[21] This problem, completely ignored by politicians, economists and to an extent by doctors, will determine the position and potential of people who live increasingly longer. See Z. Woźniak, "Profilaktyka starzenia się i starości..." [Ageing Prevention...], op. cit. The problem will be discussed in detail further in the book.

[22] In 2005 Polish standards of geriatric care were expanded; however, they are still only theoretical: J. Derejczyk, T. Grodzicki, A. Jakrzewska-Sawińska, A. Jóźwiak, A. Klich, K. Wieczorowska-Tobis, Z. Woźniak (sociological consult), "Standardy świadczenia usług medycznych w specjalności geriatria" [Service Standards in Geriatric Medicine], *Gerontologia Polska*, 2005, vol. 13, no. 2, pp. 67–83.

7. Changes in marital patterns (an increase in the number of informal, partner relationships, divorces and re-marriages, acceptance of LGBT relationships, a rising number of single parents and people who are single[23] in their old age will increase the number of elderly living on their own.

8. Rejection/questioning of dysfunctional stereotypes about the beautiful and forever young and/or the wise and experienced and about the elderly as the only ones who are just; instead:

– older and younger people learn together, from each other and about each other;

– senior citizens are invited by younger generations to act as mentors – the role of elderly people as bearers of cultural patterns, values, roles and life experience (*When I was your age, I had already..., at some point you are going to...*).

9. Care of dependent family/society members should be culturally and socially appreciated and financially supported (support, prestige and respect for carers).

10. Internalisation of the principle: *derive satisfaction from every life phase* and the attitude shift from the classic saying: *those were the days*, into: *these are the days*[24] will be an important educational task.

11. In next decades, the expected increase in the number of the elderly who will be healthier, better educated, more mobile and financially secured than today's senior citizens will challenge most prevailing stereotypes about ageing. This will help create an attitude of acceptance towards ageing and the old, and decrease ageism[25].

---

[23] This theory is based on the assumption that today's *singles* – term coined by media and adopted by some sociologists – in most cases look for long-lasting relationships as an antidote for loneliness. People living alone (also by choice) and as a result of various life events have always been a minority within social structure. Contemporary *singles*, however, include also people who prefer the model of *having oneself for oneself*. Metaphorically, we could name them "orphans and/or adopted offspring" of hedonism and consumerism, who invest in life pleasures, whose relations are mostly formal and short-term, and who feel little responsibility for others. When they grow older, they may experience the bitter taste of loneliness. If this category extends, this would herald a risk of losing our civilisation and cultural heritage. However, it seems that due to globalisation, singles will be soon outnumbered by strong family cultures and by stronger, more durable relationships based on mutual responsibility.

[24] Louis Armstrong put it succinctly: *The best age is the age you are.*

[25] In 2001 I wrote about a change in intergenerational relations: Z. Woźniak, "Present Situation and Future Prospects of Social Policy Aimed at Senior Citizens Against the Background of the Globalization of Ageing," in M. Ziółkowski (ed.), *Ludzie przełomu tysiąclecia a cywilizacja przyszłości* [The People of the Turn of the Millennium vs. the Civilisation of the Future], Wydawnictwo Fundacji Humaniora, Poznan 2001, pp. 169–197; idem, "Globalizacja problemów zdrowotnych i starzenia się a rodzina" [Globalisation of Health and Ageing Problems and the

12. Future senior citizens will become active actors on the public scene (this activity will be inversely proportional to the level of satisfaction with family life). They will be also considered a significant category of voters. Such a social position of the elderly can lead to the liquidation of intergenerational distance and mean real rapprochement of different age categories.

While the 19th century "discovered" children and their problems and the last century focused on the ageing population, the next decades will turn people's attention towards searching for individual and collective resources and reserves thanks to which children and the elderly (particularly the disabled from both social categories) will be able to function with maximum independence (normalisation) and efficiency equal to their potential. It is thus assumed that future generations will have to face transformation and restructuring of intergenerational relations, therefore internationally promoted, intergenerational solidarity should be represented in several aspects:

– emotional and territorial closeness (increased chance of interaction),

– common ideas, norms and values; mutual exchange of emotions, goods, services and support (instrumental and emotional support),

– ties between different generations,

– obligations of ascending generations to ageing generations.

Intergenerational programmes are a vehicle for effective and uninterrupted resource exchange and understanding between the old and the young with the benefit of individuals and communities, which:

– [...] *demonstrate mutual benefits for the participants,*

– [...] *establish new social roles and/or new perspectives for young and old,*

– [...] *can involve multiple generations and must include at least two nonadjacent and non familial generations,*

– [...] *promote increased awareness and understanding between the younger and older generations and the growth of self esteem for both generations,*

– [...] *address social issues and policies relevant to those generations involved [develop] intergenerational relations.*[26]

A key to the *society for all ages* are strong social structures, particularly a harmonious and strong local community and a nuclear family supported by members of dispersed extended family and other relatives.

Family], in Z. Tyszka (ed.), *Współczesne rodziny polskie. Ich stan i kierunek przemian* [Contemporary Polish families. Their Condition and Direction of Change], Wydawnictwo Naukowe UAM, Poznan 2001, pp. 281–408.

[26] See A. Hatton-Yeo, T. Ohsako, *Intergenerational Programmes: Public Policy and Research Implications an International Perspective*, The UNESCO Institute for Education, The Beth Johnson Foundation, Hamburg 2000.

An innovative idea of ageing-friendly communities[27] is the theory of successful ageing[28]. Successful ageing is based on participation and integration supported by physical, technical and social infrastructure which enables the elderly individual to perform the role of an active citizen (voluntary work of the elderly and for the elderly), building alliances and agreements beyond age boundaries, meeting the life needs of the elderly by in-home care (maintaining independence and self-reliance), and reducing to a minimum the necessity of moving the elderly with disabilities to nursery homes.

A condition of success of this scenario, however, is to find a solution within the social security system which will guarantee the balance between standards of living of retirees and those who are currently paying premium for future generations of retirees.

In such a society we do not have to be afraid of the consequences of ageing and young people do not have to be afraid of future.[29]

* * *

Without doubt, future solutions will be a result of compilations and overlapping of various proposals included in the presented scenarios, and other details yet unknown. Some elements will be certainly incorporated into the strategies and programmes of future social policy. This particularly concerns the last scenario, which will probably be combined with projects aimed at building an information society in which state authorities on a central level can construct legal and organisational framework (legislation and redistribution) for actions supporting equal treatment of all the categories of citizens/groups/communities and their development, and give access to the mainstream of social life for everyone.

Using theatrical rhetoric, we could say that during rehearsals which precede a premiere performance, actors can also introduce some modifications to the scenario. The same rule applies to the actors on the public scene. The state and its agendas, formal and informal institutions, communities, families and

[27] In various countries there are numerous innovative initiatives already functioning or in the making (in the USA, a few dozen to a few hundred) – e.g. AdvantAge Initiative, Communities for All Ages Communities for All Ages, WHO Aging-Friendly Cities, AARP Livable Communities Initiative, "Building Healthy Communities for Active Aging," Community Partnerships for Older Adults. A. Scharlach, "Creating Aging-Friendly Communities in the United States," *Ageing International*, 2012, no. 37, p. 30 and next.

[28] See R.C. Atchley, "A continuity theory of normal aging," *Gerontologist*, 1989, no. 29, pp. 183–190; J. Rowe, R. Kahn, *Successful Aging*, Random House, New York 1999.

[29] S. Harper, "Don't panic, we have nothing to fear from an ageing society," *Times* (online) 26.08.2008.

organised representatives of the elderly who follow the rule: if you are not a part of the solution, you are still only a part of the problem.

Thus, "Society for all Ages," the recent appeal for intergenerational solidarity[30] in fostering well-being of all ages, should be considered a general rule for creating the framework of social policy on ageing.

[30] 2012 was declared European Year for Active Ageing and Solidarity between Generations.

Chapter III

Multi-layered structure of gerontological programmes of social policy – a holistic view

1. Conceptual frame of gerontology programmes

> What you come from, depends on genetics – what you turn into – on politics
>
> Stanisław Jerzy Lec

It is hard to determine an all-encompassing criterion of old age, or to find one universal pattern of ageing. Also, there is more than one way to solve the problems caused by population ageing. Therefore, ageing and old age should be perceived and analysed from the perspective of social holism,[1] according to which individuals can only be analysed through studying the systems and/or institutions they live in. In some aspects, social holism is a contrast to individualism as it is based on a theological and metaphysical assumption that the actions of wholes determine the actions of individuals rather than the other way round. The concept of ageing is a lot more complex and complete when

[1] Holism (from δλος holos, a Greek word meaning all, whole, entire, total), the opposite of reductionism, is the idea that all phenomena make up systems which somehow function as wholes and that their functioning cannot be fully understood solely in terms of their component parts. The whole is greater than the sum of its parts, not only because there is synergy between the parts, but because the parts contribute to the whole, and manifest its essence, purpose or function. See T. Atlee, *Using Synergy, Diversity and Wholeness to Create a Wisdom Culture* and *Six Facets of Wholeness*, The Co-intelligence Institute, 2001; http://www.co-intelligence.org/I-wholeness.html [accessed: 25.10.2011].

considered as a whole as opposed to merely a total of anatomic body parts or mental features. It is a result of the co-dependency of mind, body and soul, rooted in social and cultural systems. Neither is it possible to understand nor to explain the behaviour of an ageing person without referring to regularities which determine the whole phenomenon (organisation of social life, culture, social infrastructure, social consciousness, family, education, socialisation, etc.). In this way, both the individual dimension of ageing on the one hand and the variety within the elderly category on the other require a holistic approach: both in description and explanation of the essence of ageing and in solving individual and macrostructural problems caused by population ageing.

Therefore, the multidimensional and all-encompassing character of ageing and its consequences demand equally comprehensive and multi-layered programmes and institutional solutions which would be adequate to the needs of senior citizens and changing structures of the ageing society. It is thus necessary to promote innovative solutions[2] which would embrace the theory and practice of introducing new ideas, initiatives, strategies and programmes, one which deeply and entirely changes current routines, resources, power transfers, policy (in general, and sectoral policies in particular) and/or beliefs which are constitutive for a given social system (similarly to nonconformity, which is aiming at the absolute change of a normative system).

Social innovations involve developing and implementing new ideas which allow people to organise interpersonal actions/social interactions in order to accomplish common aims. They generate new methods and tools of responding to social problems, becoming a catalyst of change in the face of unfavourable demographic and economic conditions and processes, exhausting environmental resources and shifts within social structure. They are also a tool to implement social reforms which aim at both solving social problems and providing services and benefits that improve the quality of life. The criterion of success is the necessity for change of a system, not its slight modification or increase in value of single indicators. Therefore, not all social innovations can be subjected to traditional measuring tools of the costs and effects of implementation.

Premises of social innovations[3] are for example: demographic changes, insufficient resources, dysfunctionality of institutions, limitations in the access

[2] Innovation is the development of new ideas/solutions which may be either introducing something new or renewing old ideas/solutions to use them in a new, better way. Innovation is a process, product, radical/immediate or accumulating change in thinking, production, services, technology, organisation which may be derived from scientific theories or following people's needs/expectations. To put it simply, innovations are new ideas which work.

[3] More on the subject: e.g. G. Cahill, "Primer on Social Innovation: A Compendium of Definitions Developed by Organizations Around the World," *The Philanthropist*, 2010, vol. 23,

to social services and benefits; inconveniences and absurdities of everyday life; escalation of social needs and unrealistic expectations that new ideas/solutions can be applied everywhere (what is good for some should be also available for others); changes in production and in particular markets; deficits in the areas inefficiently supported by the market and/or the public sector; unexpected events and increasingly better understanding of natural and social laws (new knowledge). Numerous social innovations are addressed to risk groups. Their aim is social reintegration of marginalised categories which are risked by social exclusion: the poor, the homeless, the mentally ill, the lonely, etc. Not only do social innovations involve the improvement of economic conditions, but, above all, the improvement of the quality of life. Therefore, they may be related to social policy, social security, working conditions, employment or local community development. Their main aim is to bring changes to public policy and social practice.

Thus, the new architecture of future social policy programmes addressed to the elderly (including people at high risk of losing social security and life independence) must be a combination of innovative and strategic thought with pragmatic remedies, which use international, national, regional and local resources[4] as well as the aspirations and skills of the public actors (government, self-government, private sector, NGOs, senior citizens) in a creative way in order to provide favourable conditions for ageing and a good quality of life at old age.

The three-layered structure of gerontology programmes developed by the author includes:

– social policy on ageing and the elderly (first layer) embedded in social legislation, defining the tasks of the state related to the implementation of sectoral policies which serve to anticipate events and develop social programmes addressed to specific groups on the basis of available resources;

– strategies and directional programmes of senior social policy (second layer) – including prevention of ageing and meeting the needs of the elderly;

no. 3; R. Murray, J. Caulier-Grice, G. Mulgan, *The Open Book of Social Innovation*, Social Innovator Series: Ways to Design, Develop and Grow Social Innovation, London 2010; F. Westley, N. Antadze, "Making a Difference: Strategies for Scaling Social Innovation for Greater Impact," *The Innovation Journal: The Public Sector Innovation Journal*, 2010, no. 2.

[4] Resources embrace everything which is designed to achieve aims, solve problems, and eliminate threats, and resources allow people to realise their life tasks, aspirations or values. Resources can be measurable and tangible (money, housing, food, home and institutional care, transport, clothing) or immaterial (knowledge, courage, resourcefulness, initiative, encouragement, humanism, love, etc.). Resources include both particular individuals with their personal and material values, their closest social environment (family, friends, and neighbours), formal and informal groups, organisations, associations, institutions.

– programme domains of the policy on ageing (third layer) – specifying operational goals and tasks in the areas which are important for developing the conditions and quality of life of the elderly.

The content of the first, key layer of gerontology programmes demands explaining the difference between *policy* in general and *social policy*. The former is usually defined as procedures which allow power to be exercised and/or methods of influencing those who lack this power.[5] Every policy is a structure, a certain framework for everyday actions, organisational and system operations and future events. Established rules, binding norms and accepted values are a basis for strategic aims of organisational activity[6] responsible for the quality of life of the members of groups/communities and for the development of society as a whole.

The values which are contemporarily defined as elementary from the perspective of universal political aims are: *freedom*, *dignity*, *subjectivity*, *equality*, *sustained development*, *justice* and *solidarity*. Elementary values activate the actions of the democratic state, and maintain/reproduce hopes that politicians' promises will be fulfilled.

Most generally, policy provides guidelines and support in the decision-making and execution processes. On the other hand, it forces individuals and whole social entities to act in a certain way and move in a certain direction. It serves to give continuity to actions, to set directions, plan future events and provide a basis for countless everyday decisions by using its resources.

Contemporary policies should be also perceived as a result of the influence of numerous public actors – as a reflection of group interests in a society. In the light of pluralistic theories of policy, the role of decision makers (management) should be to set the scope of influence of these interests.[7]

Policy sets responsibilities and delegates competences (power) to all organisational levels and establishes rules about the use of resources available to policy makers and users. It is a verbal, written or recommended set of rules on the basis of which decision makers determine premises and guidelines or use coercion when developing and explaining organisational missions and actions. It specifies approved directions, areas and scope of actions, covering/

[5] *Politeia* (from Greek) – society under some rule, an area of human activity related to the state and authority.

[6] The scope of rules, aims and practice of a policy are co-determined by values (including ideals, beliefs and preferences), people and social groups that can satisfy real and perceived, individual and collective needs. Values allow people to figure out what is respected, expected and desired enough to become a principle behind the choice of methods, means and aims of action.

[7] R. Sutton, *The Policy Process: on Overview*, Chameleon Press, London 1999, p. 26 and next.

surrounding the decision-making process and setting standards of managerial action.[8]

An efficient policy gives a choice to partners and opponents; it is also open to alternative ideas and it regularly stimulates them. Thus, it does not offer ready formulas once and for all. As practice demonstrates, they key to solving dilemmas of contemporary policy is to develop effective methods of gaining citizens' energy, time and interest (including the oldest generation of citizens). A necessary condition for making full use of social resources offered by programmes designed to satisfy social needs is the implementation of a strategic partnership formula, which is the most complete form of social participation. The basis of partner relations is the collaboration of various public actors in performing the analysis and prioritisation of common needs as well as planning how to meet these needs and solve the problems that appear on the way.

From a wider perspective, a general (non-specific) policy is a holistic structure composed of interrelated processes and functions and based on a synergy, that is, an optimal integration of organisational elements. It is an organisation which functions in a wider world of phenomena and processes: in a wider institutional environment.[9]

Once we add the adjective "social" before the general term "policy," we place this notion among the phenomena and processes which involve interpersonal, group and intergroup relations (the result of the mutual influence that people have on each other); we also locate the source of phenomena, processes or problems within a community or demonstrate the social dimension of other policies (e.g. land planning, transport, municipal engineering, etc.).

The term "social" can sometimes mean the opposite of the term "economic," as social policy goes far beyond the simple redistribution of income and wealth, and the domains of economic policy are not only the basis of social programmes (finances), but must also support social aims (sustained development).

In its original meaning, the term "social policy" was used to refer to the role of the state in shaping people's quality of life and to the social welfare system. Therefore, in previous decades this policy was particularly focused on issues related to economic development (labour market, financial status, income, etc.) or the improvement of the quality of life, health, education, security, etc. In this

[8] In this sense, it *is the art of opportunity*. Similar ways of understanding policy can be found in G. Terry, S. Franklin, T. McNichols, P. Haner, after F. Harrison, *Policy, Strategy, and Managerial Action*, Houghton Mifflin Co., Boston 1986, p. 2 and next; K. Kirst-Ashman, H. Grafton Hull Jr., *Understanding Generalist Practice*, Nelson-Hall Publishers, Chicago 1993, pp. 16–17.

[9] Similar stand can be found in F. Harrison, *Policy, Strategy, and Managerial Action*, op. cit., pp. 2–3.

approach, there were more elements characteristic to welfare policy (*social emergency*) than social policy *sensu stricto* (organisation of social life, quality of life), which did not always bring about the expected results due to the quite selective involvement of the members of the society (addiction to welfare institutions).

Contemporary social policy claims significant new elements to complete its definition, one of which is its increasingly stronger connection with social development. Therefore, traditional areas of social policy (heath, social security, social welfare) are today supplemented by, for instance: housing, employment and related benefits, education, labour market, culture, transport, travelling, shopping, leisure time activities.

In forthcoming decades, a new model of society is expected to emerge, in which personal and individual success will be achieved through the quality of life rather than possessions, wealth, social status, etc. Already today, in wealthy countries, social policy makers were forced by social processes and events to activate all available community resources in the process of building the sense of social security and improving areas which determine the quality of life of the citizens.

The author's proposal of social policy, presented in this book, was anchored in the theory of functional community (Focus box 2), in which organisations, regulations and institutions designed to meet the needs, aspirations and interests of individuals and groups are based on social solidarity,[10] and the agency and participation of citizens are developed according to the subsidiarity principle.[11]

The essence of the functional community is its ability to formulate and realise aims and needs in order to guarantee survival and self-actualisation to its members. Each community develops its own systems of support, which are activated whenever there is a social problem or an individual finds oneself in a difficult life situation that is impossible to overcome with their own means, possibilities or entitlements. The community attempts to build a cohesive and efficient system of institutional security to provide the citizens with the opportunity/guarantee of satisfying their individual and group needs, aspira-

---

[10] Distributing the tasks related to education, security, transport, environment, culture etc and the burden of threats posed by illness, disability, ageing, deviation, crime, between all the society members (redistribution).

[11] Subsidiarity principle means that every institution/group should help the others with tasks they cannot do on their own. It is intended not to deprive but to accompany and it requires both acting and self-constraint. Applying this rule must not lead to the minimum state which shifts full responsibility onto individuals and other actors of the public scene. The state is still responsible for organising and financing the subsidiary system and for the quality of public tasks and the choice of their implementers: I. Colozzi, "Zasada pomocniczości a trzeci sektor" [The Subsidiarity Principle and the Third Sector], *Społeczeństwo*, 1998, no. 1, pp. 129–133.

Focus box 2. Acknowledged way of understanding social policy

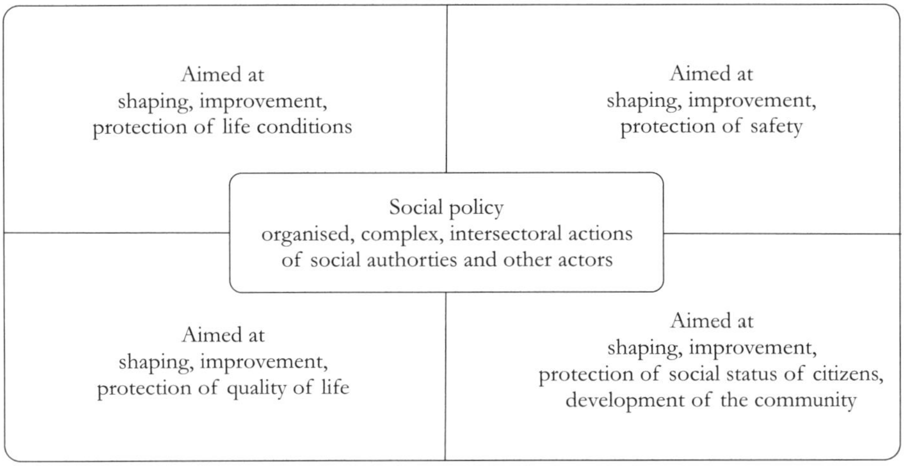

Actions which are a rational response to demographic, economic and socio-cultural changes, which provide.

Individuals and groups with:

- the possibility of harmonious development
- participation in cultural and social life, and
- the chance to lead an active and independent life.

Social policy is a guideline:

- based on declared values and rules
- determining and explaining its mission
- embracing possibilities and aims of organisational and institutional endeavours (vision)
- forcing behaviour which is appropriate from the perspective of adopted aims and tasks
- defining *distribution of responsibility* and the accompanying *delegation of competences* (power) on all organisational levels of the state and the civil society.

Source: own elaboration.

tions and expectations. The duty/task of public authorities is to take actions designed to maintain/improve/strengthen the conditions and quality of life of community members. And the elementary needs of groups and individuals as well as their priority criteria are always rooted in historical, cultural, and system background and economic conditions.

Therefore, the task of the contemporary social policy is to establish the rules of sharing, regulate the institutional structure of the social sphere, regulate financial-economic systems and their functionality and create conditions for the harmonious growth, local government and participation of the recipients. The momentum of contemporary social policy programmes should thus be the equal opportunities principle: derived from civil rights and regarded as the key criterion of the evaluation of the efficiency of social and economic structures (availability, solidarity), and the above-mentioned subsidiarity principle (not to replace people/structures in activities that they can do themselves). Both principles should be supported by the individual, obligatory/voluntary foresight.

Demographic prognoses, the health and fitness of the population, the world economy, increasing social problems, globalisation of cultures, decrease in social activity and the problems of contemporary family and non-family institutions caused by economic, adaptation and educational problems of the young generation require acknowledgement by the public scene actors four main categories of social policy programmes:

– children and the youth (the principle of the primacy of issues related to children and the young generation),

– senior citizens (the principle of intergenerational compensation and solidarity),

– people with disabilities (the principle of social integration and normalisation).

The supplement of the priority recipients of social policy are:

– emergency programmes designed for people and groups who find themselves in a difficult life situation as a result of: poverty, unemployment, addictions, chronic disease, helplessness; for former inmates, refugees, repatriates, etc. (the principle of solidarity towards individuals and groups in need) (Figure 4).

On the central, regional and local level, such a conceptual and implementational framework of social policy is, relatively speaking, the easiest way for policy makers and their social partners to determine and prioritise minimum rules which are protected and favoured in social programmes, such as:

1. Promotion of the young generation; conditions for an equal start and chances to acquire the ability to face life challenges. Social programmes should provide the generation entering adulthood with skills, social competences and independence. An independent, adult life means *real*, not only legal, *responsibility* for one's own development, future life standard and position in social structure (social stratification).

2. Protection and improvement of life standards of the dependent community members and their families.

3. Compensation of the life standard that has decreased as a result of health/intellectual deficits or life events.

4. Protection from discrimination, marginalisation and social exclusion.

<table>
<tr><td colspan="12">Social policy</td></tr>
<tr><td colspan="12">Values</td></tr>
<tr><td colspan="6">Principles</td><td colspan="6">Principles</td></tr>
<tr><td colspan="12">Domaines of social policy</td></tr>
<tr><td colspan="2">Emplyment
labour market</td><td colspan="2">Housing</td><td colspan="3">Education</td><td colspan="2">Health
Fitness</td><td colspan="3">Family
Household</td></tr>
<tr><td colspan="2">Culture</td><td colspan="2">Sport,
recreation,
relaxation</td><td colspan="3">Transport</td><td colspan="2">Security</td><td colspan="3">Deviancies</td></tr>
<tr><td colspan="12">Key strategies</td></tr>
<tr><td colspan="3">Intervention</td><td colspan="3">Assurance</td><td colspan="3">Compensation</td><td colspan="3">Participation</td></tr>
<tr><td colspan="12">Priorities</td></tr>
<tr><td colspan="4">Children, youth</td><td colspan="4">Senior citizens</td><td colspan="4">Disabled</td></tr>
</table>

Figure 4. Structure of social policy

Source: own elaboration.

5. Provision of relief to people/groups in a temporarily difficult life situation.

Such aims and priorities of social policy mean that social help *completes* the social security system and is addressed to people/groups at particular risk of being below the *social security threshold*. The package of emergency programmes should thus include mainly reliefs, emergency/support/protection programmes of the public sector and other elements of social support system, activated and implemented according to the subsidiarity principle.

Contemporary systems of social life organisation and the infrastructure of social support are based on the activity of the state and its specialised institutions and the resourcefulness and solidarity of particular people and groups (as much state as necessary – as little as possible). Implementing the subsidiarity principle and dialogue, reforming state structures and institutions, contemporary societies take over the public tasks and goods which were earlier assigned to the state (self-organisation).

The programmes designed to build and strengthen civil society are based on the strategy of incorporating bigger and bigger segments of society into the ruling (decision-making) process, increasing their possibility of action in the key areas of social life and extending mediation structures.

From the perspective of social development, individualism and free market must be supported by the practice of incorporating citizens into the ruling process and by socialising decisions. Therefore, the contemporary state and its agendas (of the government and local government), by means of various legal and financial instruments, build a quite cohesive, complementary and functional system of social support with NGOs as an important element. The most secure way of improving and maintaining the standard and quality of life is by enabling community members to make decisions about the key matters determining living conditions and quality and the factors that influence them.

The growing imbalance between the requirements of social environment and the chances to meet these expectations by individuals and social groups (resources) sets a barrier for the efficiency of the public sector. There are many signs that social policy will not be effective in near future, unless the public sector makes good use of the potential of both voluntary organisations and networks of family, friendship and neighbour ties.

Dynamic social policy means that every member of a community can and should be an architect and a catalyst of change in this sphere (particularly on a local level), because communities are strong when human potential is released. Trust and relationships are built, creativity and resources are mobilised for some future vision and the community encourages social leadership (social capital).

Citizens'involvement in solving their own problems does not, however, absolve the state and its institutions from the responsibility of realising tasks related to social policy programmes. The proportion of public sector participation in creating living conditions and guaranteeing social security and the quality of life and the resourcefulness and solidarity of citizens reveals the real character of the state and its social policy.

According to the repeatedly invoked subsidiarity principle, the burden of implementing social policy is currently shifting to different levels of local government, the private sector and primary social groups (family, friendship circles, and neighbourhood). A critical issue for post-industrial societies is economic entities taking the responsibility for the society.[12] Academic and direct practice is also increasingly interested in corporate business responsibility; moreover, there are new instruments to implement it.

The social policy tasks of public authorities go beyond providing individuals and families (particularly those living in difficult conditions) with access to the systems of social support. They also include providing resources to help reach the potential necessary for functioning independently and harmoniously. Therefore, it is necessary to expand the area of health and social security and develop the universal principle of assisting people in danger as well as to

[12] Corporate Social Responsibility assumes that responsibility means not only fulfilling all formal and legal requirements, but also an increased investment in human resources and the environment and community-oriented activities which can have real impact on the efficiency of the business activity – it is not only a cost but also an investment.

anticipate events and create conditions for development and improvement of quality of life.

In this context, social security is not social policy *sensu stricto* but only one of its tools. It does not create all conditions for generating benefits and services guaranteed by law and included in the system of social support for potential clients.

What should activate community resources in order to satisfy needs and induce changes to improve efficiency of actions in critical situations which pose a threat to social safety and/or independence, is social work, that is, aprofessional discipline that seeks to:

– identify, minimise and/or remove socio-economic imbalance between an individual and his/her social environment,

– regain/strengthen the potential of individuals, groups and communities,

– provide tools of life change,

– induce changes to improve efficiency of action in problematic (crisis) situations which can lead to insufficiency and/or helplessness of people and groups at social risk.

By activating intervention procedures, special benefits and services, social work becomes one of the significant factors of social control (fighting social deviations, protecting victims of abuse, e.g. ill-treated children, women, etc.).

What should enliven a community and its resources is the idea of advocacy of the rights, needs and interests of citizens. It focuses on the protection of equality and standard and quality of life, and is related to care and support (in the health and social sphere), and designed to protect the right to self-determination. Advocacy of individuals and groups whose position is weaker than others (usually not of their own will or fault) does not mean deciding or acting *for* a client. It is rather a protection of their rights, providing information and support which enable clients to make the best possible decision.

Responsibility for creating conditions for social development cannot rest solely in the social security system but must be spread over all departments of state administration.

Social policy on a central level, via parliamentary and governmental decisions (legislation, national and EU programmes, recommendations of international organisations):

– guarantees the protection of human rights and the rules of participatory democracy,

– determines structural and institutional directions and framework of this policy, and the protected areas and/or areas excluded from pure market game,

– declares what and who the state takes responsibility for as the creator, catalyst and guarantor of conditions which favour the development of individuals and communities,

– applies/restores solidarity in the allocation of resources through redistributive taxation and institutional forms of social support,

– distributes responsibility between different organisational levels of the of state and civil society structures and delegates competences to various state structures in the process of constructing and implementing social policy,

– defines social policy actors and principles of intersectoral cooperation.

Therefore, social policy on the central level means designing legal and organisational framework (legislation and redistribution) for actions devoted to the equal treatment and development of citizens/groups/communities, improvement of their life quality and conditions and opening a way to the mainstream of social life to them.

In the process of designing and implementing social policy on a regional level, local government authorities act as:

– spokesperson/representative for the people/groups/communities it is legally responsible for, as well as their issues, needs and problems (protection of rights, statutory responsibility),

– promoter of actions supporting sustainable development, availability, cohesion[13] and social integration,

– initiator of normative solutions on national/regional/local level (parliamentary and political lobbying in the EU forum and the international organisations that the country belongs to),

– action-planning organ which develops solutions to satisfy the needs of citizens/regional groups/local communities,

– connector and catalyst in the relations between the "centre," mediatory structures of the local government and local communities (information, rights, realising priorities, support, etc.),

– entity which financially supports statutory tasks related to social policy,

– creator of social infrastructure development according to the statutory tasks related to social policy,

– partner and consultant in solving social problems and meeting the needs of individuals/groups/communities on a given level of local government structure.

---

[13] A society is cohesive when people share responsibility and create a community in which there is mutual support, and people pursue the same aims with democratic methods. Building social cohesion is based mainly on human and civil rights and facilitation of social and economic development.

Such a social policy uses two important components – power/authority and social influence – to allow people to create conditions for life and development, to control and prevent destructive forces which pose a threat to individual and collective development; and to create conditions for various social groups so they can articulate their interests, particularly minority groups and groups at risk of marginalisation and/or social exclusion.

To meet these challenges, social policy must be an integral part of development policy, supporting sustainable development, creating cohesive and functional communities and the citizens' agency and activity. In this sense, social policy is all the public authorities (government, local government) do or deliberately refrain from doing[14] in the crucial spheres determining the quality of life, satisfying citizens' needs and solving the problems of a community.

2. Social policy as the creator and guarantor of the conditions for successful ageing

Politics is a never-ending process of correcting the world.
Sakaguchi Ango (Japanese writer)

Senior citizens with a lot of life experience are usually asked how their life has been and what they did to live to such an advanced age. The globalisation of population ageing addresses more complex questions – about the factors influencing the social position of older persons, which could be considered both constraints and opportunities. The answers to these questions will provide the data to help develop scenario(s) of successful ageing.[15]

Successful, satisfactory ageing manifests itself in the functional features (qualities) of an individual, such as: good health and psycho-physical fitness, well-being and independence, remaining productive and willing and capable of participation in social life (optimising potential), achieving personal and social integration at a level which is sufficient for social functioning, achieving

[14] Such a definition is often proposed by American authors.

[15] The term was probably first used by R. Havighurst ("Successful aging," *The Gerontologist*, 1961, no. 1, pp. 4–7). The theory has been developed since 1990s by Rowe and Kahn, Berkman et al.; Seeman et al., Palmore, Bearon, and later by Ryff, Featherman, Smith, Butler, Erlemeier and Peterson, Baltes and Baltes. See L. Bearon, "Successful Aging: What does the 'good life' look like?," *Concepts in Gerontology*, 1996, vol. 1, no. 3; M. Halicka, *Satysfakcja życiowa ludzi starych. Studium teoretyczno-empiryczne* [Life Satisfaction of the Elderly. A Theoretical and Empirical Study], Akademia Medyczna w Białymstoku, Bialystok 2004. Definitions by other Polish authors can be found in: M. Kaczmarczyk, E. Trafiałek, "Aktywizacja osób w starszym wieku jako szansa na pomyślne starzenie" [Activation of the Elderly as a Chance for Successful Ageing], *Gerontologia Polska*, 2007, vol. 15, no. 4.

the ability to constructively revise and adapt expectations (life wisdom) to the demands of reality (increasing longevity demands increasing resourcefulness), maintaining active control over life events and the possibility of making choices. Understanding ageing in such a way also significantly depends on the level and scope of the social competence of the elderly in solving life problems, and on institutional infrastructure (formal and informal institutions) in the case of an ageing person losing their independent functioning (Figure 5).

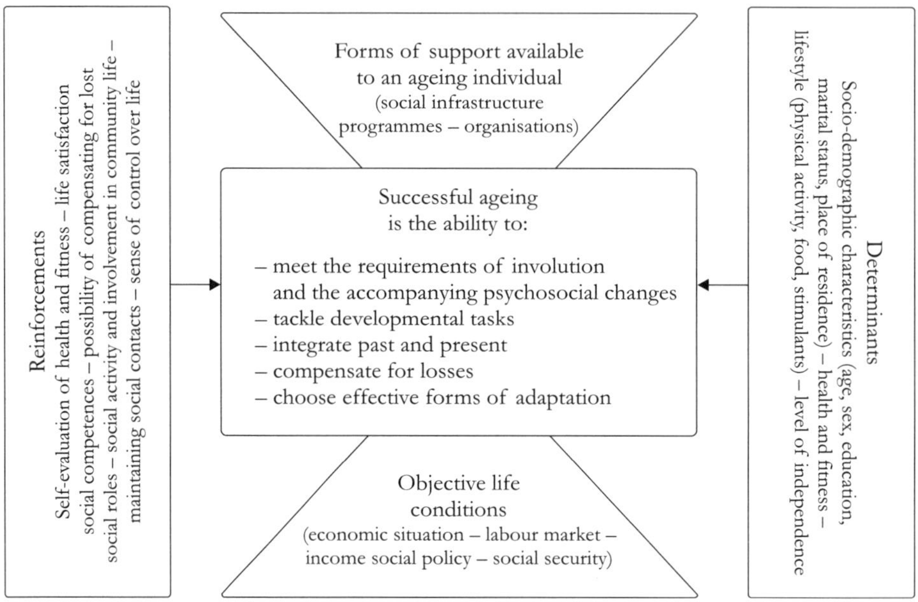

Figure 5. Determinants of successful ageing

Source: own elaboration.

Therefore, further world social and economic development will be determined by programmes which guarantee the quality of human life, based on such values as equality, social justice and solidarity and respect for human dignity.

A very useful and fruitful holistic theory of senior policy, described in detail later in the book, is the proposal of B. Szatur-Jaworska[16] to adopt a dual perspective of the two models of designing social policy[17]:

[16] B. Szatur-Jaworska, *Ludzie starzy i starość w polityce społecznej* [Elderly People and Old Age in Social Policy], Dom Wydawniczy Elipsa, Warsaw 2000, p. 119.

[17] According to Szatur-Jaworska, the proposed classification of social policy perspectives is more analytical than practical and is useful at an early stage of programming (defining goals and values) and the final stage of evaluating results. At the mid stage of planning and implementation, the difference between the two aspects is small. Ibidem, p. 125.

1. Social policy on ageing as a phase of the life cycle: it is based on the accepted understanding of ageing and its location within the whole life cycle and on the recognition of needs and threats characteristic to this life period. This model includes strategic actions of the state, its institutions, and other public actors aimed at shaping the attitudes and behaviour towards the elderly that influence their social status (equal rights, availability, transformation of social consciousness) and create optimal conditions for the elderly (infrastructural and social support systems), thereby determining their role and position in economic strategy and/or national development, etc. (labour market, contribution to GDP, consumption, etc.). The state, as the organiser of social life, performing sovereign functions such as legislation, redistribution and control (parliament, government), has the dominant role in shaping the policy on ageing. It has the duty to provide the elderly with legal security, to improve their living conditions and to integrate the elderly into the mainstream of social life in such areas as: legislation (legal valence of the subsidiarity and social status principle, health and social safety, rules and forms of social participation), health, education and employment policy, availability of the public sphere and institutional systems (decisive role of the parliament, government and its agendas), principles of legal and financial support of the elderly and the organisation of the civic sector. In democracy, local government is responsible for the development and functioning of institutional infrastructure bounded by legislation (internal and commissioned tasks: education, creating jobs in collaboration with business, culture and recreation, social security, rehabilitation, support of families taking care of the elderly), building cooperation and supporting local organisation of the civil sector. The requirement for the efficient functioning of this model (ageing as a phase of the life cycle) in social policy is monitoring the phenomena on a trans-local level (prevention of ageing) and observing social stratification of the elderly (position of the older people from different social and health categories) as well as in-depth and cyclical diagnosis of the needs, possibilities and expectations of the oldest generation (typical and specific from the perspective of social position).

2. Social policy for the benefit of the elderly (structural-categorical approach): formulating aims and performing actions aimed at the elderly as a social category in a population. It is a policy designed and implemented based on a diagnosis of needs. Its point of reference is a collection of individuals with a given health condition, efficiency and experience related to it and with qualities and indicators of their social position, problems and life course – those of universal character and those caused by the ageing process. In this approach, aims, tasks and evaluations of social policy are defined from the perspective of their influence on ageing, the elderly and their environment

(family, social circles, communities). This model is a practical interpretation and implementation of legislative solutions regulating issues related to the social position of the elderly, their living conditions and the quality of life. There are three main goals of this model of social policy: protection of income security and the quality of life; full integration into the mainstream of social life; prevention/removal of the social barriers that senior citizens must often face.[18]

> This methodological approach [...] enriches the range of problems of research and diagnosis of the process of satisfying needs oriented this way [...], given from the perspective of the position [of the elderly – Z. W.] in a society and determinants of this life phase provides a basis for a more comprehensive programme of social policy.[19]

The efficiency of such diverse action forms and types requires an organisational and conceptual framework and an implementational infrastructure. I thus propose a three-layer structure of gerontological programmes (a "tool box"), built on the social policy addressed to the elderly, embedded in social legislation, which defines the tasks of the state and its structures in implementing sectoral policies designed to anticipate events and create emergency social programmes addressed to particular groups on the basis of existing financial and organisational resources (budget and social infrastructure) (Figure 6).

Actions designed to improve or maintain the conditions and quality of life of the increasing senior population will concern the following: active and healthy ageing, advocacy of needs, problems and issues of the oldest generation, educational and training programmes aimed at ageing persons, gerontological research and dissemination of findings, and extending the international gerontological database.

I thus assume that social policy on ageing and the elderly, in the broadest sense, is a set of deliberate, organised, complex and cross-sectoral actions of public authorities and other actors in the public scene, which:

– create, improve and/or maintain the conditions and quality of life of ageing citizens,

– ensure the protection of social status and personal and social safety of the elderly,

– allow senior citizens to actively participate in culture and social life,

---

[18] There is a tension between these aims – excessive concentration on health problems may lead to ignoring factors and processes which help protect the status and position of the elderly and integrating old people into the mainstream of social life, which consequently increases the number of people at a high risk of losing social safety and independence. Neglecting the process of integrating the elderly brings feelings of being unwanted and unloved and may be the source of suffering or even lead to social isolation.

[19] B. Szatur-Jaworska, *Ludzie starzy i starość...* [Elderly People and Old Age...], op. cit., p. 125.

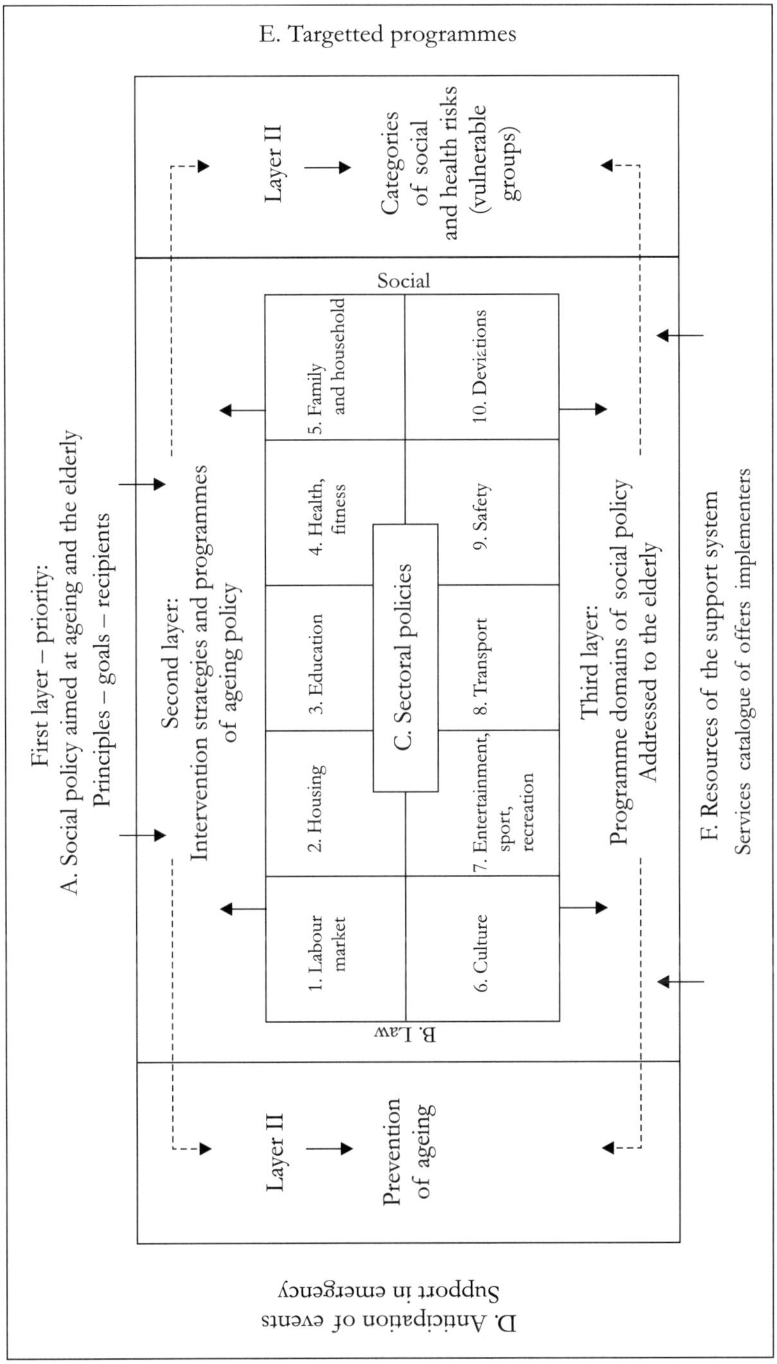

Figure 6. Conceptual frame of gerontological programmes* (three-layered "tool box")

Source: own elaboration

* Shaded boxes signalise the currently discussed layer.

– increase/maintain the potential and possibilities of the elderly to lead an active and independent life.

Therefore, actions of public authorities and their social partners following the new formula of social policy on ageing and the elderly should go beyond classic interventionist programmes and focus mainly on anticipating events, creating conditions for active and flexible performance of the elderly in the face of socio-economic changes in their environment, building people's respect and trust towards their own potential and providing possibilities to make personal choices in different phases of the life cycle. These actions are also supposed to increase the chance that the elderly will lead an independent life as long as possible, considering their health, fitness, abilities, needs and the resources of social support.

Such senior policy indicates values that should be applied in designing it, as well as goals which determine which actions and methods should or should not be taken to create decent living conditions for the elderly; it also specifies what they are and how to achieve them.

Thus, social policy on ageing and the elderly is an attempt to find a satisfactory synthesis of tradition and innovation, continuance and change, as a response to the global population ageing. It should also enable the youngest and oldest generations to satisfy their needs, which should favour the development of non-competitive intergenerational relations (Focus box 3).

The implementation of the idea of successful (healthy and active) ageing can be significantly supported by the advocacy of ageing citizens at all levels of decision-making processes and information exchange about scientific, organisational, educational and medical achievements that could accelerate/facilitate restructuring of social institutions according to the needs of the society with an increasing number of the elderly.

Therefore, the development of a well-functioning community and conditions for the quality of life of the oldest citizens through social policy should be perceived, on the one hand, as an investment by each community member (also senior) for the benefit of others, which positively affects the economic sphere and the wellbeing of all citizens, families and the state (individual and common good); on the other hand, as prevention of poverty and deviation, and promotes resourcefulness and independence in solving problems by the elderly and their social environment.

In this way, social policy – along with economic growth[20] – builds a cohesive society, a community of free, mutually supportive members of different

[20] Nowadays, economic growth is perceived as a means to achieve a more elementary goal, that is, human development. Thus, improvement of health and material situation of people (particularly dependent individuals) is the final goal of economic and social development.

groups, taking responsibility for one another and pursuing common goals with democratic methods.

Thus, social cohesion in the context of senior social policy means:

– respect of the dignity of every ageing person, recognition of their potential and right to participate in public life regardless of their culture, status, views or beliefs,

– that ageing people can choose freely to also develop in later phases of life,

– prevention of all forms of discrimination against the elderly,

– involvement in protecting and executing the rights of the elderly who are particularly exposed to discrimination and/or loss of health, physical and social safety.

Therefore, a sustainable and cohesive society with a large number of the elderly in the demographic structure must:[21]

– regard senior citizens as a valuable part of social resources,

– have scientifically-supported programmes to destroy myths and stereotypes about ageing,

– allow the elderly to be active participants in the development process,

– guarantee suitable healthcare and health promotion activities to the oldest generation,

– promote intergenerational solidarity,

– create suitable conditions and promote permanent education,

– build national and local infrastructure that supports social policy on ageing and the elderly, and special programmes addressed to senior citizens.

Social policy towards ageing and for the elderly should be implemented in all levels of of social life (national, regional, local); however, according to

---

Expenses on social goals are an investment in future sustainable economic development, not only current financial burden. This model of development is not always compatible with contemporary social values. However, democratic countries (particularly European), take on the responsibility for achieving balance between economic growth and social justice.

[21] A harbinger of the forthcoming changes were the World Health Organization recommendations, developed in the last decades of the 20th century to create a strategy for the policy on ageing based on a three-element mission: adding life to years – adding health to life – adding years to life. Also, in 1991, the UN announced something like a global constitution of the elderly, which was supposed to guarantee them the right to a dignified, safe, active and independent existence. The final version of the recommended priorities in social policy on ageing includes a 19-point Political Declaration. The Second World Assembly on Aging 2002 (04/12/2002), in its European version, was manifested in the "Berlin Ministerial Declaration: Society For All Ages" in the UNECE Region, and then specified in a detailed document, Madrid International Plan of Action on Aging 2002, with the strategic version entitled: Regional Implementation Strategy for the Madrid International Plan of Action on Aging 2002 (UN-ECE/AC.23/2002/2, 3/Rev. 2, 6, 16.09.2002).

Focus Box 3. Social policy towards ageing and the elderly

<table>
<tr><th colspan="2">Social policy towards ageing and the elderly</th></tr>
<tr><td colspan="2">Is legislative, institutional, organisational and based on a values response to the changes in socio-demographic structure of a society and, as a consequence, changes in social sub-systems, manifested in actions which are designed to:
– form general conditions for the quality of life of the oldest generation
– satisfy the needs of the elderly
– guarantee that old age has a societal position which is equal to the position of other life phases
– shape intergenerational relations
– harmonise and bring together interests of particular generations
– assist senior citizens in managing development tasks
– build a positive image of ageing in social consciousness
– create possibilities to cope with current and future situations and problems related to the ageing of community members</td></tr>
<tr><th>General principles</th><th>Global aims</th></tr>
<tr><td>– solidarity and intergenerational exchange
– agency of elderly people
– protection of the dignity of the elderly
– justice and equality in access to social infrastructure and benefits
– co-responsibility and cooperation of various actors of social policy (public authorities, social institutions, non-governmental organisations, families and the elderly)
– social participation and partnership
– universalism and selectivity in the choice of goals and actions to meet seniors' needs
– preference towards rewarding prevention rather than intervention in solving the problems of ageing
– continuity of action, durability, quality and efficiency of systemic solutions in elderly care</td><td>– protection/improvement of the conditions and quality of life of senior citizens
– strengthening the potential of the elderly and the community to support personal development, activity and self-actualisation of the oldest generation and their capacity for self-care and self-help.
– legal protection of the socio-economic status of the elderly
– addition of new social roles to the social position of the elderly
– use of the potential and experience of senior citizens in social and economic development
– creation/restoration/support of natural networks of elementary contacts and relations
– guarantee of quantitatively and qualitatively sufficient services and benefits which are adequate to needs</td></tr>
</table>

<table>
<tr><td>– state subsidiarity (public authorities delegating their entitlements to the lowest executive levels)</td><td>– anticipation of events and prevention of pauperisation, social degradation, loss of independence of ageing citizens
– change in the social image of ageing and the elderly
– intergenerational integration within society for all ages</td></tr>
<tr><td colspan="2">Priorities of senior social policy</td></tr>
<tr><td colspan="2">1. Development of institutional infrastructure supporting gerontological programmes (scientific research, social diagnosis, social work, supporting ngos, monitoring and evaluation of social security programmes)
2. Availability of education and training related to: preparation for retirement, extension of general knowledge, acquisition of new skills, neutralisation of the intergenerational cultural distance, use of new technologies, devices and institutional systems
3. Development/support of the system of institutional advocacy of the elderly (gerontological education of society, media, social organisations of the elderly, political lobby)
4. Creation of legal, institutional and material infrastructure to support independence and resourcefulness of the elderly and/or their carers
5. Elimination of/reduction in the factors contributing to marginalisation and social isolation of senior citizens and/or abuse and violence towards the elderly (biophysical, psycho-emotional and socio-economic on an individual and environmental level)
6. Development/support of various forms of actions for intergenerational integration, social participation, care and support of the oldest generation (particularly voluntary work of senior citizens and other social categories)
7. Providing infrastructural conditions for creation of actions for health and active ageing
8. "Implanting" physical environment of the elderly (removing architectural barriers, supporting independence and sense of orientation in space, house, public places and institutions, public transport)
9. Development of healthcare system and rehabilitation (revitalisation) services for senior citizens and interdisciplinary geriatric care
10. Development of various forms of long-term and hospice care (particularly environmental, familial care) and support for the carers of the chronically ill and/or disabled elderly.</td></tr>
</table>

Source: own elaboration.

Focus box 4. Role and tasks of local authorities in building foundations of legal and organisational programmes on successful ageing and satisfactory old age. Between control and influence

I. Actions at a translocal level
A. Priority and permanent tasks of local authorities:
Approaching central state organs with proposals for changes in legislation regulating status, living conditions and functioning of the elderly in society and in local communities. these tasks are based on diagnosis, social inspection and monitoring of access to social infrastructure and changes in the social position of the elderly.
B. Political and parliamentary lobbying of local authorities for:
1. Elaboration of a long-term plan to fully adjust the law regulating ageing issues to the solutions recommended by the EU. 2. An amendment to the law in order to remove barriers which hinder independent functioning of senior citizens – target: adoptation of a uniform law regulating issues of the elderly. 3. Increasing sanctions for not obeying the regulations protecting the rights, the conditions and the quality of life of the elderly (independent monitoring). 4. Real presentation of ageing in political and media discourse, including possibilities and limitations of successful ageing and satisfactory old age. 5. Elaboration and governmental support of the following programmes: – continuing education – extending the period of professional activity of senior citizens – introducing issues related to ageing and old age to professional training for the employees of central public administration and for the caring professions – creating statutory and financial conditions for operating or supporting the network of Centres for independence and quality of life of senior citizens – in future such endeavours should be connected with projects addressed to people with limited abilities.
C. Tasks initiated by local authorities:
1. Combining resources of different actors working for social integration of the elderly; annual review of the situation in this area – every year in a different region/province/county/communes. The integrator's role should be played by a council of senior citizens. In cooperation with academic institutions and at a self-governmental level. 2. Exchange of experiences and "good practices" in solving problems of the elderly as a result of international exchanges in self-government (partner towns/counties/communes).

3. Leading national programmes/contests by public authorities and the media promoting institutional solutions to maintain maximum level of independence of senior citizens. 4. Verification of existing solutions and legislation gaps and update of norms and standards specifying technical and spatial parameters of design without barriers.
II. Actions at a local level
A. Within the control and power of self-government:
General principle: Not to create entities beyond measure and needs – self-government should primarily: – make maximum use of resources and competences of existing institutions and organisations – improve the coordination of actions of particular decision-makers at all levels of the process of developing gerontological programmes and within self-governmental structures
1. Intervention actions: protection of senior citizens against discriminatory practices – particularly in healthcare and social security systems.
2. Priorities: – everything that serves the citizens and lies within the competence of self-government authorities must also be available for the ageing and the aged – new social policy programmes addressed to the elderly developed in cooperation with organisations of senior citizens and/or for senior citizens – periodical, repeating gerontological education of officials and decision-makers of different levels (compulsory training for newly employed – preferred forms: workshops, social inspections, regular assistance for at-risk groups and observations in elderly care institutions) – initiating/supporting social campaigns for "opening" social awareness for issues related to the position and needs of the elderly – expanding material resources for intergenerational integration programmes – development of an interactive information system for elderly support resources systems (website; information desks in offices, leaflets) – coordination of promotion and media activity related to ageing.
3. Successive and relatively fast introduction of the universal design principles for spatial planning, building and housing, providing the opportunity for: – significant improvement of the quality of life of all community members – overcoming the minority status of the elderly, particularly the disabled.

Universal design principles are: – evaluation criteria – tools to monitor architectural and urban projects and products intended to appear in public spaces
4. Incorporation of the representatives of senior organisations into the process of consulting and evaluating projects on social, welfare, architectural and urban solutions, at all stages of the decision and investment process, from designing to implementation.
5. Strengthening of the process of coordinating and controlling decisions about local regulation of issues related to the conditions and quality of life of the oldest members of local community.
B. Within the sphere of influence of self-government:
1. Initiation/creation/support of the projects for: – creating gerontological programmes at self-government level – monitoring housing conditions of the elderly with disabilities – disseminating information about integration and health/welfare projects addressed to the oldest citizens – disseminating information about the implementers of senior-friendly projects and programmes – starting annual contests for innovative senior-friendly projects and programmes (winners are chosen by a panel consisting of decision-makers, experts, academics, NGO – representatives, representatives of advocates of the elderly and the media.
2. Organisation of annual meetings of the public authorities with the advocates of senior citizens (presenting planned projects, evaluation of meeting the obligations).
3. Popularisation, through electronic and other media, of the lists of exemplary institutions and those which do not meet the requirements of availability for the elderly.
4. Activation/introducing of a system for collecting complaints and proposals from older citizens (electronic and traditional, written).

5.	Introducing a unit (in cooperation with architecture faculties of universities) which would give and verify the right to use an international mark of the availability of an object establishing an institution (in cooperation with architectural faculties of universities) which could award and verify the international title proving that a building is suitable for all citizens.
6.	Support given to agreements, coalitions and ad hoc solutions within the circle of advocates/organisations of and for the elderly which support real participation of the elderly in the life of a community
7.	Enabling senior non-governmental organisations to evaluate projects and organisational solutions in the self-governmental system of social security and healthcare from the perspective of the protection of the civil rights of the elderly.
8.	Informing public opinion about investors/owners of buildings who do not honour the obligation of providing public space which is available to the elderly with disabilities.
9.	Organisation of periodical press conferences with officials and senior ngo representatives about projects addressed to the oldest generation.
10.	Organisation of annual meetings of local authorities with the representatives of senior organisations and/or the advocates of the oldest members of a community; the meetings would be devoted to issues related to implementing gerontological programmes.
11.	Inspection of the availability of new buildings which are not under the rule of the self government authorities to the elderly by applicable self-governmental structures – inspections should be carried out with the participation of the elderly with disabilities and with the use of universal tool to measure architectural barriers (comparability of data from different years).
12.	Use of sanctions against self-governmental institutions which generate social, legal and architectural barriers in the public space; sanctions should be preceded and supported by repeated social campaigns.

Source: own elaboration.

the subsidiarity principle, the role of family, public actors and social organisations which are closest to the ageing persons is also significant (Focus box 4).

To conclude this part, it should be stated that the policy on ageing and the elderly is a set of systemic and legislation goals, strategies and actions, taken at a local as well as regional and national level in order to maintain and/or improve the social status and the quality of life of the elderly, unlock their potential and increase their chances for an active and independent life.

The direction, which the policy on ageing can/should follow in the next decades, will be determined by the following quotient:

$$\frac{\text{Policy}}{\text{on aging}} = \frac{\text{4P (Protection – Prevention – Promotion –Participation)}}{\text{4I (Ideologies – Interests – Institutions – Information)}}$$

The 4P formula will become a central element of long-term social policy programmes on ageing and the elderly and the following conceptual elements should be its components:

1. Protection (care) – for a dozen years or so, European experts have recommended that the members make particularly intensive efforts to provide health security and the stability of the pension system, e.g. through maintaining the ability to work (blunting the "retirement guillotine," return to work after a period of economic inactivity), increasing the employment of the elderly and the retirement contribution.[22]

Protection of the social and health status of the elderly enables elderly people to choose their way of life freely and to lead an independent life in their usual environment as long as they want to and for as long as possible, with:

– housing that corresponds to their needs and their state of health, or adequate help to fit their house,

– medical care and services corresponding to their state,[23]

– the circulation of information concerning existing services and facilities for elderly people and the possibility for them to have access to them,

---

[22] Member countries should remain responsible for the modernisation of social security and social welfare systems but the effects of these reforms should be a common concern. The role of EU is to support the modernisation efforts of member countries, see: *Paper on Relevance to EU Social Objectives*, European Commission, Research Directorate-General; Programme: Quality of Life and Management of Living Resources – The Aging Population and Disabilities, Brussels, 11.04.2000.

[23] Over 20 years ago, Scandinavian countries counted that the cost of living of one resident of a nursery home is equal to the cost of 2 hours of nursing care and 3 hours of other care services provided for the whole year.

– appropriate care for elderly people who live in institutions, respecting their private life and participation in determining the living conditions in the institution.[24]

The protection of the social status and health of the elderly includes: access to adequate food and nutrition, safe housing and physical amenities, safe use of medication and household chemicals, and the availability of medications and various amenities, devices and prostheses which allow the elderly to lead an independent life. Public authorities should take steps to protect elder consumers from aggressive advertising and sales promotions, which diminish their already limited financial resources.

2. Prevention – preventive actions are taken to identify, minimise and/or remove *imbalance* between ageing individuals and their social environment and to regain or strengthen their potential and the potential of groups and communities they belong to. Programmes on active ageing, which support senior citizens in performing significant, *productive* social roles, e.g. acknowledgment and appreciation of senior voluntary work, are also preventive actions. Their main aim is to stop and reverse the process of attributing the status of people without social roles to the elderly.

Moreover, preventive actions incorporate interventionist procedures in the case of social deviations among the elderly and the protection of the victims of abuse and violence. Ageing prevention includes important interventionist elements which influence the life stabilisation of the elderly – actions of social security institutions and NGOs complete the social security system and are addressed to circles/groups of people at particular risk of falling below the minimum social security level (overcoming shortages, correcting deficiencies).

All promotional and preventive programmes should be oriented towards:

– an individual: by helping to develop personal skills and knowledge, change attitudes, behaviour and relationships with other people,

– a community and its institutional environment, social system, organisations and other social actors that aim to support/protect health, fitness and activity of the community members, and to reorient the benefits addressed to senior citizens.

Promotional strategies aim at changing the functioning of a group (e.g. family or a group of friends) or the state, the social system, an institution and/or an organisation (authorities, social system, neighbourhood, school, workplace, etc.).

[24] In EU countries, 4.0–5.0% of the elderly live in nursing homes. In the USA the number of people aged 85 or more is estimated to increase 6-fold by 2050 compared to 1980 (in Poland: less than 1.0%). http://users.skynet.be/delperee/NICOLE/European_social_policy.pdf [accessed: 10.05.2012].

3. Promotion of ageing (propagating active ageing, education, change of the social image of ageing and the elderly) – requires mobilisation of non-traditional actors such as: science, the media, the private sector, young people and children. The media and the education system play a particularly important role in raising social awareness and overcoming ageing stereotypes and prejudice.[25]

Children and young people are quite a new priority for the programmes on ageing and are subject to the following assumptions:

– childhood as the cradle of longevity – individual capacity to start the process of adaptation to ageing early in life is thus a condition of the change of social attitudes towards ageing and the elderly,

– Both individual behaviour and national policy (affecting different age groups, particularly young people) will have an effect on the real position of the elderly in the coming years,

– the contemporary youth is a significant target group of social policy – they need new knowledge and skills, and need to learn behaviour which will allow them to enter their old age with health, fitness, a sound financial situation, sufficient income, a habit of saving money and the support of family and the community.

Promotion of ageing also means using the inherent potential and resources of an individual and their environment. Active ageing, supported by ingenuity and initiative and building resourcefulness demands a favourable environment; multifaceted capital created over a lifetime (money, natural environment, people and their skills, cohesion of the community, social bonds, etc.) and the ability of families, local communities and the social system to adapt to changes related to population ageing. What can foster this process, particularly in local communities, is developing centres for initiatives and counselling which address their work to people of middle and more advanced ages.

4. Participation (participation of senior citizens in social life and the process of making the decisions that affect them) – participation presumes intergenerational integration: each generation contributes rare and specific resources to the community and thus strengthens both the community and individual partners. In future, the position of the elderly in relations with other generations will strengthen; senior citizens will be the ones who possess and carry cultural patterns, values, role models and life experience.

Participation also means involving retirees in the process of satisfying their own needs and solving individual and social problems. Social programmes that

[25] Attempts to conduct gerontological research on a European level have been coordinated, as well as dissemination their results and promotion and exchange of best practices on international, national, regional and local level – e.g. 5th Framework Program of EU.

focus on increasing the participation of the elderly in the life of a community should include all aspects of social life (also the labour market) and foster self-education, civil education and attitudes of acceptance of different life phases. They should also consider social space (group, community space) as one's own. Experience of the countries with a long democratic history demonstrates that older people should and must have their own say in their own matters and participate in making the decisions that concern them – otherwise social programmes will belittle and ignore the issues, needs and problems of this growing social category.

Councils and committees composed of senior citizens (silver-haired legislature) play a significant role in establishing the equal social position of the elderly. They have influence over the course of events which are important for the local community, including the oldest generation.

The possibility for initiation and efficient realisation of the 4P formula (protection, prevention, promotion, participation) is determined by the 4I (ideologies, interests, institutions, information[26]):

Ideologies. They are rooted in the assumptions and views about the individual and social life, the role and function of the state, institutions, etc. Values, connected with ideas, generate diverse systems of beliefs about ageing, old age and the elderly (e.g. the position of senior citizens in the social system, the role of the state and family in the care of the elderly, etc.). Values, which underlie the surface of ideologies, mobilise public authorities and maintain/reproduce hopes that politicians' promises will be fulfilled. Ideas filter political and social programmes; decisions and actions are taken according to ideological positions of both decision-makers and social partners (regulative ideas).

Interests. The contest of interest groups in a society is called politics. It is articulated by:

– elites, parties in political coalitions – a subset of the political system, composed of groups with stable, close relationships and connections, restricted membership, having interests in the same political area. They focus on macro-political effects (system, power, maintaining political hegemony over other actors), are privileged in decision-making and policy implementation; political players often compete against each other regardless of their beliefs or preferences, using their resources and position in the professional hierarchy to attempt to control the process of information exchange and the access to key decision makers;

[26] The relationship: *interests – ideologies – information – institution* and its role in creating the image of public policy. See C. Weiss, "Research-policy Linkages: How Much Influence Does Social Science Research Have?," in *World Social Science. Report 1999*, UNESCO Publishing, Elsevier, Paris – London 1999, s. 198.

– expert groups and advisory bodies - define and explain problems concerning certain political areas, provide decision makers and public opinion with a communicatively simplified explanation of alternative solutions (decisions); disseminate results of diagnoses and proposed methods of solving problems which are at the centre of politicians' attention. Experts and advisors have a privileged position in the access to information and significant people. They are also let into debates about ideas, presumptions, goals and strategies of a certain policy. Experts' involvement in direct political decisions which is too intense may jeopardise their ideological neutrality and/or may result in subjectivisation and politicisation of expertise and real influence on the decisions of public authorities which go beyond the stage of formulating policies (power beyond the throne[27]);

– bureaucracy – public administration is involved in conflicts and negotiations between different actors inside the systemic *machinery*. Bureaucrats use these conflicts to increase the influence of their office, win the support of constituents and advance their own careers. The individual goals of these players conflict with the priorities of groups, organisational structures and governmental institutions which attempt to maintain control over the public scene through administration;

– local communities and citizens – due to the increasing dependence of individual citizens on policies, political plans, necessities, successes and failures have a direct impact on individual fates. Therefore, social participation is believed to be a chance for the real expression of people's interests and needs as well as citizens' empowerment. The emphasis that the state and social actors put on the principles and goals of the social policy (with the leading role of the institutions of civil society) is supposed to reduce the *state-society* dichotomy. The subsidiarity principle plays an important role in this process as it alleviate tensions, reduces the areas of potential conflict of interests between individuals/groups/communities and different levels of the organisation of social life.

Values often clash with interests, become instrumentalised (state interest, class interest, public interest, etc.) and are contrasted with individual interests. Thus, decision makers (management) should mark out the real game field for these divergent interests[28] and focus their attention-influence-resources on reaching balance rather than optimising effects.

Institutions. Institutional systems should be a response to recognised needs and social problems. They should also have a social control function (encouragement, giving an impulse towards desired behaviour to power structures, administration, organisation and citizens). Political players who function in

[27] Ibidem, p. 194.

[28] R. Sutton, *The Policy Process...*, op. cit., p. 26 and next.

organisational structures use infrastructural resources to compete against each other and achieve their aims (ideological, political) – not necessarily according to the real needs of the society or the statutory tasks (institutional dysfunctionality). In this way, they create dependency paths in access to particular social services and benefits (law, money, influence). In the pursuit of political success, decision makers sometimes only adapt new laws for the sake of it[29] and avoid making decisions which go beyond the term of office of elective bodies or the time of performing a political function. Such tendencies can be strengthened by limited resources which result in congestions of institutional systems and lead to the deformation of statutory tasks and goals (risk of the juridisation of the public life and erosion of law).

4. Information. Contemporary policy is a communicative process, and the most elementary and universal sources of power and influence are information and knowledge.[30] This political ammunition helps to create and disseminate ideologies, allows decision makers to define developmental interests and facilitates the decision process. For many organisational structures and institutions, particularly for bureaucracy, the source of power and political influence is the control over information and transfer of knowledge between different organisational levels of a system.[31] Thus, the distribution of information and knowledge is often more important than the redistribution of other resources – this does not always, however, serve individual or group interests. This way of policy making or exercising power may be perceived by citizens as a tool to manipulate social consciousness and a source of creating false images of meeting social needs and representing the interests of all social categories on the same level and in a similar way.[32]

Each "I" element interacts with all the others, which may lead to the emergence of new policy directions.

To conclude: Rationality and efficiency of strategies and programmes of the policy designed for senior citizens (4P) depend on the impact of interest groups (e.g. producers of medical equipment and medications, senior organisations), rooted in certain ideologies (leftist-central-rightist, social movements, civil society), on the principles behind financing gerontology programmes and organisational structures which support them (systemic solutions, politi-

[29] N. Luhmann, *Political Theory in the Welfare State*, de Gruyter, Berlin 1994.

[30] A. Toffler, *Powershift: Knowledge, Wealth and Violence at the Edge of the 21st Century*, Bentam Books, New York 1990.

[31] N. Luhmann, *Political Theory...*, op. cit.; A. Toffler, *Powershift: Knowledge, Wealth and Violence...*, op. cit.

[32] T. Atlee, *Transformational Politics*, London 1999, www.co-intelligence.org/CIPol_TransformPol2.html, p. 1 [accessed: 25.10.2011].

cal priorities, social infrastructure), and on the system of sharing information with partners (using or ignoring/marginalising expert knowledge) on all levels of planning and realising political programmes (initiating and controlling role of the civil society). The greater the unfavourable role of the "4I" elements (4I = infrastructure of decisions), the fainter the possibility of increasing the elements of "4P" (4P = strategic goals), which can translate into a domination of interventionist programmes in policies addressed to ageing and the elderly (instrumental and bureaucratic management of the problems of ageing) with little participation of senior citizens in decisions regarding their generation (difficulties in implementing the theory of the society for all ages).

The possibilities of increasing social resources in a "traditional way," that is, by simply increasing funding for a given field are shrinking, both on a local and a global level. As a result, human resources are now perceived as the most important resource for further social and economic development. Therefore, the role of contemporary social policy actors must change: their participation in creating medical and social safety for the elderly must increase.

Society is based on human relationships, repeated/continued within various mediatory structures – family, neighbourhood, local communities, economic, social, political and cultural unions – which are all autonomous subjects. Many years ago, mass societies shifted their initiative and responsibility for satisfying numerous, more or less important needs to institutions, mostly public. Now, the time has come to take over (re-vindicate) the competences in many life issues, particularly self-care and care of others, which were once given away (lost) by citizens.

For all these reasons, the future system of support and care addressed to the elderly (particularly from vulnerable groups) will demand careful, subtle forms of the evaluation of potential benefits and risks, which result from greater variety and complexity, and accessibility of solutions (apart from the family system and public institutions, an expanded, commercialised market of services and benefits will emerge). These changes must be accompanied by an integrated, inter- and over- departmental approach to economic and social planning.

The integrated, holistic model of social policy addressed to the elderly is being developed more slowly than the models used in healthcare, social security, education, tourism, etc. It is often a result of imbalanced sectoral policies (health, culture, education, etc.), which can be an obstacle in the integration of different projects addressed to the elderly and social programmes within the general social policy and developmental policy.[33]

[33] See *Report of the World Assembly on Ageing*, Vienna 26 July – 6 August 1982 (UN publication, no. E.82.01.16, VI, A, par. 49).

It should thus be acknowledged that global population ageing creates the opportunity and the necessity to face up to the needs of the society in which the proportion of the oldest generation in various structures (family, local communities, larger social groups) is increasing, which demands a synchronisation of different policies (demographic, economic, health, social) and requires that the state elaborate programmes of equal access to institutional resources, their fair distribution, the choice of appropriate intervention methods, a subsystem of long-term care (availability, duration, voluntary and professional care, public and private funding) and the protection of the civil rights of senior citizens (particularly poor and disabled).

3. Strategies and emergency programmes of the policy on ageing

A person who is wise uses more opportunities than he is given.
Francis Bacon

There is no policy without a strategy related to decision-making and goal-achievement.[34] A strategy includes important action patterns, necessary to achieve goals, and involves methods of allocating resources and making decisions which are adequate for the needs of the policy implementation. Policy provides a structure, that is, a conceptual and implementational frame so that a given strategic vision[35] can be formulated and implemented in the name of the adopted mission[36] and the organisational goals. The mission aims at reducing uncertainty and the likelihood of unexpected events as well as gaining the

[34] Strategy – Greek στϱατηγία: stratēgia, generalship, the art of distributing and applying military means to destroy enemies), in business, a way of action in a situation when the available resources are not enough; the task of strategy is an efficient use of the available resources for the achievement of a competitive advantage and capitalisation on the realised and accepted risk.

[35] Vision is the idea of the desired result after completing designed actions based on values. It may result from dissatisfaction with the current state of affairs. It should be realistic, it should design courageous/risky solutions and have a motivational function. A vision is based on a good diagnosis and contains an idea of solutions which guarantee the durability of proposed changes and self-regulatory tools and the projected institutional order.

[36] Mission is a general idea of the way to achieve the state of affairs which was articulated in the vision. Mission defines what is necessary to achieve the ultimate goal and includes general information about the method of making changes. It is a bridge between what is there and what should be. Mission does not involve direct influence on all the identified aspects of reality but places the emphasis on changes which will entail the greatest number of desired results (cost-effectiveness requirement – aim-achievement with the use of available resources).

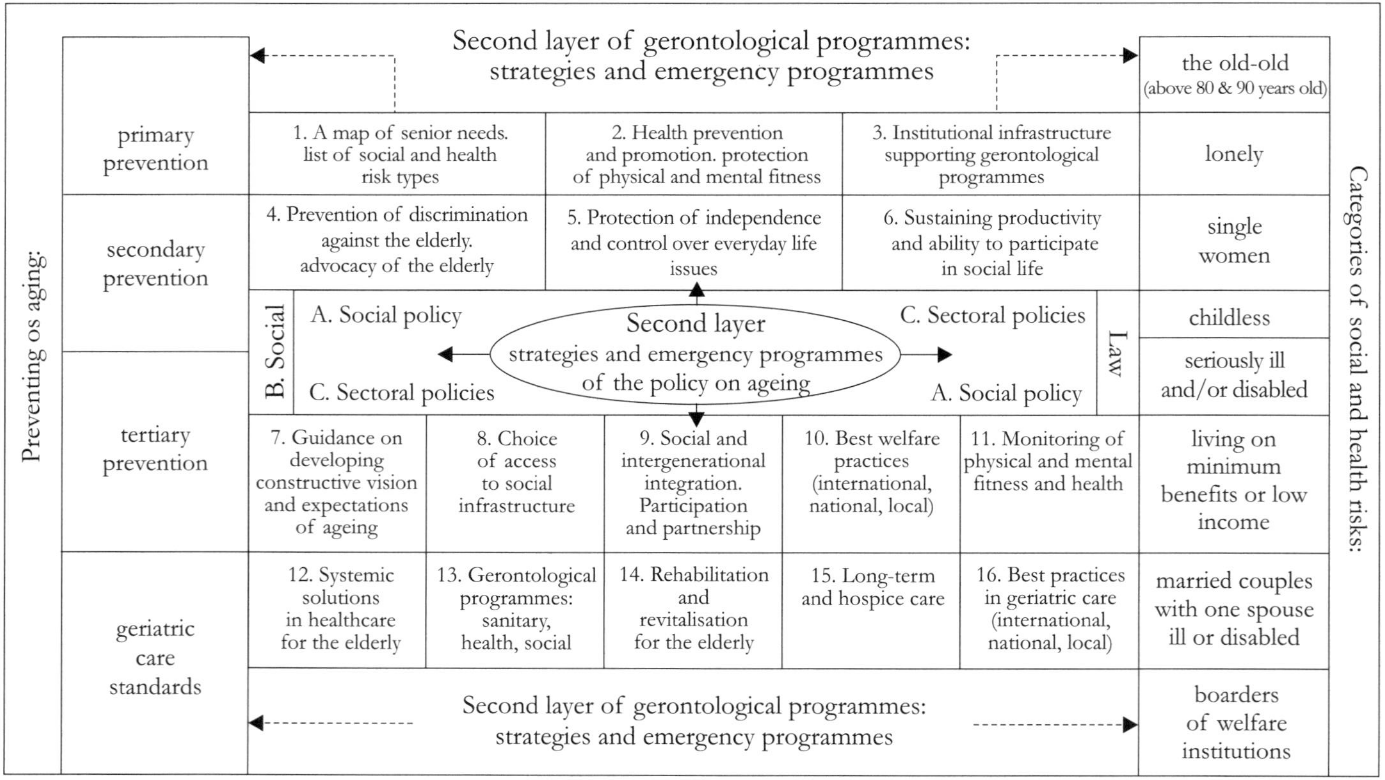

Figure 7. Conceptual frame of gerontology programmes. "Tool box" – second layer

Souce: own elaboration.

ability to cope with externally induced changes by means of actions undertaken mostly within the external organisational structure.

Therefore, the second layer of the structure of gerontology programmes consists of, on the one hand, strategies of the policies on ageing, and, on the other hand, emergency programmes of the social policy on ageing: from the actions focused on ageing prevention and the protection of the social status of the elderly to the support of the groups at high risk of losing personal, health and social safety.

Emergency programmes addressed to particular groups include diagnosis (health and social position of the elderly), infrastructure (resources and functioning of the geriatric care system) and the best practices of senior policy on a local, national and global level (Figure 7).

The processes of planning and implementing social policy on ageing should include – depending on local circumstances – the following four key strategies:[37]

– support in an emergency (intervention – elimination of deficiencies, resolution of current problems, satisfaction of needs after recognition of the problem);

– anticipation of events (security – prediction of what can happen to an individual or a group and prevention of these events; definition of the area of activity and life independence of senior citizens);

– equation of chances/lost opportunities (compensation – protection of development and/or protection/reparation of financial and social status according to the existing rules of social policy and legislation);

– co-operation (participation – social integration, improving conditions, supporting growth and participation of people and institutions in decision-making and the implementation of goals and tasks) (Figure 8).

The proposed four basic strategies of social policy on ageing and the elderly involve the following actions:

[37] The proposed model of the support of strategic social decisions was inspired by Tadeusz Szumlicz's four models of social policy: social intervention (elimination of shortages, deficiencies and negative social phenomena; release of social tensions), social anticipation (actions which anticipate threats), social distribution (access to social goods and services according to social preferences) and social integration (support of the factors which foster integration and elimination/alleviation/neutralisation of social disintegration). See T. Szumlicz, *Modele polityki społecznej* [Models of Social Policy], Monografie i Opracowania nr 376, SGH, Warsaw 1994. Having acknowledged basic theoretical assumptions of T. Szumlicz, however, I decided that the models proposed by the author should instead be seen as strategies which are a part of an integrated theory of social policy for a community/region/state with a certain scope and intensity (determined by resources, system, and social infrastructure).

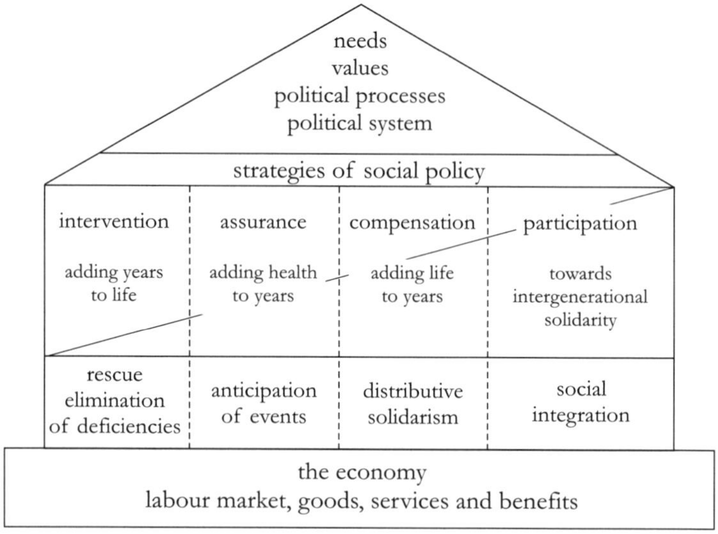

Figure 8. Model strategies of social policy on ageing and the elderly

Source: own elaboration.

1. Adding years to life[38] – a short-time, intervention-and-security strategy, focused on eliminating shortages, completing deficiencies and social emergency. Welfare completes the social security system and is addressed to people/groups at particular risk of income below the social security level. The rescue package should include diverse ad-hoc, emergency/safety/security programmes of the public sector and other elements of the social security system, launched and implemented according to the subsidiarity principle.[39] The goal of this strategy is to protect the life standard and functioning of the dependent elderly and their families, as well as providing emergency help to people/groups who are temporarily in a difficult life situation – particularly to the elderly living in poverty, the helpless, and those at risk of exclusion or marginalisation. The strategy includes actions which provide the elderly with access to sufficient amounts and quality of food, safe appliances, safe use of medications, household chemicals, and accessibility of medications and various devices, appliances and prostheses which allow the elderly to lead an independent life. It also involves restructuring/developing a complex but common and

[38] Titles of the strategies are derived from the names of programmes promoted by the UN between 1991 and 2011.

[39] Public authorities focus on tasks which cannot be passed over to other subjects and which should be fulfilled by the public sector in the name of the broadly defined public interest. The remaining authorisations (bills, regulations, resolutions of local authorities) should be delegated by public authorities to the lowest level of execution.

physically, territorially and financially accessible healthcare system adequate for medical development. Preventive measures are focused on senility prevention and are addressed to the elderly with illnesses that speed up the ageing process and/or lead to the loss of life independence. They also involve launching interventionist procedures in the case of social deviations among the elderly and the victims of abuse and violence, etc.

2. Adding years to life – medium-term security-and-compensation strategy (5–10 years), based on preventive and promotion programmes designed to anticipate age-unfriendly phenomena, events and processes, particularly in the area of health. Elements of intervention are also present, although modified. Their role is to identify, minimise and/or remove the imbalance between ageing individuals and their social environment as well as to help the elderly regain/strengthen their potential and the potential of groups they belong to (social work). The goal of this strategy is to provide the elderly with a free choice and independent way of living in their familiar social environment. Preventive measures include preventing premature and pathological ageing and are addressed to healthy, middle-aged people at risk of premature ageing (protection from disease and/or their complications). The strategy also includes a new priority within the programmes for the elderly – children and the youth. Childhood is considered the cradle of longevity and the contemporary youth is a significant target group of social policy – they need new knowledge and skills and need to learn behaviour which will allow them to enter their old age in health, fitness, with a sound financial situation, sufficient income, the habit of saving money and the support of family and the community. An individual can only adapt to the long ageing process in timely fashion when social attitudes towards ageing and old age change.

3. Adding life to years – a long-term compensation-participation strategy developed on the basis of the effects of previously launched and still functioning prevention programmes on creating healthy and active ageing, foresight, resourcefulness and the ability of self-care. The strategy involves enabling senior citizens to perform significant and productive social roles. The actions are designed to improve/keep the quality of life of senior citizens, particularly "the old-old," guarantee health safety and maintain the ability to work, increase employment among the elderly, and increase pension and stability of the pension system. They also involve providing the boarders of nursing homes with proper care, respect of privacy and participation of the boarders in defining life conditions in these institutions.

4. Developing intergenerational solidarity – a long-term, participation-integration strategy, which is expected to soon be predominant. It is based on the idea of society for all ages, which will adapt its structural

functions, policy and planning to the needs, abilities and skills of all citizens, unlocking and using generational potential to the benefit of all age categories, according to the mutuality and equity rule. In the process of intergenerational integration, every generation brings their own unique resources and skills, strengthening the community and social partners. The elderly should benefit from relations with the youth, being appreciated as those who carry culture patterns, values, role models and life experience. Senior citizens are included into the process of satisfying needs and solving individual and social problems. The elderly speak for themselves and take part in making the decisions that concern them. Participation of the elderly in community life embraces all aspects of social life, particularly the labour market, self-education and civil education. The goal of this strategy is to develop attitudes which foster acceptance and satisfaction derived from all life phases and to promote the idea of social space as *one's own* by older citizens.

Although particular strategies should be implemented on all the levels of social life organisation, there are differences between local levels and "the centre."

1. The lower the level of social life organisation, the more actions related directly to satisfying the needs of the elderly and solving problems of a community caused by the growing number of the elderly; the more tools are provided to the recipients of social policy which help them change their lives or help individuals and/or families lead independent lives (more tasks to be done by social policy and social security).

2. The higher the level of the state organisational structure (centre, region), the more often social policy includes actions designed to equalise chances of development and develop the potential of particular administrative structures which are the infrastructure of gerontological programmes (broadly defined social policy dominates).

Therefore, security-and-compensation strategy is the domain of the state on a parliamentary and governmental level, while intervention and participation-integration strategy, according to the subsidiary principle, is implemented mostly by local government agencies and the institutions and organisations of the local community.

According to experts, the lifestyle choice of healthy and active ageing[40] should begin in the earliest phases of human development (from the prenatal period) and include participation in family and social life; a balanced and healthy

[40] Vital, healthy and active ageing is a process *of optimising for physical, social and mental wellbeing at every level of individual development, to extend life expectancy* (I would add: and its quality, according to accepted standards). *The International Journal of Public Health*, Bulletin of the World Health Organization, Geneva 26.10.1999, p. 1.

diet; physical activity adequate to abilities; avoiding smoking; avoiding alcohol abuse. What supports healthy and active ageing are pro-health lifestyle programmes, development of conditions fostering good health and revitalisation, use of individual and environmental resources and minimising the dependence of the elderly, as well as promoting a positive image of ageing.

Youth is the most important category from the perspective of anticipatory educational influence, as young people need new knowledge, abilities and skills and if they want to enter their old age in good health, with a sound financial situation and with the support of family and the community. The young generation needs permanently updated information about the long-term influence of lifestyle, distress and environmental pollution on the health condition of an ageing individual.[41] Problems related to building foundations of healthy and satisfactory ageing and preventing premature ageing were included in global and local action proposals of a WHO programme,[42] which, for the first time, had made ethical values (human rights) the foundation of this policy. The motto of the programme: protect people's health throughout their lives, is translated by many countries (mainly wealthier countries) into programmes for developing complex actions, initiated in early life stages, for active and healthy ageing.

All this should help to develop social (attitudes towards ageing, protection of the social status of the elderly, etc.) and institutional conditions (law, policy, support system) for activity and flexibility in response to changes, to increase the sense of dignity and trust to one's own potential and the ability to make personal choices at different life stages.[43]

Considering the diverse pace, scope and intensity of changes in the functioning of an ageing body and the social and economic determinants of health and social status of the elderly, it is necessary to design diverse preventive[44] programmes for different categories of ageing citizens. These programmes should provide the basis of intervention in emergency situations (tertiary prevention); however, anticipatory and protective actions (primary prevention),

---

[41] Ibidem.

[42] "[...] the improvement of the health and well-being of people is the ultimate aim of social and economic development," *Health for All in the 21st Century*, p.4.

[43] Experts point out that it is necessary to maintain balance and be careful in the promotion of active ageing and the choice of actions designed to prevent separation and isolation of the elderly. One should avoid extreme activism, which may be beyond the capabilities of some old people. This remark particularly concerns work after retiring and physical activity.

[44] Prevention involves actions which obviate phenomena, situations and events which are disadvantageous, threatening to the development and the efficient functioning of individuals and communities. Preventive measures aim at stopping negative state of events, both the ones that are about to happen and those which are already at an early stage (anticipate events).

Table 5. Gerontological prevention I° – recipients, goals and actions

Primary prevention		
Recipient	Goal	Actions
Two types of recipients: 1. Society as a whole – partly diverse actions addressed to all citizens (productive age) and people close to the retirement age (50–60 years)	1. Increased social sensitivity and awareness of: – rules and consequences of population ageing – equal rights of older people, particularly their right to fully participate in public life – threats to the social position and role of the elderly, having their source in physical and social infrastructure and legislation 2. Formation and popularisation of a healthy lifestyle among all age categories (health promotion). 3. Identification of main health threats in a population and their sources, with particular focus on people of working age. 4. Increased psycho-physical health potential of the population, particularly in productive age. 5. Decreased general morbidity, including chronic diseases. 6. Foundations of financial security in old age – reduction and/or elimination of social inequalities. 7. Public space for organisations aimed at the elderly. 8. Infrastructure and basis for the social opposition to manifestations of the discrimination of the elderly.	1. Creation of real image of ageing in social consciousness (promotion programmes for education institutions, socialisation in peer groups, NGO activities, media, activities of parish communities, etc.). 2. Restructuring of educational institutions and labour market to allow the elderly to continue working after retiring. 3. Development of thematically and categorically diverse (age, status, gender, etc.) forms of adult education (lifelong learning). 4. Legal protection of the social status of the elderly, quality and conditions of their life, guarantee of the equal participation of the elderly in public life (anti-discrimination legislation; institutional advocacy of senior citizens). 5. Popularisation and implementation of preventive programmes and health promotion (chronic diseases, debilitating diseases; addictions; health at school, living environment and workplace): – evaluation and reduction of health risk factors (cutting down on and/or giving up drugs, detection of hypertension, prevention of inactivity and decline in psychophysical condition, vaccination)

		– modification of lifestyle (diet, active lifestyle, physical activity, etc.) – monitoring of health problems in a population (cardiovascular disease, stroke, certain tumours, poor nutrition, osteoporosis, influenza, pneumococcal disease, tetanus) – prevention of accidents, injuries and suicide.
2. Healthy people in middle age, but at risk of premature ageing	9. Elaboration on/implementation of procedures for estimating health risk of particular age categories (medical monitoring, screening tests, tests of early changes in the health and fitness). 10. Reduction/elimination of sources of health risks and deficits (in particular, the risk of chronic diseases and loss of efficiency) – development/ implementation of programmes to reduce health risks at workplace. Protection from complications from middle age diseases – development/implementation of screening tests for early detection of disease. Prevention of premature/pathological ageing.	6. Counselling to change lifestyle, provide tools – promoting active recreation, hobbies, relaxation intellectual activity, etc. 7. Education to: – help citizens to increase/maintain the control over one's life (self-control, self-care, self-help) – expand the understanding of the role of mental and physical help in different life phases. 8. Elaboration on/implementation of preventive programmes to reduce health risks at workplace. 9. Periodical health check (plus self-control) – promotion of preventive health behaviour of middle-aged people (particularly with groups at high health risk). 10. Gerontological education (preparation for retirement).

Source: own elaboration.

or those stabilising health and fitness of the elderly (secondary prevention) seem to be more important.

For many years, numerous European countries have been developing programs fostering complex actions for healthy ageing, initiated at early developmental stages. Primary prevention is not possible without health promotion[45] oriented towards developing and strengthening health potential. Health promotion allows people to increase their control over their health and to achieve the highest possible level of well-being, which in consequence helps people/groups identify, control and solve their health problems. It also results in postponing and overcoming diseases – the basis of promotion programmes is developing sufficient social and economic conditions which are favourable for improving health in a society.

Contemporary understanding of ageing prevention also includes lifelong learning to create an educated population of senior citizens and to popularise the habit of permanent learning through extending permanent education at the workplace and providing the opportunities to be trained in new technologies, social services and ensure a secure income in older age.

Preventive programmes are based on the theory, verified by representative research, that biological ageing is quite universal and most of its symptoms are modifiable. Ageing symptoms such as systolic blood pressure, cardiac reserve, osteoporosis, impaired glucose tolerance, problems with physical strength and endurance, decreased lung capacity, increased cholesterol level, tooth decay, longer response time, decrease in memory capacity and IQ level can be corrected with the use of proper diet, physical exercise, regular control of body weight and health condition, and mental exercises.[46]

Primary preventive programmes are addressed to the whole of society and particularly the middle-aged, who should be more aware of the problems of an ageing population and health risks in old age (Table 5).

Most contemporary diseases result from individual choice (knowledge, attitudes, behaviour: lifestyle) and/or social, common choices (living conditions – both poverty and excess, natural environment; social life organisation, social security institutions – including healthcare). A healthcare model which is efficient in curing acute diseases has little use in the prevention and treatment

[45] Health promotion involves the whole population (participation, developing citizens' co-responsibility), therefore close inter-departmental cooperation is necessary, as well as the responsibility of government and/or local government for providing pro-health life conditions. Healthcare in this process has the role of a spokesperson on health issues and is the key subject in heath education.

[46] Key findings were reported by American geriatricians, Fries and Crapo, who proved that only a few ageing symptoms are not modifiable. See J. Fries, L. Crapo, *Vitality and Aging. Implications of the Rectangular Curve*, W. H. Freeman and Co., San Francisco 1981.

Table 6. Gerontological prevention II° – recipients, goals and actions

Secondary prevention (so called: early prevention)		
Recipient	**Goal**	**Actions**
The elderly with diseases: – accelerating the ageing process – leading to the loss of life independence	1. Health monitoring of population in post-productive age – objectification of health potential and fitness of the elderly. 2. Early detection/inventory of diseases, dysfunctions and disabilities in psycho-physical and social context – socio-medical profiles of high risk groups. 3. Classification of barriers which limit the functioning of people who are chronically ill and/or have dysfunctions, deficits or some other disability. 4. Reduction in the effects of disease or preventing disease relapses. 5. Legal protection of the access of the elderly to medical care and social support – anti-discrimination actions. 6. Analysis of the social position of the elderly, estimation of social resources and support system. 7. Development/implementation a system of guidance and geriatric care.	1. Regular mental health (particularly, tests for depression and cognitive disorders) and physical health (particularly, periodical vision and hearing tests, mammography for women, screening for prostate in men) checks in all phases of ageing – estimation and analysis of bio-psycho-social determinants of health and fitness disorders of the elderly. 2. Elaboration of diverse activating and preventive actions and programmes for at least two categories of senior citizens: – people aged 60–74 – people aged 75 and over. 3. Development/implementation of the screening test system for early detection – particularly of diseases leading to efficiency loss. 4. Profiling of health and social programmes for senior citizens with high risk of independence loss (therapeutic, rehabilitation, revitalisation). 5. Programmes supporting senior citizens who experience events threatening their life and health or prolonged adversity. 6. Prevention of incorrect, ungrounded decisions to place senior citizens in nursing homes. 7. Gerontological education.

Source: own elaboration.

of chronic diseases, as an increasing number of constitutive elements of health and quality of life go beyond the area of medicine – they are found in the areas of culture and economy, as well as in the evolving goals and strategies of local, national and international social (incl. health) policy addressed to the elderly. Therefore, previous geriatric programmes, focused mostly on abnormal aspects of ageing, could not be fully efficient, as the causes of most diseases and disabilities of the elderly appear long before they enter the path of involution. The pathogenetic model explaining health changes in old age is not capable of to meeting the challenges posed by the aging of the global population. What is more, it can lead to strengthening of the conviction shared by wider social circles (also among doctors and politicians) that demographic changes in social structure will only be a source of problems. Such pessimism is as unfounded (senior citizens are also a value) as it is harmful, as it inhibits the development of effective social and health policy programmes (therapeutic nihilism) and related benefits and services (including rehabilitation and revitalisation).

Therefore, medicine must be reoriented, and new preventive measures need to be implemented. Early detection or reduction of conditions conductive to diseases is not enough[47] – it is necessary to predict and prevent what may happen. This is the aim of the secondary ageing prevention programmes aimed at the elderly with diseases that accelerate the ageing process and/or lead to the loss of life independence (Table 6).

WHO experts[48] recommend that preventive actions addressed to senior citizens aged less than 75 should aim at optimally prolonging the period of life activity in all its dimensions: biological, psychological and social. Preventive measures should also minimise factors which lead to disability and discomfort caused by long-term, unfavourable biological, psychological and social conditions and initiate preparations for retirement before it comes.

---

[47] S. Flanzer, S. Lash, *The Role of Prevention in an Aging and Disability Resource Center*, Aging and Diability, An Initiative of the U.S. Department of Health and Human Services, Technical Assistance Exchange, 2010, www.adrc-tae.org [accessed: 1.09.2012].

[48] Basic tendencies related to developing health programmes for the elderly have been analysed e.g in R. Chernoff, D. Lipschitz, *Health Promotion and Disease Prevention in the Elderly*, Raven Press, New York 1988; A. Stabb, M. Lyles, *Manual of Geriatric Nursing*, Gleneview, London 1990; J. Michel, P. Hof, "Management of Aging. The University of Geneva Experience," *Interdisciplinary Topics in Gerontology*, 1999, vol. 30, pp. 1–11; C. Estes, K. Linkins, "Critical Perspectives on Health and Aging," in C. Harrington, C. L. Estes (eds.), *Health Policy*, Jones & Bartlett Publishers, Boston 2008, pp. 97–101; G. L. Albrecht, L. Verbrugge, "The global emergence of disability," in G. L. Albrecht, R. Fitzpatrick, S. C. Scrimshaw (eds.), *Handbook of Social Studies in Health and Medicine*, London 2000, p. 154 and next; C. Michaud, "The Global Burden of Disease and Injuries in 1990," *International Social Science Journal. Health Policies and Social Values*, 1999, no. 161, pp. 287–296.

Table 7. Gerontological prevention III° – recipients, goals and actions

Tertiary prevention		
Actions aimed at individuals: – with functional disorders – with chronic diseases – with disabilities – with symptoms of psycho-social dependence – characterised by helplessness – functioning outside the social mainstream (marginalisation, exclusion, isolation)	1. Area of health: – prevention of secondary effects of illnesses and/or disabilities (preventing the transformation of primary disability into the secondary one) – prolongation of the period of real activity and ability to lead an independent life – prevention of the institutionalisation of the disabled with efficiency losses – prevention of hospitalisation – development of diverse forms of care of the terminally ill – decline in the number of premature deaths 2. Social area: – reduction in the risk of social deviation among senior citizens – decrease in the number of the elderly threatened by social exclusion, marginalisation and/or isolation – support of the carers of people with chronic/permanent afflictions	1. Promotion/support/implementation of programmes and actions designed to: – minimise passivity and mental discomfort resulting from chronic illnesses – protect health and provide therapy for the old-old – extend help in a crisis for senior citizens and their family/carers – provide the terminally ill and their family/carers with institutional and emotional help 2. Periodical orthopaedic check-up, visibility and hearing tests, tests for dementia and addictions (mainly alcoholism). 3. Implementation of programmes designed to maintain life independence, including the necessary and possible level of self-control, self-care and self-help 4. Regular visits to the households of people severely ill/disabled (priority: households of the old-old, particularly those living on their own). 5. Counselling for senior citizens and their families to prepare them for living with illness/disability.

Source: own elaboration.

Strategic preventive actions aimed at people aged 75 or over should focus on optimal prolonging of the period of real activity and the ability to live independently for as long as possible without the necessity of institutionalisation. They should minimise passivity and discomfort resulting from chronic diseases, provide conditions for minimising physical and mental distress in the case of terminal illness (providing emotional support to patients and their families – hospice care). The above-mentioned goals of health prevention should be accompanied by numerous specialist health services and benefits of geriatric programmes (which are a standard for many countries).[49]

The responsibility of individuals, families and communities for their own health and prevention from illnesses does not mean that the state should be absolved from the duty of providing conditions which determine the quality and life and the sense of health safety of an individual – particularly in key areas such as: economy, work, education, food and nutrition, sport and recreation. Therefore, the development and management of preventive programmes should be based on the strategy of acquiring not only senior citizens but also all possible partners who are statutorily obliged to protect health, and particularly with potential "competitors" (on the micro- and macro- social level).

Although tertiary ageing prevention (prevention III°) includes everything within the concept of good geriatric care,[50] this area of preventive actions also contains non-health programmes, such as prevention of marginalisation and exclusion of the elderly with severe health problems and serious efficiency losses, as well as creating conditions for taking care of the elderly at high risk of losing life independence (Table 7).

Institutions and organisations of European communities recommend that gerontological programmes provide the elderly with a choice of the form of care: either at their home, or at the home of friends or relatives, or, if necessary/desired, in a proper nursing home.[51]

---

[49] See A. Somers, "Preventive Health Services for the Elderly: Growing Consensus," in R. Chernoff, D. Lipschitz (eds.), *Health Promotion and Disease Prevention in the Ellderly*, Aging Series, vol. 35, Raven Press, New York 1988, p. 22.

[50] A. Jain, A. Bhatt, *Care of the Elderly in General Practice: A Guide to Geriatric Care,* 2010, oldagesolutions.blogspot.com/2010/02/prevention-of-disease-in-elderly.html [accessed: 20.09.2012].

[51] Polish geriatricians in 2003–2005 elaborated on standards of medical services for the elderly, but this is still only a project and not a working structure in the healthcare system. The barriers to this are problems with the definition of the role of internists and geriatricians in the care of the elderly. See J. Derejczyk, T. Grodzicki, A. Jakrzewska-Sawińska, A. Jóźwiak, K.Wieczorkowska-Tobis, Z. Woźniak (sociological consult), "Standardy świadczenia usług medycznych w specjalności geriatria" [Service Standards in Geriatric Medicine], stanowisko Polskiego

Considering the so-called rolling costs, preventive and promotion programmes related to health almost always bring significant benefits – also in financial terms.[52] Despite numerous arguments, often quoted in the literature, which justify health promotion and prevention programmes, most adversaries of these programmes, particularly of ageing prevention, are economists, but there are also critics among decision-makers of different levels of power, insurance officials, academicians and doctors, particularly those attached to the rules of conventional, interventionist medicine.[53] Discussions on this subject too often include the idea of the cost-benefit analysis, intended to prove that prevention does not decrease and actually increases expenses, which exceeds the costs of current treatment procedures.

Critics of preventive programmes usually use two simple economic arguments. First of all, it cannot be proved that any money will be saved. Second of all, even if it can, this process may be too long to be financially viable.[54] These practices effectively block the implementation even of cheaper projects, for their authors cannot always gather evidence that their actions are efficient (short application deadlines).

One of the additional but hidden barriers which make it impossible to gain wider support of health promotion and preventive programmes is the fact that public authorities, particularly at lower levels of state structures, serve only one term. It is not democracy itself that creates an impediment to reform but rather the inability/unwillingness of politicians to implement reforms over a period of time longer than the term of their office. Why introduce a reform that cannot bring direct political profit to its author?

All the above-mentioned barriers, which make it difficult or impossible to implement the principle that "prevention is better than cure," become formidable when it comes to the implementation of promotion and preven-

---

Towarzystwa Gerontologicznego, Kolegium lekarzy specjalistów geriatrii w Polsce i konsultanta krajowego w dziedzinie geriatrii, *Gerontologia Polska*, 2005, vol. 13, no. 2, pp. 67–83.

[52] D. Goldman, D. Cutlery, B. Shangz, G. Joyce, "The Value of Elderly Disease Prevention," *Forum for Health Economics & Policy*, 2006, vol. 9, no. 2, art. 1 (Biomedical Research and the Economy); R. Besdine, *Approach to the Geriatric Patient: Evaluation of the Elderly Patient*, 2009, www.merckmanuals.com/professional/sec23/ch340/ch340c.html [accessed: 14.11.2011].

[53] Critics of health promotion and prevention can be also found among fundamentalists-intercessors of freedom and civil rights who perceive them as interfering in the free choice of actions – not necessarily pro-health from the medical perspective (freedom of choice without responsibility). Cynics ironically add that the only value of promotion and prevention is that people die healthier.

[54] A. Somers, *Preventive Health...*, op. cit., p. 17; R. Kane, "Empiric Approaches to Prevention in the Elderly: Are You Promoting Too Much?," in R. Chernoff, D. Lipschitz (eds.), *Health Promotion...*, op. cit., p. 161.

tive programmes aimed at the elderly. It is a "vicious circle" – the elderly fall ill more often and for longer periods than others, which seriously increases the costs of healthcare; at the same time, no actions are taken which could decrease these costs by changing lifestyle and implementing health protection at earlier life stages.[55]

A strategy needs a diagnosis based on synthesised indicators and data, which contributes to creating an opening balance that helps to define operational aims and tasks of senior policy and its domains. Therefore, preparatory works on the new architecture of social policy on ageing should focus on research and analysis in order to create of the map of needs of the oldest generation and and to classify diverse categories of senior citizens, particularly the vulnerable groups, and to define their individual/family potential as well as the support of the local community.

The process of objectifying the picture of ageing is, however, too often interrupted by a one-dimensional, polar perception of both senior citizens and the ageing process. Ageing and old age are treated and presented either as a personal drama, a time imbued with suffering and hopelessness, a period analysed only from the perspective of deficiencies and pathologies, increasing costs of living, treatment and care of the oldest generation (medical image of ageing), or their image is dominated by a model of ageing (characteristic of the organisations of and for the elderly) that is too optimistic, which does not really help to objectify the position and potential of senior citizens. Neither way of defining and presenting ageing and old age is suited to creating rational programmes for improving/maintaining conditions and quality of life at the last stage of human life.

Thus, considering the diversity among senior citizens should take precedence over attempts to treat the elderly as a homogenous category. The former approach entails studying socioeconomic and health profiles of older people and the resources, potential and barriers which have to be considered to solve various problems related to ageing.

The worse the health and fitness of the elderly from "vulnerable groups," the more often interventionist strategies need to be implemented by social policy. Besides, compensatory and participatory strategies should be addressed to senior citizens at risk of marginalisation and social isolation, and security-compensatory strategies to the poorest elderly.

New architecture of future gerontologist programmes must be anchored in social policy addressed to future generations of the elderly and should include

[55] The above quoted WHO experts estimate that the decrease in morbidity and mortality from cardio-vascular diseases and tumours, as a result of health promotion, and the prevention of accidents and injuries would increase life expectancy of the elderly by 3 to 5 years.

pragmatic remedies for today's retirees. The minimum programme on equal social position of the elderly is proposed to include advisory groups, committees and senior counsels (silver legislatures) which can influence issues that are important for local communities, particularly if they concern older people.

Needless to say, priority is given to endeavours which aim at improving the economic position of the elderly (the main task of the political/decision-making "centre"), particularly programmes which make use of the skills and abilities of numerous citizens over 50 years old[56] to keep them in employment (also part-time), and those focusing on diverse methods of saving (e.g. cooperatives) and initiatives which use new technologies to increase the productivity of an ageing individual and the national income. Tasks of the "centre" also include introducing a pro-natalist policy that promotes a high birth rate, or a pro-immigration policy.

Whenever it is right and desired, it will be necessary to introduce financial solutions, alternatives to formal systems of social insurance, which would support attempts to generate the income of ageing people from sources other than pension systems, so as to help the elderly to maintain financial independence. It is also necessary to implement legal and organisational solutions to enable the elderly to re-enter the labour market after the period of economic inactivity. What is more, a long-term programme to protect the standard of living of the elderly in general, and to give systemic support to the poorest senior citizens is necessary. It can be complemented with the implementation of a flexible labour market policy, e.g. by creating jobs for the elderly on a local scale (services), flexibility of retirement age (blunting the "retirement guillotine"), enabling gainful employment with the right to receive full pension (pension as a rightful benefit earned in the period of economic activity) etc.

Ageing societies face the necessity of restructuring and creating a complex but common, physically, territorially and financially accessible healthcare system, diversified according to needs, which guarantees a high quality of service. It is particularly necessary to integrate geriatric care into the system of medical institutions and to develop prevention, rehabilitation and revitalisation services for the elderly, financed from the public health budget. The increasing number of the elderly, particularly *the old-old* and senior single households is accompanied by a decreasing circle of relatives which will make elderly care a priority task of the social policy on ageing. Growing disproportion between demand and supply for the care of dependent elderly persons creates the need to develop different forms of individual and collective action to alleviate and solve problems related to elderly care. The carers of the elderly should be

---

[56] Communication from the Commission to the Council. The European Parliament: The Economic and Social Committee and the Committee of the Regions, Brussels, 5.12.2001.

supported by diverse organisational forms of long-term care for the ill and disabled senior citizens (taxes, benefits, training, personal leaves, etc.).

Consideration must be given to the growing need for all – institutional and environmental – forms of support of the family care of the chronically and terminally ill and dependent and disabled senior citizens. Future gerontological programmes should offer a choice to older persons for care, either in their own home, in the home of a relative or friend, or if necessary and desirable, in an institution. It is also advisable to provide support systems which enable families to continue being care providers for dependent older persons. This may take the form of local, intergenerational community support centres which cater to the needs of both young and old (educational, social, recreational, economic, health, etc.). The best way to guarantee the elderly to remain in their own homes for as long as possible is to provide a high standard of services to the dependent elderly in their living environment. We should thus strive to ensure the provision of good quality and gender-sensitive services for dependent older persons as a continuum, from in-home household help to visiting nurses and day care to institutional care and social services.

The aim of social security reforms planned for the next decade is to spread effective solutions to the problem of long-term care,[57] including the potential costs of care for future pensioners (long-term care insurance) and basing a pension system on stable rules guaranteeing due benefits to successive generations passing into economic inactivity.

Family care of senior citizens needs employment policy and personal policy at the workplace which are adequate to the care needs of the elderly. Family friendly and gender-sensitive workplace policies aimed at reconciling work and caregiving for both men and women carers should include: establishing flexible work arrangements, improving pay scales in the caring professions as a clear signal regarding the true value of caregiving to society, expanding parental leave to family leave in order to include care for other dependent family members, providing workplace care services for older persons, providing workplace stress management training for caregivers.[58]

To support the caring function of a family, public policy should introduce the following:

---

[57] 15–20 years ago, the average length of care of the terminally ill lasted 4.5 months, today it is 15 years. See *Aging in OECD Countries. A Critical Policy Challenge*, OECD Publishing, Paris 1996, p. 51.

[58] Based on *Caregiving and Older Persons – Gender Dimensions. Expert Group Meeting*, International Institute on Ageing, United Nations, Division for Social Policy and Development, Programme on Ageing United Nations Division for the Advancement of Women, Malta, 30.11–2.12.1997.

"– target and publicise available care services more specifically to reach care givers who are also in paid employment,

– provide payments and benefits in cash and/or in kind to either care givers or receivers in order to ensure choice of services by either party,

– award social security credits to carers for periods devoted to care giving,"

– provide care givers with options with respect to work and retirement[59] (flexible, phased and partial retirement programmes, telework),

"– expand tax deductions for carers by expanding the dependent category which would include care for the dependent elderly,"[60]

– expand the range of services for the carers of dependent relatives, including housekeeping help, respite care, self-help groups, care giving instruction, and specialised counselling,

– enable women to perform roles other than traditional roles and tasks, and enable men to be care givers,

– build supportive, barrier-free environments enhancing intergenerational relations, integration, and better intergenerational dialogue,

– invest in the development of civil society, particularly organisations gathering different generations and organisations of the elderly in order to enrich social resources,

– provide healthcare packages and social services based on a stable system of social security – e.g. by creating holistic systems of geriatric care in the local community (homecare, ambulatory and stationary care of private and public sector and NGOs), and to provide good quality and gender-sensitive services for dependent older persons as a continuum, from in-home household help to visiting nurses and day care to institutional care,

– integrate the activity of day care and institutional care facilities with the local community, and involve residents and their families in planning and providing services,

– give efficient support to actions which provide dignity in death (hospice care), support in mourning and respecting the will of the elderly for issues related to death and dying,

– promote and implement foster care programmes for the elderly living alone, as a way to maintain their functioning within a community.

For many years, official UN documents (recently also EU programmes) have paid special attention to social categories such as elderly women, people with different sexual preferences, emigrants, refugees, people with AIDS, and the oldest citizens who were usually outside the mainstream of social

[59] Ibidem.

[60] Ibidem.

and economic development.[61] It is necessary to make efforts to expand upon three different types of counselling for families with elderly who require help:

– individual counselling – the goal is to teach family members to cope with stress caused by the social position and health of the oldest generation and to create the conviction that an ageing person has a right to control their own life issues. Individual counsel requires elaborating a culturally and environmentally diverse model of carer, particularly preparing potential carers for additional requirements related to chronic diseases and disabilities of the elderly and providing preventive measures and/or emotional support;

– group counselling – the goal is to redefine roles and responsibilities for dependent, chronically ill, disabled oldest relatives; create conditions for exchanging information, ideas and good practices between members of dispersed extended family and peers who experience similar situations (functioning similar to self-help groups);

– family counselling – advisable when family members need to regain the ability to create "buffers" in order to cope with stress and conflicts caused by chronic disease and/or disability of senior citizens (a possibility to get a periodical leave from "ER"). In such cases, the family needs tools to keep a balance between the needs of family members taking care of the dependent, ill and/or disabled elderly (maintaining/rebuilding relations with neighbours and friends) and the outside pressure (work, education).

To conclude, it should be stated that the new architecture of programmes addressed to the elderly must combine a strategic approach about future generations of the elderly with pragmatic remedies for today's retirees. A strategic approach demands creative methods, use of local and national resources, aspirations and skills of public actors (government, local government, private and non-governmental sector, the elderly) to implement the idea of active and healthy ageing and society for all ages, in particular:

1. Acknowledgement of ageing problems as a global priority, which demands integration of economic processes and social policy on a global, national and local scale.

2. Teaching citizens to derive satisfaction from every life phase – this task is for all levels and stages of education and all socialisation agents. Without it, we will be powerless in the face of media and advertising pressure promoting youth as the only interesting part of human existence.

---

[61] The document quoted earlier does not include direct references to elderly rights but acknowledges "the right of everyone to social security, including social insurance." This commentary was intended to help member countries understand their duty to respect the rights of the elderly when implementing social policy projects, International Covenant on Economic, Social and Cultural Rights Resolution 2200 A (XXI), annex.

3. Lifelong learning leading to:

– development of educated senior population and cultivating the habit of lifelong learning by all members of the society, also at the workplace,

– the opportunity for the elderly to be trained in how to use new technologies,

– use of the potential of the knowledge and experience of the elderly in counselling and education for the elderly and for other generations,

– gerontological education for politicians, journalists, advertisers, architects, employers, social workers, healthcare workers, volunteers, and state officials at all levels,

– extension of educational offers for senior citizens through (i) reduced or free admission to regular courses and (ii) special training for the elderly directly related to ageing problems such as health, income security and changing images of the elderly; involving senior citizens into elaborating local plans and educational programmes addressed to retirees and their families,

4. Promotion of a healthy lifestyle which results in:

– delaying and overcoming illnesses,

– implementation of programmes developed to help understand and popularise factors, phenomena and processes responsible for good health of individuals and societies,

– placing of emphasis on using individual and environmental resources in health promotion,

– elaboration and introduction to the market of a wider and more attractive range of pro-health goods and services for all age groups, beneficial for the elderly,

– taking steps to protect older consumers from aggressive advertisement and promotion which results in shrinking their modest income,

– taking action to provide the elderly with access to sufficient amounts and quality of food, safe appliances, safe use of medications, household chemicals, and accessibility of medications and various devices, appliances and prostheses which allow the elderly to lead an independent life; also to create real image of ageing in social consciousness.

Therefore, perspective gerontological programmes should focus on promoting active retirement, involving senior citizens in the network of intergenerational relations,[62] developing networks of support and care in local

[62] A good example is the programme elaborated by the Centre for Applied Gerontology, Birmingham University: Design for the young and you exclude the old; design for the old and you include the young. I. Hamilton, *The Psychology of Ageing: An Introduction*, Jessica Kingsley Publishers, London 2002, p. 218.

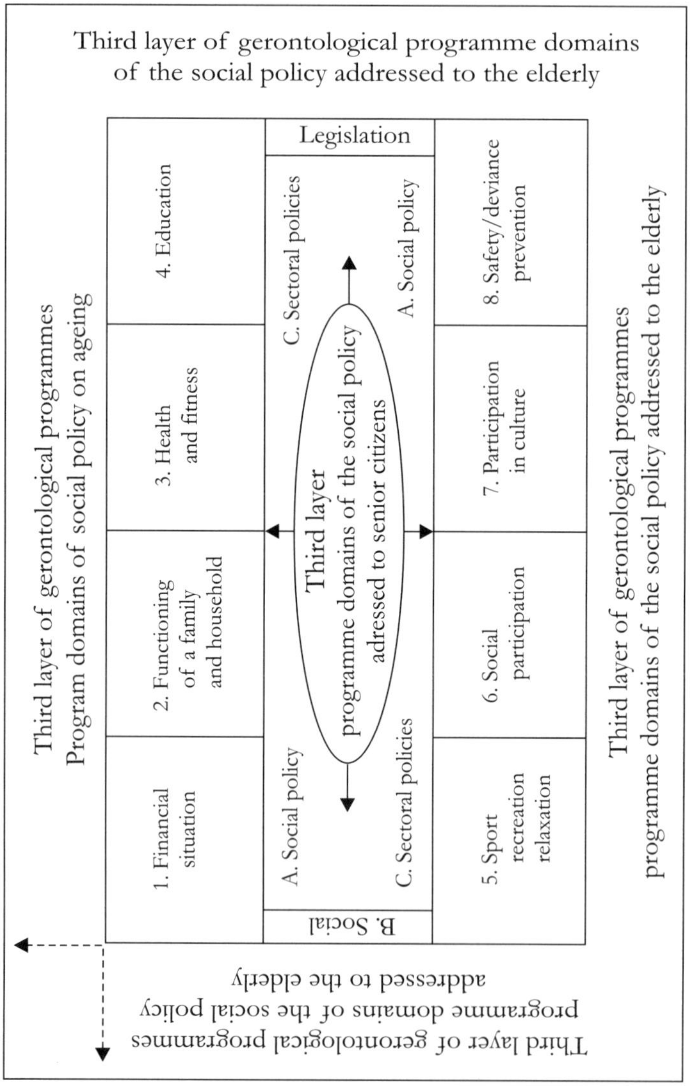

Figure 9. Conceptual framework for gerontological programmes "toolbox" – third layer

Source: own elaboration.

communities, balance between individual needs and the demands of particular situations of the elderly.

To guarantee efficient actions of European social policy addressed to the elderly, a good idea would be to establish a European Institute of Gerontology (EIG) in the near future, an institution to diagnose and foresee the problems of the elderly, to train staff, to exchange experiences of member countries and to become a centre for creating strategies for solving the significant problems of the elderly. Such an institution would gather interests of the elderly, objective knowledge about ageing and governmental ideas, and offer a chance of a synthesis of European gerontological research findings.[63]

4. Program domains and tasks of social policy addressed to the elderly

A few new directions wait around every corner.

Stanisław Jerzy Lec

Domains of ageing policy programmes belong to the third layer of the gerontological programme package and include materialisation of operational goals and tasks in the significant areas related to the conditions and quality of life of the elderly (Figure 9).

Demographic prognoses, health and fitness of ageing citizens and family difficulties caused by increasing needs of the elderly, limited capacity of institutions and deteriorating economic situations in many countries argue for adopting the following operational goals of social policy:

– family and its functioning (primacy of family in creating individual and collective satisfaction),

– work and income (foundation of a dignified human existence and the possibility of satisfying needs),

– children and the youth (primacy of the affairs of the young generation as the source of potential for society and state development),

– senior citizens (intergenerational solidarity, agency of the oldest generation),

– people with limited efficiency (subjectivity, citizen rights, integration and normalisation),

– health (potential of the economy, social structures and individual quality of life),

[63] The seat of EIG could be a member country with research experience and the experience in elaborating gerontological programmes within the framework of social policy.

Table 8. Operational goals and tasks of the local social policy addressed to the elderly

Domain of social policy: I. Family and household		
Operational goals	**Tasks**	**Implementors**
Enabling elderly people to choose their way of life freely and to lead an independent life in their usual environment for as long as they want and for as long as possible	1. Preparation of a report about the living conditions of the elderly and their families (socio-demographical profiles, regular examination of the standard and quality of life). 2. Development/strengthening of social and service infrastructure for the households of the elderly. 3. Creation of social service centres with different forms of payment (personal hygiene, laundry, cleaning, catering, hairdresser, etc.). 4. Introduction of reduced rents/taxes for economic entities which offer preferential rates of social services for the elderly. 5. Development of the support system for families (or their particular members) which take care of their dependent, elderly relatives. 6. Introduction of diverse forms of support for carers (training, information; medical, psychological and legal counselling). 7. Development of/support for local information, educational, advisory and therapeutic infrastructure, which supports families in understanding and solving problems related to the functioning of the elderly.	In order of importance: public sector, family, neighbourhood, parish, school, volunteers, social organisations. The role of public sector institutions: initiation of programmes, information about resources, competitive selection of projects, coordination of actions. Lobbying for: – introduction of protective insurance, – introduction of tax solutions which favour the carers of the elderly – award social security credits to carers for periods devoted to care giving.

	8. Initiation, promotion, support for senior citizens' cheap/free access to the INTERNET – co-financing monitoring of the homes of the disabled elderly..	
A. Creation of a housing programme offering diverse options to the ageing citizens	1. Creation of local housing resources for the elderly (foundations, donations, flats in return for care, etc.). 2. Simplification and acceleration of the procedure of flat exchange. 3. Counsel/support for the elderly in their efforts to regain the ability to pay rent and avoid eviction as a result of debt accumulation. 4. Adjustment of housing offers to financial resources, age and needs of the elderly (social housing, e.g. council flats, senior housing communities, boarding houses, independent flats, assisted living residences). 5. Development of/support for aid programmes for the disabled elderly which help improve technical standards of living, removal of architectural barriers in the home environment. 6. Development of diverse forms of services to support the elderly in their living environments (priority: lonely, chronically ill and disabled elderly). 7. Development of a system of rewarding families and other people who create housing communities with the elderly (priority: the elderly and their families who, having constituted a housing community, pass their houses over to local authorities).	In order of importance: public sector, housing cooperatives, private sector, resources of the elderly and their families, social organisations; international programmes (particularly EU). The role of public sector institutions: elaborating a prospective housing programme, cooperation with other entities of the housing market to adjust living environment to the needs of the elderly and financing council flats for the elderly. Lobbying for a prospective, governmental housing programme for the elderly, which would support local government actions.

Operational goals	Tasks	Implementors
B. Development of a system of early detection of changes in health condition and social position of the elderly	1. Permanent monitoring of the households of the old-old (priority: regular home visits in the households of people aged 80 and over). 2. Equipment of the living environment of the elderly with senior-friendly, safe appliances which allow the elderly to lead an independent life (priority: telephone availability, telephone discount programmes for the elderly, visual and phonic aid in space orientation). 3. Information exchange between different public institutions and cross-departmental cooperation on projects addressed to senior citizens.	In order of importance: family, neighbourhood, parish, volunteers, social organisations, Państwowy Fundusz Rehabilitacji Osób Niepełnosprawnych [State Fund for the Rehabilitation of the Disabled], police and telecommunications network operators. The role of public sector institutions: coordination, information, as a guide to social support system, granting projects through the system of tender.
C. Prevention of accidents involving the use of household appliances (consumer accidents)	1. Registration, analysis and monitoring of domestic accidents suffered by the elderly. 2. Development of a local programme of protecting senior consumers from accidents involving domestic appliances, in collaboration with healthcare and the Office of Competition and Consumer Protection. 3. Taking of action in order to integrate counties (powiat)/towns/communes (gmina) into the European programme of prevention of domestic accidents.	In order of importance: public authorities, healthcare (particularly hospitals), local representatives the Office of Competition and Consumer Protection, European aid programmes, non-governmental consumer organisations, local organisations of the producers of household appliances. The role of public sector institutions: Applying for European funds from the local programme on preventing accidents in homes of the elderly; preparing applications to institutions protecting consumer rights.
Strategic preferences: 1. Interventionist programmes addressed to groups at high risk of institutionalisation (oldest, lonely, disabled). 2. Domination of security-compensation programmes to minimise the risk of loss of independence by senior citizens. 3. Target: local programmes (within the framework of housing policy) allowing the elderly to stay in their familiar social environment and foster social integration in diverse housing forms for the elderly.		

II. Financial condition		
A. Protection of social security of the oldest citizens.	1. Creation/update of a map of needs of the elderly in particular counties/communes. 2. Implementation of the statutory tasks of protecting the financial condition of the elderly – evaluation of social security programmes aimed at the elderly at risk of poverty. 3. Publication of a guide about income-generating activities which could be undertaken by the elderly – with help and counsel of local business clubs and organisations which can provide good practices and support. 4. Development of counselling on how to rationally manage the household budget. 5. Evaluation of social service programmes addressed to people at risk of poverty. 6. Compensation for financial deficiencies to improve/maintain the life standard and independence of senior citizens.	In order of importance: social service centres, NGOs, family and neighbour resources, academic institutions, private sector, central and international aid programmes for the elderly. The role of public sector institutions: leading role of the public sector: implementation of statutory tasks, social diagnosis, support for aid programmes by academic experts, searching for partners and resources to aid programmes, informing about programmes to prevent poverty among the elderly. Lobbying for maintenance of pensioners' right to earn without losing their social benefits.
B. Compensation for financial deficiencies to improve/maintain the life standard and independence of senior citizens	1. Encouragement of the efforts to maintain secondary labour market for the elderly (preferential conditions for enterprises employing the elderly, handyman services programmes, brochures informing about neighbourly services, etc.). 2. Support at the early stages of economic endeavours undertaken by ageing persons (particularly those launched in or around senior care institutions).	

Operational goals	Tasks	Implementors
	3. Aid addressed to risk groups (e.g. housing allowance, reduced cost of medications, covering health insurance).	
Strategic preferences: 1. Prioritisation of interventionist, emergency and assurance for the elderly at risk of poverty. 2. Compensation for financial deficiencies (internal and external tasks). 3. Increase in the share of local government in central taxation should be accompanied by the development of local programmes on equalising financial standards for ageing community members who use their potential and experience and foster their active participation in public, cultural and social life (prevention/elimination of the financial sources of marginalisation, exclusion and isolation).		
III. Education		
A. Embedding of gerontological module into the system of lifelong learning for all generations	1. Implementation of immediate training programmes offering support for the elderly in their functioning within institutional systems of the country, region and local community. 2. Pre-retirement counselling as preparation for the role of a pensioner. 3. Support for educational institutions and programmes which serve to extend the knowledge of senior citizens (priority: development of the Universities of the Third Age). 4. Organisation of training/workshops for employers, social workers, healthcare providers, volunteers and the representatives of local government on the subject of the consequences of ageing and the possibility of meeting the needs of the oldest members of the community.	In order of importance: educational and training services in all sectors, non-governmental organisations, public sector institutions. The role of public sector institutions: initiating actions, catalysing ideas, coordination, support and advice.

	5. Extension of education for the elderly through: – reduced or free admission to regular courses and – special training for the elderly directly related to ageing problems, such as health, income security and changing images of the elderly – use of the experience of senior education NGOs and solving the problems of the elderly. 6. Elaboration, publication and promotion of brochures containing a compendium of existing legal solutions, rights and privileges, available benefits and services, operating NGOs, rehabilitation, education, health care, labour, tourism and sports facilities, etc. 7. Support for educational programmes which introduce the elderly to the information society (priority: "familiarising" with new technologies facilitating everyday functioning).	
B. Use of the knowledge and experience of the elderly	1. Organisation of shows/competitions of professional skills of senior citizens. 2. Launch of a facility which would allow the elderly to perform the role of advisors from various fields. 3. Publishing/popularising of a list of senior citizens who wish to share their skills and support local, regional, national and international development actions. 4. Organisation of regular lectures given by the elderly for the elderly – for instance: a psychologist lecturing on relationships in a family; a farmer on improv-	In order of importance: educational and training services in all sectors, non-governmental organisations, public sector institutions. The role of public sector institutions: initiating action, catalysing ideas, coordination, support and advice.

Operational goals	Tasks	Implementors
	ing the quality of garden crops, an accountant on financial planning; a physiotherapist on physical exercise, a doctor on nutrition; a pharmacist on the principles of medicine, a police officer on security and protection against criminal assault, a lawyer on writing a will and applying to the court in the case of fraud, etc. 5. Creation of opportunities for the involvement of older people in the creation and implementation of development programmes addressed to the commune/county/town.	
Strategic preferences: 1. Focus on the initiatives which foster and help in social activation of senior citizens and support intergenerational integration (adding life to years). 2. Assurance (rather than intervention) programmes for individuals facing retirement and to help the elderly function more effectively in their everyday life.		
IV. Social participation/activity		
A. Recognition of the elderly as a valuable and significant part of social resources	1. Cooperation in creating the conditions for change of social images and stereotypes of ageing and older people (local newspapers, radio and TV, advertisement and graphic agencies, public relations companies, etc.). 2. Initiation of/support for actions which promote the idea of intergenerational solidarity through dialogue held in schools, on social forums and in local media about principles and values of intergenerational	In order of importance: NGOs (particularly of the elderly), schools, academic and research institutions, media, public authorities. The role of public sector institutions: initiating action, catalysing ideas, coordination, support and advice.

	exchange, family help, equitable distribution of tasks within the family, particularly regarding the care of dependent family members, and about the cases of elderly abuse within family and close environment. 3. Creation of an advisory group in the local government, made up of senior citizens, dealing with matters affecting the community and the oldest generation. 4. Integration of daily care facilities into the community in which they function, involving residents and their families in planning and providing services in the facility and outside.	
B. Elaboration on programmes and tools to implement the idea of society for all ages on the local level	1. Creation of conditions for maintenance of intergenerational relations and provision of equal access to generational resources (in health care, culture, education, etc. 2. Arrangement/support/development of initiatives to promote mutually beneficial exchange. 3. Promotion and implemention of a foster families programme or community living for the elderly as a way to keep them functioning within the society.	In order of importance: public sector, NGOs, neighbourhood, family, schools, universities. The role of public sector institutions: initiating integration actions, education, encouragement for intergenerational integration in the closest environment of the elderly. Lobbying for elaborating organisational and financial foundations for active ageing and intergenerational integration programme and implementation of the programme.
Strategic preferences: Exclusivity for programmes, procedures and tools which lead to the development of intergenerational integration.		

V. Participation in culture		
A. Self-creation and self-realisation of the elderly in the area of culture	1. Support for various forms of creativity and artistic movement of the elderly; finding sponsors for this activity in private sectors and NGOs. 2. Taking an initiative to launch a magazine published for and with the elderly; financing the purchase of paper, lower charges for printing, delivering papers (e.g. editorials) and trainings in marketing and running a newspaper (narrow version). 3. Support for the initiative of a regular supplement-gerontological magazine added to a local newspaper (wider version). 4. Support/promotion of the initiative of senior programmes in local TV and radio channels.	In order of importance: NGOs, private sector, cultural institutions, public authorities. The role of public sector institutions: patronage, supporting institution.
B. Increase in the availability of cultural institutions for the elderly	Finding sponsors for projects aimed at promoting culture among the oldest generation. Subsidies for participation in a culture of older people with a lower socio-economic status (Senior cards).	
VI. Sport – recreation – relaxation		
A. Implementation of the active ageing programme.	1. Support for the initiatives aimed at creating diverse tourist-recreation offers for the elderly. 2. Organisation of sport, exercise and competitions for the elderly and other age categories (intergenerational integration). 3. Provision of sport and recreation facilities for the elderly on lower charges.	In order of importance: sport and tourist organisations, private sector, public authorities. The role of public sector institutions: initiating action, organisational and infrastructural support (local resources).
Strategic preferences: Programmes aimed at activating the elderly and fostering their social participation and integration.		

VII. Health and fitness		
A. Launch and development of a system of preventive health care complementary to insurance packages	1. Provision of encouragement and financial incentives to support the creation of a complete system of geriatric and gerontological care in local communities, involving public and private sectors and NGOs. 2. Incorporation of more medical check-ups recommended by the WHO into the health promotion package (priority: screening for cancer and cardiovascular). 3. Initiation of/support for the rehabilitation programmes and training about pro-heath lifestyles addressed to the elderly. 4. Support for mental health prevention programmes 5. Expansion of the rental of rehabilitation equipment and devices necessary in care of the chronically ill. 6. Initiation of/support for gerontological education programmes addressed to medical staff and carers of the elderly.	In order of importance: public health insurance institution, public and private healthcare institutions, central budget, NGOs, local authorities, support for international programmes. The role of public sector institutions: corporate governance over medical institutions, control of the standards of medical procedures, encouragement and support for elderly care promotion programmes. Lobbying for increasing central funds for preventive gerontological programmes.
B. Increase in the access to local hospice care	1. Sufficient support for actions aimed at creating a situation of dignity and respect for dying elderly patients, supporting them in mourning, respecting the older persons' decisions about the matters related to death and dying. 2. Support for educational programmes for the carers of the terminally ill.	
Strategic preferences: Apart from interventionist programmes, it is necessary to design a local system of health prevention addressed to senior citizens and specialised geriatric programmes.		

VIII. Safety – deviance prevention		
A. Prevention and treatment of addictions in old age	1. Diagnosis of the size of addiction among the elderly. 2. Development of and support for the prevention and treatment of substance abuse among the elderly. 3. Support for educational programmes about the risk of addictions in old age, addressed to professional and non-professional carers of the elderly.	In order of importance: anti-alcohol fund, NGOs.
B. Protecting the elderly from threats related to crime and deviant behaviour	1. Development of a programme of senior safety at home and in the street, in collaboration with police, municipal police and fire brigade. 2. Diagnosis of the size of deviance among the elderly and abuse of the elderly. 3. Launch of an information/application point where abuse and violence can be reported. 4. Development and implementation of interventionist programmes for senior victims of crimes, abuse, accidents, and catastrophes, which also help them to regain stability after such events.	In order of importance: professions which protect the citizens from criminal attacks and other threats to personal safety, NGOs, social security, academic and research institutions. The role of public sector institutions: inspiring and initiating actions, intervention in emergency, support for interventionist programmes.
Strategic preferences: Rescue and assurance, prevention as a priority		

Source: own elaboration

– education (basis of equal start and social position of individuals, development potential of a society),

– recreation and relaxation (individual development and regeneration of labour force resources),

– social problems – poverty, unemployment, addictions, chronic diseases, helplessness, released prisoners, refugees, repatriates, etc. (solidarity principle applied to individuals and groups in need),

– development of social infrastructure (availability of services and benefits).

The starting point for specifying the goals and principles of the social policy addressed to the elderly on a local level are questions related to the four dimensions of the quality of life, that is:

– living, learning and working environment,

– interpersonal relations,

– participation and involvement in community life,

– stability/durability of legal and organisational solutions regarding the social sphere.

The duty/task of public authorities is to undertake actions to maintain/improve/strengthen the conditions and quality of life of community members. Therefore, local government is the only subject responsible for meeting elementary needs related to the areas determining the quality of life of ageing persons such as:

– information – the elderly must know the resources of the local system of support,

– counsel – support for self-help and peer help, professional advice for individuals, groups, families,

– housing – proper and sufficient place to live for the elderly,

– technical support – appliances in public space which reduce dependency,

– personal help – support for self-care; assistant network for the disabled – trainings, certifications, professional supervision,

– social service – benefits, services and financial support for the at-risk eldest citizens,

– transport – so that the elderly "could move wherever they feel like,"

– availability – so that the elderly could "go where they want and get what they need."

To sum up, it should be emphasised that social policy addressed to the elderly, according to the proposed conceptual framework for the general social policy, is an integral part of said policy and the foundation of developing gerontological programmes. A matrix of goals and tasks was developed to help to create such programmes; it includes the principles, norms and strategies which are necessary/helpful for social integration of senior citizens, solving their problems and encouraging their participation in public life (Table 8).

The proposed list of gerontological programmes and tasks attached to various operational goals of the social policy addressed to the elderly is:

1. A resource: source of ideas which can be implemented as political decisions by decision-makers, in accordance with constitution and national legislation.

2. A basis for planning the direction and scope of actions undertaken by social policy addressed to senior citizens:
   - for a particular budget year,
   - in long-term planning,
   - over a longer period of implementation.

3. A back-up, useful in many editions of works on evaluation, and an update of gerontological strategies and programmes.

I propose to use a "zipper formula" (Figure 10) to define the range of choices of goals/directions and their hierarchy according to the accepted value system as well as the role and involvement in the social policy implementation of diverse social actors.

Shifts on the scale of standard-deficits, participation-exclusion, development-degradation, rights-limits, dependence-independence, etc. are then made in reference to:

1. Statutory tasks attached to organisational structures of the political centre (ministries, central offices) and self-government (region, county, commune).
2. Principles of social policy accepted/agreed with strategic partners.
3. Recommendations of international organisations and European structures, whose documents are ratified or politically approved by a particular country (UN, European Council, European Union, OECD, World Bank, etc.).
4. Political preferences/programmes of current elites (arrangements made within the structures of local government concerning the adoption and implementation of social policy).

The advantage of this solution is that the choice of directions/goals of social policy can be made by horizontal shifts (options to values and tasks), without violating/ignoring the principles in the figure below (directions/goals).

The proposed zipper system:

1. Objectifies and clarifies the criteria of goal/direction choices in social policy, providing a chance to make them less likely to be the subject of political wrangling as the sole criterion for decision-making.
2. Enables the use of a similar technique in defining principles and goals of specific policies, e.g. educational policy, health policy, etc.

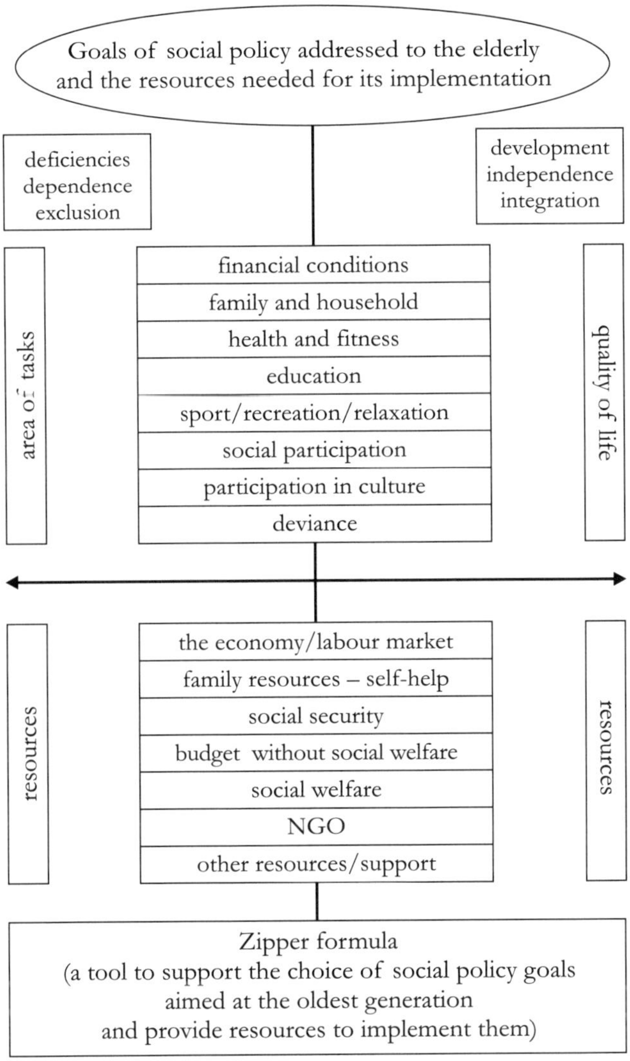

Figure 10. Goals of social policy addressed to the elderly and the resources needed for its implementation

Source: own elaboration.

3. Facilitates administrators of public funds to define the promoted and secured areas of social policy and start preparing sufficient funds to implement social programmes and use the resources in a sensible way (also outside the public sector).

4. Provides a chance to maintain continuity and stability of the market of providers and other entities in realising the social policy in its most sensitive areas.

5. Allows for fast and reality-adapted responses of public authorities to economic, health, demographic, social and cultural changes in the country, region, county and commune (up-to-date corrections of social service programmes).

6. Allows for the construction of social policy programmes which also include regional and particularly local problems (diversity of the emphasis in choosing courses, goals and objectives in social policy).

In the first years of implementing the new, complete concept of social policy addressed to the elderly, the burden of solving the problems of ageing must continue to rest on emergency, interventionist action, especially in developing countries. However, the priorities of gerontological programmes should soon shift, as should the expenditures on prevention, particularly the primary prevention embracing actions aimed at increasing social awareness and sensitivity to problems and needs caused by population ageing and creating conditions for successful ageing and development of institutions dealing with the elderly.

The author is aware that every model solution must include both the potential and limitations related to preparation and implementation of given tasks. In this case, the limitations can be alleviated by flexible structuring of the strategy and its openness to social and economic changes that can appear on the way, as well as the numerous variants of senior policies which partly belong to public tasks and are partly practically without cost (participation, volunteering), and some – particularly those which are innovative – can be realised in a private-public partnership or by NGOs.

Summary

> By three methods we may learn wisdom: First, by reflection, which is noblest; Second, by imitation, which is easiest; and Third by experience, which is the bitterest.
>
> Confucius

We cannot escape from biology (physiological ageing of human body), or demography (ageing of human population) – as we can neither exchange the population nor "generate" the required number of children to fill the widening generational gap on the labour market and, in consequence, decrease the risk of the collapse of the social security system for the elderly.

Nevertheless, demographic and biological perspectives, however significant for the social policy attempting to tackle population ageing, are insufficient. The process of ageing is not isolated from other factors of change (technology development, market) which necessitate a rapid reconstruction of production and consumption patterns and changes in savings and investment models. These causative factors may prove to be significant, but their impact on various areas of economic and social life can be predicted within a decade at most.

A belief that ageing is a pathological condition belongs to the past. Nowadays, it is widely believed that ageing is a natural process of change (every living matter changes its structure and functions over time) and a response to what happens in the social environment of an individual.[1]

However, one should not ignore negative consequences of population ageing[2] such as chronic diseases (particularly those caused by dementia), a grow-

---

[1] Although these statements seem to be simple common sense, they are not a part of the mass imagination, which is occupied by stereotypes and myths of ageing.

[2] K. Dychtwald, *The 10 Physical, Social, Spiritual, Economic, and Political Crises the Boomers Will Face as They Age in the 21st Century*, http://www.asaging.org/am/cia/dychtwald.html [accessed: 8.02.2012].

ing number of disabled elderly (particularly, sensory and mental disorders), inefficiency of many institutional systems and the pauperisation of the elderly (especially in developing countries and/or countries in the process of political and economic reconstruction[3]). All in all, societies, state structures and most institutions, particularly the family, will face a serious challenge.

Therefore, on the one hand, ageing is a biological, psychological and social fact which is hard to deny, but on the other hand, it is a balance, crisis or triumph of science and technology (particularly medical technology); therefore, it is interpreted as a value, challenge and/or task – for some it will be an expected event (deserved relaxation), predicted process (science), or a tragedy and barrier to development (politicians, financiers, labour market, healthcare).[4]

One should not forget that every generation of the elderly, a generation that is usually focused on the past, must live in a world focused on the future. Therefore, the caution culture represented by the elderly and the advantages of late maturity (equipped with experience and life wisdom) become unsuitable under new social and cultural conditions. Considering the pace and intensity of changes in the operation of modern societies, it is increasingly difficult to find a satisfactory basis for a synthesis of tradition and innovation in forming the relationship between the elderly and younger generations.

Thus, one could say that ageing has a "double nature" – it should not be perceived as only negative or positive, as it is neither a good nor a bad phenomenon. What our ageing society needs is a competent debate and adequate actions to protect the resources of the elderly and to help citizens become aware of their own potential, which can be developed in every life phase.

An open and difficult issue remains. It is the question about dealing with the costs of elderly care: who will benefit and who will pay?[5] Nevertheless, we already need to look for ways to switch from today's restrictions to tomorrow's possibilities in social policy aimed at the oldest generation.

Ageing societies need appropriate political decisions to be implemented in order to reconstruct their social and economic infrastructure. It is thus necessary to develop and expand gerontological programmes.

---

[3] Only 30.0–35.0% of the rapidly growing category of the oldest citizens of the world use funds from the public old-age programmes (WHO and OECD data).

[4] Defeatists call the risks of global ageing a *geriatric tsunami* or a *geriatric Pearl Harbour*, warning that they can lead to a *Gerasic Park*.

[5] In reality, the expected consequences of population ageing which worry the world so much concern young people and not the elderly.

The most general principle of developing social policy aimed at the elderly is the creation of well-being for all ages.[6] However, global implementation of the idea of a society for all ages will require:

– effort/investment by the elderly,[7]

– unlocking potential/resources: skills, abilities and possibilities accumulated throughout life (development and exchange of generational capital),

– development of mutually rewarding intergenerational relationships in families and communities,

– adaptation of the country's infrastructure to demographic changes and other social, cultural and economic changes.

Most countries with an ageing demographic structure (particularly those in the process of political transition) face the necessity of restructuring and developing a complex, common and physically, geographically and financially viable system of public services.[8] This is because economic development today must serve to satisfy an increasing number of non-economic needs which determine the conditions and quality of life of the citizens. However it would be impossible to set an upper limit for some of these needs (e.g. health needs), therefore they cannot all be met according to the expectations of citizens.

Lack of commonly agreed principles and goals of social policy and public services as its essential part results in the instability of legal solutions in this field, the dispersion of suppliers, increasing costs and reduced access to social benefits and public services, as well as the stoppage/restriction/withdrawal from the process of satisfying the individual and social needs. Without doubt, the far-reaching economisation of public services, disregard of social values and goals, and the growing inefficiency of this sector requires not only a re-

[6] Outline of the concept can be found in the *Brasilia Declaration on Aging* (1996), later developed into an international plan and strategy for ageing societies – UN GA resolutions 37/51, 47/86 and 50/141.

7 When developing programmes aimed at reconstructing/strengthening the social position of the elderly, we should speak of "re-activation" (re-integration of the elderly to the mainstream of social life) rather than of "making the elderly active."

[8] I distinguish three main categories of public services: (1) relating to the areas which determine the development, conditions and quality of life of individuals and societies (education, care of children under 5 years old, healthcare, culture, sport and recreation, public media); (2) providing the citizens with the sense of security – public safety (army, police, fire brigade, security in public buildings, events, etc.), social security (social assistance, social protection, care of the dependent, council houses); (3) meeting the basic needs of citizens and performing tasks which are essential to the operation of the community and the state as an institution (general administrative services, transport infrastructure, public transport, postal services, energy, water supply and sanitation, telecommunications, environmental protection, waste management and the maintenance of order and cleanliness).

definition of the policy in this sector (rules, norms, values, goals), but also implementation tools (strategies, priorities).

In response to limited resources, public authorities increasingly focus on the maximum use of the existing potential of institutions, organisations, benefits and services in all sectors – recently, a new partner has emerged: NGOs, which in many cases proves to be quite effective. The institutionalised system of satisfying needs, monopolised by professions, also witnessed the intensifying process of rebuilding lost subjectivity and the citizen's role. Citizens (including senior citizens), as taxpayers and consumers, increasingly often demand improved efficiency in the management of public goods and public sector resources[9] and the introduction of factual responsibility of policymakers for the decisions they make.[10]

Policymakers today are trapped between expectations and necessity. On the one hand, they cannot ignore social expectations, especially the needs and demands of those who most depend on public services (in this case, the elderly). On the other hand, too many sacrifices of citizens and the expanding gap between social demands and policy capabilities ruin political ideologies and destroy trust of potential allies and voters.[11]

Challenges presented in this book and directions in social policy towards aging and older people proposed by the author require public approval. It is not an easy task and will never be, as, in addition to financial barriers, the lack of understanding of the necessity of these projects and excessively high demands of individual benefits may be an obstacle to social approval for changes, long-term solutions, and reforms in the social security system.

Conflicts in expectations and tension between citizens and decision-makers result in a growing demand for three virtues forgotten by the consumer society: restraint, predictability and subsidiarity. Therefore, in many countries, social policy aimed at ageing and the elderly arrived at the Bermuda Triangle,

---

[9] In everyday life, the word "public" was used as a synonym for "non-private," "shared." Since the word was appropriated by economic, legal and political discourse, it has lost this meaning. Here is how "public," which used to be "ours," became "ours and not ours" and fell under the control of the state. Services are not accessed by everyone and an increase in their cost may be accompanied by the necessity of additional fees.

[10] After voting, taxpayers lose real influence on the way, as well as scope and volume of public services. Moreover, the incompetence of policymakers, their errors and bad management of public resources are not held liable. The Geneva Charter on Quality Public Services of 2011 is a symbol of institutionalised criticism of consumer and employee movement.

[11] This is because the theories which allowed modern, constitutional states to emerge are now helpless in the face of situations caused by them. N. Luhmann, *Political Theory in the Welfare State*, de Gruyter, Berlin 1994.

torn between political promises, social expectations and the actual financial and infrastructural capacities of the state.

Solving social problems caused by population ageing is neither easy nor painless and will never be. If we are to start developing a comprehensive system of support in old age, waiting for a better economic situation is the worst solution. Delaying change usually results in even more difficult solutions in the future, more expenses for taxpayers and a burden for next generation of grandchildren and even great-grandchildren.[12] In particular, withdrawal from funding, preventive and promotional gerontological programmes or from developing an effective system of community care for the dependent elderly may prove to be expensive, as it may result in an avalanche of caring needs which neither family nor the weak network of specialised institutions can meet.

Wealthy, highly developed countries are much better prepared to face the challenges posed by population ageing, having become rich in infrastructure, goods and services before they entered the spiral of demographic aging. These countries have already responded to the challenges of population ageing: rebuilding the healthcare system, reforming the system of social benefits and adapting employment policy to current and future trends in the labour market. The next changes will concern the education system, leisure activities and information policy in the media, and if necessary, other areas of social life.

Countries with an ageing social structure which are in the process of political and economic transition will encounter much more severe problems in this matter, struggling with poverty-related issues – the demographic structure of these countries aged before they reached a level of economic development which would be adequate to demographic challenges.

Depending on legal regulations, infrastructure of the support and care system for the elderly, public projects aimed at senior citizens in different countries, and the level of economic and social development for gerontological programmes are stretched between the survival and isolation policy (countries of political transition, developing countries) and the welfare and integration policy[13] (highly industrialized countries). It should be emphasised that what was done in recent years for the benefit of modern geronto-

---

[12] An example of the repercussions of postponing a reform and a lack of public debate was the social resistance to passing the bill for raising the retirement age and making it equal for men and women.

[13] The terms were coined by B. Szatur-Jaworska (ed.), *Stan przestrzegania praw osób starszych w Polsce. Analiza i rekomendacje działań* [Respecting the Rights of the Elderly in Poland. An Analysis and Recommendations for Action], Biuletyn Rzecznika Praw Obywatelskich – Materiały, Warsaw 2008, pp. 143–144.

logical programs resulted to a large extent from the openness and innovation of civil society institutions.

Although a raise in the socio-economic gap between generations in the next decades cannot be ruled out (which means that young people are not likely to gain the material resources which would guarantee significant support for the older generation), pessimistic prognoses for societies with an ageing demographic structure seem to be exaggerated. One should rather expect that forthcoming decades will be a time of social innovation, numerous experiments, reforms, and gerontological programs as a response to the global socio-demographic situation. We should definitely expect strategic social policy, which will attempt to:

– strengthen the foundations for economic growth,
– improve the work efficiency of the economically active population,
– encourage citizens to extend the period of economic activity,
– increase individual savings into pension funds during the period of economic activity,
– increase the fertility rate,
– strengthen family ties and intergenerational solidarity,
– create reasonable social assistance, adequate to real needs (targeted support),

Ideological conversion surrounding social policy decisions in recent years, noticeable in many countries (the left wing closer to the centre, the right wing more sensitive about social issues) may weaken the blade of political debate on subjects related to population ageing and thus facilitate solving the forthcoming social problems.

One of the significant obstacles to social approval for changes, long-term solutions, and reforms in the social security system (apart from the lack of understanding of their necessity) is the global financial crisis: the simplest way to reduce the budget deficit is to decrease the financial support for social programmes. This process is accompanied by institutional barriers which partly grow out of a stereotypical belief that the population of retirees generates only costs, and lead to cutting funding as the only strategy to solve the problem of ageing. Besides, many necessary reforms need more time to be implemented than the term of office of policymakers. Therefore, in spite of their declarations, politicians are not interested in introducing them.

General or specific policies cannot ignore social expectations, particularly the needs and demands of the victims of processes and transitions in a given society. Too many sacrifices of citizens and the expanding gap between social demands and policy capabilities ruin political ideologies and destroy the trust of potential allies and voters.

Thus, it is important to examine the question of whether politicians and policymakers[14] are ready to begin the process of reforms and whether the social consciousness is prepared for the change. If the world does not soon find a *modus vivendi* for the process of transformation of the social service system to guarantee decent retirement, sooner or later taxpayers in pre-retirement age will propose (demand?) a radical but not irrational solution: deal with our needs and problems for as long as you can – once you are no longer able to, give us back our money and reduce the state structures.

A warning signal of the limited social acceptance of the state withdrawing from its obligations should be the determination of a growing number of citizens in rich European countries who use democratic principles to defend their living standards and who increasingly often employ violent forms of protest and communicate their civil refusal to bear the costs of bad economic decisions made by the state authorities.[15]

Any new idea is only half the response to the challenges of reality. Creative leaders are in fact the beginning and the end of the innovation process. However, they should take many other people into account, including those who are interested in maintaining the status quo. Here, I recall a very apt observation by G. Bernard Shaw, who said that progress is impossible without change, and those who cannot change their minds cannot change anything.

For many years, gerontologists, sociologists and social policymakers have been providing information about the problems which global population ageing is going to bring and suggesting strategic directions for social policy. That the decision-makers ignored this information should therefore not be considered an oversight, but rather an intentional and too-often committed sin of omission (current political interests and intellectual arrogance), resulting in the sin of negligence which opens the way to intergenerational conflicts. Those who are responsible should be aware that it is also their relatives who will atone for their political sins.

[14] In the circles of decision-makers there is a popular belief that one usually knows what to do about finances and public funds but no one knows how to win the election afterwards.

[15] For instance, the Indignants Movement.

Bibliography

A Global Response to Elder Abuse and Neglect: Building Primary Health Care Capacity to Deal with the Problem Worldwide: Main Report, World Health Organization Ageing and Life Course Family and Community Health, WHO Press, Geneva 2008.

Abelin Th., Schlettwein-Gsell D., "Behinderungen und Bedurfnisse Betagter," *Schweizerische Medizinische Wochenschrift*, 1986, no. 116, pp. 1524–1542.

Active Ageing and Solidarity Between Generation. A Statistical Portrait of the European Union 2012, Eurostat, Publications Office of the European Union, Luxembourg 2011.

Active Ageing. A Policy Framework, A Contribution of the World Health Organization to the Second United Nations World Assembly on Aging, Madrid, April 2002.

"Ageing and Health," *The International Journal of Public Health*, Bulletin of the World Health Organization, Geneva, 26.10.1999.

Aging in OECD Countries. A Critical Policy Challenge, OECD Publishing, Paris 1996.

Ageing Report 2009: Economic and Budgetary Projections for the EU-27 Member States (2008–2060), Joint Report prepared by the European Commission (DG ECFIN) and the Economic Policy Committee (AWG).

Albrecht G. L., Verbrugge L., "The global emergence of disability," in G. L. Albrecht, R. Fitzpatrick, S. C. Scrimshaw (eds.), *Handbook of Social Studies in Health and Medicine*, London 2000.

Atchley R. C., "A continuity theory of normal aging," *Gerontologist*, 1989, no. 29, pp. 83–190.

Atchley R. C., Barusch A., *Social Forces and Aging. Introduction to Social Gerontology*, Wadsworth Publishing Co., Belmont, Ca 2005.

Averting the Old Age Crisis, World Bank, New York 1994.

Baltes M., "The psychology of the oldest-old: the Fourth Age," *Current Opinion in Psychiatry*, 1998, no. 11, pp. 411–415.

Baltes M., Carstensen L., "The Process of Successful Ageing," *Aging and Society*, 1996, no. 16, pp. 397–422.

Baltes P., "On the Incomplete Architecture of Human Ontogeny: Selection, Optimization, and Compensation as Foundation of Developmental Theory," *American Psychologist*, 1997, no. 52, pp. 366–380.

Baltes P., Baltes M. (eds.), *Successful Aging: Perspectives from the Behavioral Science*, Cambridge University Press, New York 1990.

Baltes P., Mayer K. (eds.), *The Berlin Aging Study: Aging from 70 to 100*, Cambridge University Press, New York 1999.

Baltes P., Smith J., *New Frontiers in the Future of Aging: from Successful Aging of the Young Old to the Dilemmas of the Fourth Age*, George Maddox Lecture Series, Duke University, Durham 2002.

Baltes P., Smith J., "Toward a Psychology of Wisdom and its Ontogenesis," in R. Sternberg (ed.), *Wisdom: Its Nature, Origins and Development*, Cambridge University Press, Cambridge 1990, pp. 87–120.

Banks J., Breeze E., Lessof C., Nazroo J., *Living in the 21st Century: Older People in England – The 2006 English Longitudinal Study of Ageing (Wave 2 and 3)*, Institute for Fiscal Studies, London 2006.

Barnes M., Blom A., Cox K., Lessof C., Walker A., *The Social Exclusion of Older People: Evidence From the First Wave of the English Longitudinal Study of Aging (ELSA). Final Raport*, Office of the Deputy Prime Minister (Creating Sustainable Communities), London 2006.

Bartlett H., *Ageing Well and Maintaining Independence into the Future*, Australasian Centre of Aging, University of Queensland, Brisbane 2007.

Bartlett H., Harper P., *Intergenerational Relations Research Workshop. Report*, Research Network in Ageing Well, University of Queensland, Brisbane 2006.

Bearon L., "Successful Aging: What Does the 'Good Life' Look Like?," *Concepts in Gerontology*, 1996, vol. 1, no. 3.

Beers D., Mršnik M., *Global Aging 2010: A Worldwide Challenge*, Standard & Poor's Financial Services, McGraw-Hill, New York 2010.

Belsky J., *The psychology of aging. Theory, Research, and Practice*, Monterey 1984.

Bengson V., "Is the Contract 'Across Generation' Changing? Effects of Population Aging on Obligations and Expectations Across Age Gorups," in V. Bengtson, W. Achenbaum (eds.), *The Changing Contract Across Generations*, Aldine de Guyter, New York 1993.

Bengston V., Oyama P., *Intergenerational Solidarity: Strenghten Economic and Social Tie. Expert Group Meeting*, United Nations Headquarters, Department of Economic and Social Affairs, Division for Social Policy and Development, New York 2007.

Bijnen F., Feskens E., Caspersen C., Mosterd W., Kromhout D., "Age, Period, and Cohort Effects on Physical Activity Among Elderly Men During 10 Years of Follow-up: The Zutphen Elderly Study," *Journals of Gerontology Series A: Biological Sciences and Medical Sciences*, 1998, vol. 53 (3), pp. 235–241.

Binstock R., George L. (eds.), *Handbook of Aging and the Social Sciences*, Academic Press, San Diego, Ca 2001.

Błędowski P., "Polityka społeczna wobec osób starszych w UE i w Polsce" [Social Policy Towards the Elderly in the EU and in Poland], in K. Głąbicka (ed.), *Społeczne skutki integracji Polski z Unią Europejską* [Social Consequences of the Integration of Poland into the EU], Elipsa, Warsaw 1999, pp. 138–161.

Boersch-Supan A., Heller G., Reil-Held A., "Is intergenerational cohesion falling apart in old Europe?," *Public Policy & Aging Report*, 2011, vol. 21, no. 4, pp. 17–21.

Bonnie R., *Elder Mistreatment: Abuse and Neglect, and Exploitation in an Aging America*, National Academies Press, Washington, D.C. 2003.

Brockmann H., Gampe J., *The Cost of Population Aging: Forecasting Future Hospital Expenses in Germany*, Working Papers of the Max Planck Institute for Demographic Research, Rostock 2005.

Bromley D., *The Psychology of Human Ageing*, Penguin, London 1966.

Brzezińska A., Stolarska M., Zielińska J., "Poczucie jakości życia w okresie dorosłości" [The Sense of the Quality of Life in Adulthood], in K. Appelt, J. Wojciechowska (eds.), *Zadania i role społeczne w okresie dorosłości* [Social Tasks and Roles in Adulthood], Wydawnictwo Fundacji Humaniora, Poznan 2001, pp. 103–126.

Brzezińska A., Woźniak Z., *Wielkopolska przyjazna seniorom. Projekt systemowy dla województwa wielkopolskiego: Budowanie psychospołecznych warunków pomyślnego starzenia się (propozycje wstępne)* [Senior-Friendly Wielkopolska. Systemic Project for Wielkopolskie Region: Developing Psychological and Social Conditions for Successful Ageing (Initial Proposals)], Regionalny Ośrodek Polityki Społecznej, Poznan 2011 (photocopied material).

Butler R., Lewis M., *Aging and Mental Health. Positive Psychosocial and Biomedical Approaches*, C.V. Mosby Company, London 1986.

Cahill G., "Primer on Social Innovation: A Compendium of Definitions Developed by Organizations Around the World," *The Philanthropist*, 2010, vol. 23, no. 3.

Caregiving and Older Persons – Gender Dimensions. Expert Group Meeting, International Institute on Ageing, United Nations, Division for Social Policy and Development, Programme on Ageing United Nations Division for the Advancement of Women, Malta, 30.11–2.12.1997.

Chandler M., Holliday P., "Wisdom in a Post Apocaliptic Age," in R. Sternberg (ed.), *Wisdom: Its Nature, Origins and Development*, Cambridge University Press, Cambridge 1990.

Chernoff R., Lipschitz D., *Health Promotion and Disease Prevention in the Elderly*, Raven Press, New York 1988.

Clemen-Stone S., Eigisti D., McGuire S., *Comprehensive Family and Community Health Nursing*, McGraw-Hill, St. Louis 1991.

Colozzi I., "Zasada pomocniczości a trzeci sector" [The Subsidiarity Principle and the Third Sector], *Społeczeństwo*, 1998, no. 1, pp. 129–133.

Confronting Demographic Change: a New Solidarity Between the Generations, Green Paper: Commission of the European Communities. Brussels, 16.03.2005, COM(2005) 94 final.

Coni N., Davison W., Webster F., *Ageing*, Oxford University Press, Oxford 1998.

Corry J., Cimbolik P., *Drugs. Facts, Aternatives, Decisions*, Belmont, Ca 1985.

Cowgill D., "Aging and Modernization: A Revision on the Theory," in J. F. Gubrium (ed.), *Late Life. Communities and Environmental Policy*, Thomas, Springfield, Ill 1974.

Cowgill D., *Ageing Around the World*, Wadsworth, Belmont, Ca 1986.

Dankwarth G., Puschel K., "Suizide im Senium," *Zeitschrift fur Gerontologie*, 1991, vol. 24 (1), pp. 12–16.

Davidson K., Arber S., "Older Men: Their Health Behaviours and Partnership Status," in A. Walker, C. Hagan Hennessy (eds.), *Growing Older: Quality of Life in Old Age*, McGraw-Hill, Maidenhead 2004, pp. 127–148.

Derejczyk J., Grodzicki T., Jakrzewska-Sawińska A., Jóźwiak A., Klich A., Wieczorowska-Tobis K., "Standardy świadczenia usług medycznych w specjalności geriatria" [Service Standards in Geriatric Medicine], *Gerontologia Polska*, 2005, vol. 13, no. 2, pp. 67–83.

Dychtwald K., *Speculations on the Future of Aging*, INSIDE Magazine, 21st Century Publishers, Hawaii 1997.

Dychtwald K., Kadlec D., *The Power Years: A User's Guide to the Rest of Your Life*, John Wiley and Sons, New Jersey 2005.

Edlin R., Round J., McCabe Ch., Sculpher M., Claxton K., Cookson R., *Cost-effectiveness Analysis and Ageism: a Review of the Theoretical Literature*, Institute of Health Sciences, Leeds University, Leeds 2008.

Edwards P., *Active Ageing. A Policy Framework*, World Health Organization to the Second United Nations World Assembly on Ageing, Madrid 2002.

Elder Abuse and Neglect: In Search of Solutions, Aging Issues, Public Interest – APA on Line, American Psychological Association, Washington, D.C. 2008.

Ellinger-Weber P., "Medikamentengebrauch und Medikamentenabhangigkeit im Alter – unter besonderer alterer Frauen," in *Alter und Sucht*, Hamburg 1990.

Estes C., Linkins K., "Critical Perspectives on Health and Aging," in C. Harrington, C. L. Estes (eds.), *Health Policy*, Jones & Bartlett Publishers, Boston 2008, pp. 97–101.

Eyde D., Rich J., *Psychological Distress on Aging. Family Management Model*, Rockville 1983.

Field M., Cassel C. (eds.), *Approaching Death: Improving Care at the End of Life*, National Academy Press, Washington, D.C. 1997.

Fikus M., "Moja, twoja, nasza starość" [Ageing: Mine, Yours, Ours], *Wiedza i Życie*, 1998, no. 11.

Flanagan J., "A Research Approach to Improving Our Quality of Life," *American Psychology*, 1978, no. 33, pp. 138–147.

Franklin S., Hickie J., "Strategies for Housing Policy Action in an Aging America," *Public Policy & Aging Report*, 2011, vol. 21, no. 4, pp. 22–25.

Fries J., Crapo L., *Vitality and Aging. Implications of the Rectangular Curve*, W. H. Freeman and Co., San Francisco 1981.

Future Ageing. Inquiry into Long-term Strategies to Address the Ageing of the Australian Population over the Next 40 Years, The House of Representatives Standing Committee on Health and Ageing, Canberra 2005.

Giannakourris K., "Aging Characterizes the Demographic Perspectives of European Societies," *Eurostat. Statistics in Focus*, 2008, no. 72.

Global Aging. The Challenge of the New Millenium, Watson Wyatt Data Services, New York 2000.

Goban-Klas T., Sienkiewicz P., *Społeczeństwo informacyjne: Szanse, zagrożenia, wyzwania* [The Information Society – Opportunities, Threats, Challenges], Wydawnictwo Fundacji Postępu Telekomunikacji, Cracow 1999.

Goldman D., Cutlery D., Shangz B., Joyce G., "The Value of Elderly Disease Prevention," *Forum for Health Economics & Policy*, 2006, vol. 9, no. 2, art. 1 (Biomedical Research and the Economy).

Halicka M., "Człowiek stary jako ofiara nadużyć" [Older people as victims of abuse], *Gerontologia Polska*, 1996, vol. 4, pp. XXXVI–XL

Halicka M., "Elder Abuse and Neglect in Poland," *Journal Elder Abuse and Neglect*, 1995, vol. 6, no. 3–4, pp. 157–169.

Halicka M., *Satysfakcja życiowa ludzi starych. Studium teoretyczno-empiryczne* [Life Satisfaction of the Elderly. A Theoretical and Empirical Study], Akademia Medyczna w Białymstoku, Bialystok 2004.

Halicka M., Halicki J., *Zostawić ślad na ziemi. Księga pamiątkowa dedykowana Profesorowi Wojciechowi Pędichowi w 80. rocznicę urodzin i 55. rocznicę pracy naukowej* [To Leave a Trace in the World. Collected works dedicated to Prof. Wojciech Pędich], Wydawnictwo Uniwersytetu w Białymstoku, Bialystok 2006.

Halicka M., Halicki J. (eds.), *Nadużycia i zaniedbania wobec osób dorosłych. Na przykładzie badań środowiskowych w województwie podlaskim* [Adult Abuse and Neglect. The Example of Field Research in Podlaskie Region], Temida2, Bialystok 2010.

Halicka M., Kramkowska E., "Uczestnictwo ludzi starych w życiu społecznym" [The Participation of the Elderly in Social Life], in J. Hrynkiewicz (ed.), *O sytuacji ludzi starszych* [About the Situation of the Elderly], Rządowa Rada Ludnościowa, GUS, Warsaw 2012, pp. 33–50.

Hamilton I., *The Psychology of Ageing: An Introduction*, Jessica Kingsley Publishers, London 2002.

Hank K., *Spatial Proximity and Contacts Between Elderly and their Adult Children: A European Comparison*, University of Mannheim, Mannheim 2005.

Harper P., *Generations and Life Course: The Impact of Demographic Challenges on Education 2010–2050*, Institute of Aging, Oxford 2008.

Harrison F., *Policy, Strategy, and Managerial Action*, Houghton Mifflin Co., Boston 1986.

Hatton-Yeo A., Ohsako T., *Intergenerational Programmes: Public Policy and Research Implications an International Perspective*, The UNESCO Institute for Education, The Beth Johnson Foundation, Hamburg 2000.

Havighurst R., "Successful aging," *The Gerontologist*, 1961, no. 1, pp. 4-7.

Hayflick L., *How and Why We Age*, Ballantine Books, New York 1996.

"Health Promotion and Disease Prevention," United Nations Economic Commission for Europe (UNECE), *Policy Brief on Ageing*, 2010, no. 6.

Heikkinen E., "Health Implications of Population Aging in Europe," *World Health Statistics. The Impact of Demografique Trends on Health*, 1987, vol. 40, no. 1, pp. 22–40.

Henry P., *Active Ageing and Intergenerational Solidarity: Findings, Issue and Perspectives*, Institute for Quality of Daily Life SODEXO, 2011.

Hodgins M., McKenna V., D'Eath M., *Enhancing the Quality of Life of Older People in Poverty (With Particular Reference to Those Living Alone)*, Health Promotion Research Centre – NUI Galway: Combat Poverty Agency Research Seminar: 30 January 2007.

Holzmann R. R., Stiglitz R. (eds.), *New Ideas About Social Security*, World Bank, Washington, D.C. 2001.

Hrynkiewicz J. (ed.), *O sytuacji ludzi starszych* [About the Situation of the Elderly], Rządowa Rada Ludnościowa, GUS, Warsaw 2012.

Huber J., Skidmore P., *The New Old. Why Baby Boomers Won't Be Pensioned off?*, Demos, London 2003.

Hubert A., *Empowering People, Priving Change: Social Innovation in the European Union*, The Bureau of European Policy Advisors at the European Commission, Brussels 2010.

"Intergenerational Solidarity," *The Flash Eurobarometer*, 2009, no. 269.

Intergenerational Solidarity the Way Forward. Proposals from the NGO Coalition for a 2012 European Year for Active Ageing and Intergenerational Solidarity, NGO Coalition on Intergenerational Solidarity, Brussels 2010.

Jeune B., Christensen K., "Biodemography and Epidemiology of Longevity," in M.L. Johnson (ed.), *The Cambridge Handbook of Age and Aging*, Cambridge University Press, Cambridge – New York – Melbourne – Madrid – Cape Town – Singapore – São Paulo 2005.

Johnson M.L. (ed.), *The Cambridge Handbook of Age and Aging*, Cambridge University Press, Cambridge – New York – Melbourne – Madrid – Cape Town – Singapore – São Paulo 2005.

Józwiak J., "Teorie przejścia van de Kaa" [Van de Kaa's Theory of Transitions], *Gazeta SGH*, 2003, no. 174.

Kaczmarczyk M., Trafiałek E., "Aktywizacja osób w starszym wieku jako szansa na pomyślne starzenie" [Activation of the Elderly as a Chance for Successful Ageing], *Gerontologia Polska*, 2007, vol. 15, no. 4, pp. 116–118.

Kalache A., "WHO Aging and Health Programme," in J.P. Michel, P.R. Hof, *Management of Aging. The University of Geneva Experience*, Basel 1999, pp. 247–260.

Kalache A., Barreto S., Keller I., "Global Aging. The Demographic Revolution in All Cultures and Societies," in M.L. Johnson (ed.), *The Cambridge Handbook of Age and Aging*, Cambridge University Press, Cambridge – New York – Melbourne – Madrid – Cape Town – Singapore – São Paulo 2005, pp. 30–46.

Kalmijn M., *Intergenerational Solidarity: A Review of Three Theories and Their Evidence*, Department of Social Cultural Sciences, Tilburg University, Tilburg 2005.

Kane R., "Empiric Approaches to Prevention in the Elderly: Are You Promoting Too Much?," in R. Chernoff, D. Lipschitz (eds.), *Health Promotion and Disease Prevention in the Elderly*, Raven Press, New York 1988.

Kapella O., Liedekerke A.-C. de, Spence L., Radunovich H., *Developing intergenerational relationships*, University of Florida, Florida 2010.

Kearney M., "The Local and Global: Anthropology of Globalisation and Transnationalism," *Annual Review of Anthropology*, 1995, no. 24.

Kenny R., "Mobility and falls," in M.L. Johnson (ed.), *The Cambridge Handbook of Age and Aging*, Cambridge University Press, Cambridge – New York – Melbourne – Madrid – Cape Town – Singapore – São Paulo 2005.

Kędziora-Kornatowska K., Grzanka-Tykwińska A., „Osoby starsze w społeczeństwie informacyjnym" [The Elderly in the information Society], *Gerontologia Polska*, 2011, no. 19 (2), pp. 107–111.

Kirkwood T., "The Biological Science of Human Ageing," in M.L. Johnson (ed.), *The Cambridge Handbook of Age and Aging*, Cambridge University Press, Cambridge – New York – Melbourne – Madrid – Cape Town – Singapore – São Paulo 2005.

Kirkwood T., *Time of Our Lives: The Science of Human Aging*, Oxford University Press, New York 1999.

Kirkwood T., Austad P., "Why Do We Age?," *Nature*, 2000, no. 408, pp. 233–238.

Kirst-Ashman K., Grafton Hull H. Jr., *Understanding Generalist Practice*, Nelson-Hall Publishers, Chicago 1993.

Kluczyńska S., "Aby chciało się chcieć. Teoria wyuczonej bezradności" [Care to Care. The Theory of Learned Helplessness], *Niebieska Linia*, 1999, no. 5.

Kocemba J., "Biologiczne wyznaczniki starości" [Biological Determinants of Ageing], in A. Panek, Z. Szarota (eds.), *Zrozumieć starość* [Understanding Old Age], Test, Cracow 2000, pp. 107–110.

Kowaleski J. (ed.), *Ludzie starzy w polskim społeczeństwie w pierwszych dekadach XXI wieku* [Old People in Polish Society in the First Decades of 21st Century], Wydawnictwo Uniwersytetu Łódzkiego, Lodz 2006.

Krug E., Dahlberg L., Mercy J., Zwi A., Lozano R. (eds.), *World Report on Violence and Health*, World Health Organization, Geneva 2002.

Leońska L., Woźniak Z. (eds.), *Profile starości* [Profiles of Old Age], Wydawnictwo Miejskie, Poznan 2000.

Lifelong Preparation for Old Age in Asia and the Pacific, ESCAP, New York 1996.

Lindenberger U., Baltes P., "Intellectual Functioning in Old and Very Old Age: Cross-sectional Results from the Berlin Aging Study," *Psychology and Aging*, 1997, no. 12, pp. 410–432.

Lisowski A., *Badanie potrzeb społecznych* [Studying Social Needs], Warsaw 1996.

Lowenstein A., "Solidarity-conflict and Ambivalence: Testing Two Conceptual Framworks and Their Impact on Quality for Older Family Members," *Journal of Gerontology Social Science*, 2007, no. 62, pp. 100–107.

Luhmann N., *Political Theory in the Welfare State*, de Gruyter, Berlin 1994.

Lundström F., *Supporting Grandparents Caring for their Grandchildren*, A Comhairle Social Policy Report: Social Policy Series, 2005.

Macura M., MacDonald A., Haug W. (eds.), *The New Demographic Regime. Population Challenges and Policy Responses*, United Nations: Economic Commission for Europe and Population Fund, New York – Geneva 2005.

McClearn G., Petrill S., "The Genetics of Behavioural Ageing," in M. L. Johnson (ed.), *The Cambridge Handbook of Age and Aging*, Cambridge University Press, Cambridge – New York – Melbourne – Madrid – Cape Town – Singapore – São Paulo 2005.

Meulen R. ter, *Are There Limits to Solidarity with the Elderly?*, Hastings Center Report, Sept-Oct 1994.

Michaud C., "The Global Burden of Disease and Injuries in 1990," *International Social Science Journal. Health Policies and Social Values*, 1999, no. 161, pp. 287–296.

Michel J., Hof P., "Management of Aging. The University of Geneva Experience," *Interdisciplinary Topics in Gerontology*, 1999, vol. 30, pp. 1–11.

Mommaerts S., Devlin W., Greef M. de, Grignoli D., Paolo M. di, Rupprechter M., *Reflections and Contents of the Project EASY (European Activation for Seniors and Youth)*, Vrijzinnig Studie, Anwerpen 2008.

Moody H., *Four Scenarios for an Aging Society*, Hastings Center Report, Sept-Oct 1994.

Moor N., Komter A., *Demographic Changes, Intergenerational Solidarity and Well-being in Europe: A Comparative Approach*, UE Multilinks: Position Paper, 2008.

Mossakowska M., Więcek A., Błędowski P. (eds.), *Aspekty medyczne, psychologiczne, socjologiczne i ekonomiczne starzenia się ludzi w Polsce* [Medical, Psychological, Social and Economic Aspects of Ageing in Poland], Termedia Wydawnictwo Medyczne, Poznan 2012.

Mulgan G., "The Process of Social Innovation," in *Innovation. Technology. Governance. Globalization*, MIT Press, Boston 2006.

Murray R., Caulier-Grice J., Mulgan G., *The Open Book of Social Innovation*, Social Innovator Series: Ways to design, develop and grow social innovation, The Young Foundation. A Centre of Social Innovation, London 2010.

Narodowa Strategia Integracji Społecznej dla Polski [National Strategy of Social Integration for Poland], Ministerstwo Pracy i Polityki Społecznej, Zespół Zadaniowy ds. Reintegracji Społecznej, Warsaw 2003.

Nauck B., Steinbach A., *Intergenerational Relationships*, German Council for Social and Economic Data (RatSWD), Working Paper, 2009, no. 116.

Nusberg Ch., *Strategies for a Society for All Ages*, American Association of Retired Persons, Washington, D.C. 1998.

Older People in Transition Economies: An Overview of their Plight in the ECA Region, Environmentally and Sustainable Development, World Bank, Washington, D.C. 1999.

Olshansky S., Carnes B., Désesquelles A., "Prospects for Longevity," *Science*, 2001, no. 291, pp. 1491–1492.

Opatz J., *Primer of Health Promotion. Creating Healthy Organizational Cultures*, Oryn Publications, Washington D.C. 1985.

Paper on Relevance to EU Social Objectives, European Commission, Research Directorate-General; Programme: Quality of Life and Management of Living Resources – The Aging Population and Disabilities, Brussels, 11.04.2000.

Peterson P., *Gray Dawn: How the Coming Age Wave will Transform America and the World*, Times Books – Random House, New York 1999.

Phillipson C., Scharf T., *The Impact of Government Policy on Social Exclusion Among Oder People*, Office of the Deputy Prime Minister, Social Exclusion Unit, London 2004.

Phillis J. A. Jr., Deiglmeier K., Miller D. T., "Rediscovering Social Innovation," *Stanford Social Innovation Review*, 2008, vol. 6, no. 4.

Pierce M., Timonen V., *A Discussion Paper on Theories of Ageing*, Centre for Ageing Research and Development in Ireland, Dublin 2010.

Piotrowski J., *Miejsce człowieka starego w rodzinie i społeczeństwie* [The position of the elderly within the family and the society], PWN, Warsaw 1973.

Pitt B., *Psychogeriatrics*, Churchill Livingstone, Edinburgh 1976.

Poggeler F., "Zwischen Isolation und Emantzipation – Zur Zeitfreizeit im Alte," *Freizeit-Padagogik. Zeitschrift fur Kritische Kulturarbeit, Freizeitpolitik und Tourismusforschung*, 1990, no. 3–4, pp. 114–118.

Powell J. L., Edwards M. M., "Policy Narratives of Aging: The Right Way, the Third Way or the Wrong Way?," *Electronic Journal of Sociology*, 2002.

Pruszyński J. J., Gębka-Kuczerowska A., "Niebezpieczna starość" [The Dangers of Old Age], *Niebieska Linia*, 2006, no. 6, pp. 8–10.

Racław M. (ed.), *Publiczna troska, prywatna opieka. Społeczności lokalne wobec osób starszych* [Public Concern, Private Care. Local Communities Towards the Elderly], Instytut Spraw Publicznych, Warsaw 2011.

Rathbone-McCuan E., Hashimi J., *Isolated Elders. Health and Social Intervention*, An Aspen Publication, London 1982.

Report of Secretary General International Year of Older Persons 1999: Activities and Legacies. Highlights of an Expert Consultation on Developing a Policy Framework for a Society for All Ages, From the Annex of A54/268 – międzyregionalna konsultacja ekspertów w Seulu [Inter-regional Expert Panel in Seul], 11–16 June 1999.

Report of the World Assembly on Ageing, Vienna 26 July – 6 August 1982 (UN publication, no. E.82.01.16, VI, A, par. 49).

Rowe J., Kahn R., *Successful Aging*, Random House, New York 1999.

Rudnicka-Drożek E., Latalski M., "Rodzaje przemocy wobec kobiet po 65. roku życia" [Types of Violence against Women over 65], in J. Kowaleski, P. Szukalski (eds.), *Starość i starzenie się jako doświadczenie jednostek i zbiorowości ludzkich* [Ageing and Old Age as a Personal and Collective Experience], Zakład Demografii Uniwersytetu Łódzkiego, Lodz 2006.

Scanaill C., Garattini Ch., Greene B., McGrath M., "Technology Innovation Enabling Falls risk Assessment in a Community Setting," *Ageing International*, 2011, no. 36, pp. 217–231.

Scharf T., Phillipson C., Smith A., "Poverty and Social Exclusion – Growing Older in Deprived Urban Neighbourhoods," in A. Walker, C. Hagan Hennessy (eds.), *Growing Older: Quality of Life in Old Age*, McGraw-Hill, Maidenhead 2004, pp. 81–106.

Scharlach A., "Creating Aging-Friendly Communities in the United States," *Ageing International*, 2012, no. 37, pp. 25–38.

Schmidtke A., Weinacker B., "Suizidraten, Suizidmethoden und unklare Todesursachen alter Menschen," *Zeitschrift fur Gerontologie*, 1991, vol. 24 (1), pp. 3–11.

Schoenmaeckers R. C., *Population Ageing and its Challenges to Social Policies. Disaster Scenario or Success Story?*, Keynote speech on European Population Conference 2005. Palais de l'Europe, Strasbourg 2005.

Seligman M., *Learned Optimism: How to Change Your Mind and Your Life*, Knopf Doubleday Publishing Group, New York 2011.

Serrat O., "Sparking Social Innovation," *Knowledge Solutions*, 2010, vol. 15, no. 2.

Settersten R. Jr., Angel J. L. (eds.), *Handbook of Sociology of Aging*, Springer, New York – Dordrecht – Heidelberg – London 2011.

Silver H., "Reconceptualizing Social Disadvantage: Three Paradigms of Social Exclusion," in G. Rogers, Ch. Gore, J. B. Figueiredo (eds.), *Social Exclusion: Rhetoric Reality Responses*, International Institute for Labour Studies, International Labour Organization, Geneva 1995, pp. 74–75.

Silverstein M., Bengtson V. L., "Intergenerational Solidarity and the Structure of Adult Child–Parent Relationships in American Families," *American Journal of Sociology*, 1997, vol. 103, no. 2.

Silverstein M., Burholt V., Bengtson V. L., "Parent-Child Relations Among Very Old Parents In Wales and the United States," *Journal of Aging Studies*, 1998, vol. 12, no. 4, pp. 387–409.

Sohail I., "Ageing: Alternative Futures and Policy Choices," *Foresight*, 2003, no. 5–6, pp. 8–17.

Somers A., "Preventive Health Services for the Elderly: Growing Consensus," in R. Chernoff, D. Lipschitz (eds.), *Health Promotion and Disease Prevention in the Ellderly*, Aging Series, vol. 35, Raven Press, New York 1988.

Spence L., Radunovich H., *Developing Intergenerational Relationships*, University of Florida, Gainesville 2010.

Spicker P., *Solidarity Between Generations: A Conceptual Account. 4th International Research Conference on Social Security: Social Security in a Long Life Society*, Antwerp, 5–7 May 2003.

Spangenberg J., *Scenarios and Decision Making: Finding Integration Synergies, Avoiding Risks*, Presentation at the SEIT anniversary, Tallinn, Estonia, 8 November 2007.

Staab A., Lyles M., *Manual of Geriatric Nursing*, Gleneview, London 1990.

Stadelhofer C., *Dialog Between Young and Old*, Active Citizenship Training Initiative for Volunteers in Europe, Venice 9–13 December 2008, session 5.

Steel R., *Involving Marginalised and Vulnerable People in Research: A Consultation Document*, Promoting Public Involvement in NHS, Public Health, and Social Care Research, Involve 2004.

Sternberg R., "A Balance Theory of Wisdom," *Review of General Psychology*, 1998, no. 2, pp. 347–365.

Sternberg R. (ed.), *Wisdom: Its Nature, Origins and Development*, Cambridge University Press, Cambridge 1990.

Sternberg R., Grigorenko E., "Intelligence and Wisdom," in M. L. Johnson (ed.), *The Cambridge Handbook of Age and Aging,* Cambridge University Press, Cambridge – New York – Melbourne – Madrid – Cape Town – Singapore – São Paulo 2005.

Steyaert S., Eggermont S., Vandebosch H., *Towards the Desired Future of the Elderly and Information and Communications Technology (ICT): Policy Recommendations Based on a Dialogue with Senior Citizens*, Second International Seville Seminar on Future-oriented Technology Analysis: Impact of FTA Approaches on Policy and Decision-making – Seville 28–29 September 2006.

Stuckelberger A., "Networking in the 21st Century: GINA – International Network on Aging," in J. P. Michel, P. R. Hof, *Management of aging*, Karger, Basel – Freiburg – Paris – London – New York 1999, pp. 236–245.

Stuckelberg A., Vikat A. (eds.), *A Society for All Ages. Challenges and Opportunities*, United Nations Economic Commission for Europe, New York – Geneva 2008.

Stutz H., Bauer T., Schmugge P., *Inheritance in Switzerland. An empirical analysis with special consideration of ambivalent generational relations*, Summary of research project Childhood, Youth and Intergenerational Relationships in a Changing Society, Berne 2006.

Sutton R., *The Policy Process: on Overview*, Chameleon Press, London 1999.

Synak B. (ed.), *Polska starość* [Polish Old Age], Wydawnictwo Uniwersytetu Gdańskiego, Gdansk 2002.

Szarfenberg R., *Marginalizacja i wykluczenie społeczne* [Marginalisation and Social Exclusion], Instytut Polityki Społecznej, Uniwersytet Warszawski, Warsaw 2008.

Szatur-Jaworska B., *Jakość życia w fazie starości – próba diagnozy* [Quality of Life in Old Age: Diagnosis], Instytut Polityki Społecznej, Uniwersytet Warszawski, Warsaw 2006 (photocopial materials).

Szatur-Jaworska B., *Ludzie starzy i starość w polityce społecznej* [Elderly People and Old Age in Social Policy], Dom Wydawniczy Elipsa, Warsaw 2000.

Szatur-Jaworska B. (ed.), *Stan przestrzegania praw osób starszych w Polsce. Analiza i rekomendacje działań* [Respecting the Rights of the Elderly in Poland. An Analysis and Recommendations for Action], Biuletyn Rzecznika Praw Obywatelskich – Materiały, Warsaw 2008.

Szumlicz T., *Modele polityki społecznej* [Models of Social Policy], Monografie i Opracowania nr 376, SGH, Warsaw 1994.

Szydlik M., "Intergenerational Solidarity and Conflict," *Journal of Comparative Family Studies*, 2008, vol. 39, no. 1, pp. 97–114.

The World Aging Situation 1991, United Nations, New York 1991.

Thomae H. (ed.), *Patterns of Aging. Findings from the Bonn Longitudinal Study of Aging*, Basel 1976.

Tibbitts C. (ed.), *Handbook of Social Gerontology. Societal Aspects of Aging*, University of Chicago, Chicago 1960.

Tobiasz-Adamczyk B., "Jakość życia w starości – definicja, pojęcia" [Quality of Life in Old Age: Definition and Concepts], in A. Panek, Z. Szarota (eds.), *Zrozumieć starość* [Understanding Old Age], Test, Cracow 2000, pp. 69–78.

Tobiasz-Adamczyk B. (ed.), *Przemoc wobec osób starszych* [Violence Against the Elderly], Wydawnictwo Uniwersytetu Jagiellońskiego, Cracow 2009.

Toffler A., *Powershift: Knowledge, Wealth and Violence at the Edge of the 21st Century*, Bentam Books, New York 1990.

Toward a Europe for All Age. Promoting Prosperity and Intergenerational Solidarity, Commission of the European Communities, Brussels 1999, COM 221 final.

Toward a European Society for All Ages, Age Statement for The European Year of Equal Opportunities for All, The European Older People's Platform, Brussel 2007.

Tulle E., "The Ageing Body and the Ontology of Ageing: Athletic Competence in Later Life," *Body & Society*, 2008, vol. 14, no. 3, pp. 1–19.

Understanding and Combating Elder Abuse in Minority Communities, Archstone Foundation and the National Center on Elder Abuse, Long Beach, CA 1998.

Valliant Higginson M., *Management Policies I: Their Development as Corporate Guide*, AMA Research Study 76, New York 1966.

Verbrugge L., "Disability in Late Life," in R. Abeles, H. Gift, M. Ory (eds.), *Aging and Quality of Life*, Springer, New York 1994, pp. 79–98.

Walker A., Barnes M., Bloom A., Lessof C., Cox K., *New Horizons: The Social Exclusion of Older People, Policy Directions*, prepared for the Office of the Deputy Prime Minister, 2006.

Wallace P., *Agequake: Riding the Demographic Rollercoaster Shaking Business, Finance and Our World*, Nicholas Brealey Publishing, Boston – London 2001.

Wan K. P., *An Exploratory Study of the Elderly People's Perception of Quality of Life*, Department of Social Work and Social Administration, University of Hong Kong, Hong Kong 1997.

Wattenberg B., "European Union? European Ostrich!," *Jewish World Review*, 2000, no. 6.

Wehr P., "Die Freizeit der 'Neuen Alten'. Daten Fakten," *Freizeit-Padagogik. Zeitschrift fur Kritische Kulturarbeit, Freizeitpolitik und Tourismusforschung*, 1990, no. 3–4, pp. 103–113.

Wenger G., Davies R., Shahtahmasebi S., Scott A., "Social Isolation and Loneliness in Old Age: Review and Model Refinement," *Ageing and Society*, 1996, no. 16, pp. 333–358.

Weiss C., "Research-policy Linkages: How Much Influence Does Social Science Research Have?," in *World Social Science. Report 1999*, UNESCO Publishing, Elsevier, Paris – London 1999.

Westley F., Antadze N., "Making a Difference: Strategies for Scaling Social Innovation for Greater Impact," *The Innovation Journal: The Public Sector Innovation Journal*, 2010, no. 2.

Wiggins R., Netuveli G., Hyde M., Higgs P., Blane D., "The Evaluation of a Self-enumerated Scale of Quality of Life (CASP-19) in the Context of Research on Ageing: A Combination of Exploratory and Confirmatory Approaches," *Social Indicators Research*, 2008, no. 89, pp. 61–77.

Woźniak Z., "Centrum Wspierania Jakości Życia Seniorów jako aktywna forma integracji społecznej najstarszego pokolenia" [Support Centre for the Quality of Life of the Elderly as an Active Form of Social Integration of the Oldest Generation], in A. Jakrzewska-Sawińska (ed.), *Multidyscyplinarne aspekty opieki geriatryczno-gerontologicznej* [Multidisciplinary Aspects of Gerontological and Geriatric Care], Wielkopolskie Stowarzyszenie Wolontariuszy Opieki Paliatywnej "Hospicjum Domowe," Poznan 2007, pp. 101–111.

Woźniak Z., "Edukacja i poradnictwo dla seniorów jako narzędzia przeciwdziałania i wychodzenia z bezradności" [Education and Counseling for Senior Citizens as a Tool for Prevention and Recovery from Helplessness], in P. Sałustowicz (ed.), *Przeciw bezradności społecznej* [Against Social Helplessness], Materiały II Konwencji Ruchu Przeciw Bezradności Społecznej w Krakowie [Materials from the II Convention of the Movement against Social Helplessness in Cracow], 25 January 2003, Biuro Rzecznika Praw Obywatelskich, Warsaw 2003, pp. 80–95.

Woźniak Z., "Globalizacja problemów zdrowotnych i starzenia się a rodzina" [Globalisation of Health and Ageing Problems and the Family], in Z. Tyszka (ed.), *Współczesne rodziny polskie. Ich stan i kierunek przemian* [Contemporary Polish families. Their Condition and Direction of Change], Wydawnictwo Naukowe UAM, Poznan 2001, pp. 281–408.

Woźniak Z., "Globalne cele polityki społecznej wobec seniorów priorytetem programów gerontologicznych" [Global Aims of Social Policy aimed at the Elderly as a Priority for Gerontological Programmes], in *Jesień, moja ulubiona pora roku – sprawdzone pomysły na twórczą i aktywną starość* [Autumn, my Favorite Time of Year – Proven Ideas for Creative and Active Ageing], Akademia Filantropii, Warsaw 2003, pp. 21–24.

Woźniak Z., *Kluczowe elementy systemu opiekuńczego w świetle lokalnej polityki społecznej* [Key Elements of the Welfare System from the Perspective of Local Social Policy], conference materials, Torun 2004, pp. 14–15.

Woźniak Z., *Najstarsi z poznańskich seniorów. Jesień życia w perspektywie gerontologicznej* [The Oldest of Poznan Senior Citizens. The Autumn of Life from Gerontological Perspective], Wydawnictwo Miejskie, Poznan 1997.

Woźniak Z., *Niepełnosprawność i niepełnosprawni w polityce społecznej. Społeczny kontekst medycznego problemu* [Disability and Disabled in Social Policy. Social Context of a Medical Problem], Wydawnictwo Szkoły Wyższej Psychologii Społecznej "Academica," Warsaw 2008.

Woźniak Z., "Present Situation and Future Prospects of Social Policy Aimed at Senior Citizens Against the Background of the Globalization of Ageing," in M. Ziółkowski (ed.), *Ludzie przełomu tysiąclecia a cywilizacja przyszłości* [The People of the Turn of the

Millennium vs. the Civilisation of the Future], Wydawnictwo Fundacji Humaniora, Poznan 2001, pp. 169–197.

Woźniak Z., "Priorytety w programach gerontologicznych i struktur europejskich jako przesłanka budowy polityki społecznej wobec starości i osób starszych" [Priorities in Gerontological and European Programmes as a Condition for the Construction of Social Policy Aimed at Aging and the Elderly], in M. Szlązak (ed.), *Starzenie się populacji wyzwaniem dla polityki społeczne* [Ageing Population: a Challenge for Social Policy], Regionalny Ośrodek Polityki Społecznej, Cracow 2003, pp. 14–33.

Woźniak Z., "Problemy starzenia się i starości wyzwaniem dla polityki społecznej na progu III tysiąclecia" [Problems of Ageing and Old Age: a Challenge for Social Policy on the Threshold of the Third Millennium], *Ruch Prawniczy, Ekonomiczny i Socjologiczny*, 1999, no. 1, pp. 285–306.

Woźniak Z., "Profilaktyka starzenia się i starości – mrzonka czy konieczność?" [Ageing Prevention: Fantasy or Necessity?], *Ruch Prawniczy, Ekonomiczny i Socjologiczny*, 2011, no. 1, pp. 231–254.

Woźniak Z., "Solidarność międzypokoleniowa w starzejącym się świecie – perspektywy i zagrożenia" [Intergenerational Solidarity in the Aging World – Prospects and Risks], *Ruch Prawniczy, Ekonomiczny i Socjologiczny*, 2012, no. 3, pp. 21–63.

Woźniak Z., "Status społeczny i prawny polskich seniorów na tle programów polityki społecznej wobec osób starszych" [Social and Legal status of Polish Senior Citizens against the Background of Social Policy Programs for the Elderly], *Praca Socjalna*, 2002, no. 3, pp. 64–99.

Woźniak Z., "Teraźniejszość i perspektywy polityki społecznej adresowanej do seniorów na tle procesu globalizacji starzenia się" [Present Situation and Future Prospects of Social Policy Aimed at Senior Citizens Against the Background of the Globalization of Ageing], in M. Ziółkowski (ed.), *The People of the Turn of the Millennium vs. the Civilisation of the Future*, Wydawnictwo Fundacji Humaniora, Poznan 2001, pp. 169–197.

Woźniak Z., "The state and family in the provision of social services for older persons in economies in transition – continuity and change: the Polish case," in *Sustainable social structures in a society for all ages*, United Nations, New York 2002, pp. 83–88.

Woźniak Z., Cichocki R., Jabkowski P., Siatkowski A., *Jakość życia mieszkańców Poznania zagrożonych marginalizacją i wykluczeniem społecznym (badania wybranych kategorii wysokiego ryzyka wykluczenia).* Raport z badań wykonanych na zlecenie Urzędu Miasta Poznania [Quality of Life of Poznan Citizens at Risk of Marginalisation and Social Exclusion (the study of selected high-risk categories of exclusion). Research report on the studies conducted for the Poznan Municipal Office], Centrum Badania Jakości Życia Uniwersytetu im. A. Mickiewicza w Poznaniu, Poznan 2009.

Zelenev P., Zelenev S. (eds.), *Intergenerational Solidarity Strengthening Economic and Social Ties*, Macmillan, Hampshire 2011.

Zych A., *Człowiek wobec starości. Szkice z gerontologii społecznej* [Facing old age. Outlines of social gerontology], Warsaw 1995, ed. 2, BPS, "Śląsk", Katowice 1999.

Żakowska-Wachelko B., *Zarys medycyny geriatrycznej* [An Outline of Geriatric Medicine], Wydawnictwo Lekarskie PZWL, Warsaw 2000.

Websites

"3. Steps Toward a Society form All Ages," in *Preparation for 1999 – Toward a Society for All Age*, United Nations, 1999, www.un.org/esa/socdev/iyop/iyoppre3.htm [accessed: 5.09.2003].

Atlee T., *Transformational Politics*, London 1999, www.co-intelligence.org/CIPol_TransformPol2.html [accessed: 25.10.2011].

Atlee T., *Using Synergy, Diversity and Wholeness to Create a Wisdom Culture* and *Six facets of Wholeness*, The Co-intelligence Institute, 2001; http://www.co-intelligence.org/I-6partswholeness.html [accessed: 25.10.2011].

Besdine R., *Approach to the Geriatric Patient: Evaluation of the Elderly Patient*, 2009, www.merckmanuals.com/professional/sec23/ch340/ch340c.html [accessed: 14.11.2011].

Definition of quality of life – Perception to Factors of Good Life, http:/www.ln.edu.hk/apias/ageing/flash/qol_def_f2.htm [accessed: 12.12.2006].

Dychtwald K., *The 10 Physical, Social, Spiritual, Economic, and Political Crises the Boomers Will Face as They Age in the 21st Century*, http://www.asaging.org/am/cia/dychtwald.html [accessed: 8.02.2012].

Dychtwald K., *The Path to a Successful Retirement: Lessons from the trailblazers*, Healthy Living. AOL Lifestyle, 2011, www.huffingtonpost.com/...dychtwald/the-path-t [accessed: 8.02.2012].

Elder Abuse Fact Sheet, Administration on Aging and National Center on Elder Abuse, 2009, www.prodevmedia.com/.../elderAbuseFactSheet [accessed: 1.10.2011].

Flanzer S., Lash P., *The Role of Prevention in an Aging and Disability Resource Center*, Aging and Diability, An Initiative of the U.P. Department of Health and Human Services. Technical Assistance Exchange, 2010, www.adrc-tae.org [accessed: 1.09.2012].

Future Scenarios, Brussels, Family Platform, http://www.familyplatform.eu.

Gontarek D., Mech C., *Globalizacja starzenia się – skutki. Kryzysowa sytuacja demograficzna* [Globalisation of Ageing – Consequences. Critical Demographic Situation], 2010, www.globalizacja.org [accessed: 5.11.2011].

International Plan of Action on Aging, 2002, www.un.org/esa/socdev/ageing/waa/ [accessed: 5.08.2003].

International Policy on Ageing and Older Adult, www.ifsw.org/p38000214.html [accessed: 15.10.2010].

Jain A., Bhatt A., *Care of the Elderly in General Practice: A Guide to Geriatric Care*, 2010, oldagesolutions.blogspot.com/2010/02/prevention-of-disease-in-elderly.html [accessed: 20.09.2012].

Lenhart J., *Seven Secrets of Anti-aging*, www.antiagingrevolution.com/book_chap4.html [accessed: 5.08.2007].

Pacala J., *Prevention of Disease and Disability in Elderly*, 2009, www.msd-trinidadtobago.com/mmpe/sec23/ch342/ch342e.html [accessed: 5.08.2003].

Paying for the Past, Providing for the Future: Intergenerational Solidarity, OECD Ministerial Meeting on Social Policy, Paris, 2–3 May 2011, Session 3., www.oecd.org/social/ministerial [accessed: 26.06.2011].

Preparing for the 21st Century. Focusing on Quality in a Changing Health Care System, http://www.nas.edu/21/health.html [accessed: 23.09.2009].

Raport o kapitale intelektualnym Polski [Report on the Intellectual Capital in Poland], Zespół Doradców Strategicznych Prezesa Rady Ministrów, Warsaw 2008, www.slideshare.net/Polska2030/raport-o-kapitale- [accessed: 12.05.2009].

Tackling the Demographic Challenge. The Survey of Health, Ageing and Retirement in Europe, 2009, www.share-project.org [accessed: 13.06.2010].

The National Elder Abuse Incidence Study, U.P. Department of Health and Human Services, Administration on Aging, 1998, www.aoa.dhhs.gov/abuse/report/default.htm [accessed: 14.09.2008].

Thomas R., *Open he Arts, Open Mind*, 2005, www.edenmidwest.com/principles/principle1b.html [accessed: 2.09.2006].

Towards a Society for All Age, www.osc.govt.nz/positive-ageing-strategy/publication/towards-a-society.html [accessed: 9.05.2008].

What is Normal Aging?, www.agingcarefl.org/aging/normalAging [accessed: 5.08.2006].

Index of persons

* References to footnotes are in italics.